D1164434

JAPANESE CULTURE

The East Asian Institute of Columbia University

The East Asian Institute of Columbia University was established in 1949 to prepare graduate students for careers dealing with East Asia, and to aid research and publication on East Asia during the modern period. The faculty of the Institute are grateful to the Ford Foundation and the Rockefeller Foundation for their financial assistance.

The Studies of the East Asian Institute were inaugurated in 1962 to bring to a wider public the results of significant new research on modern and contemporary East Asia.

Recent and Forthcoming Publications of the East Asian Institute

Studies

Imperial Restoration in Medieval Japan, by H. Paul Varley. New York: Columbia University Press, 1971.

Japan's Postwar Defense Policy, 1947–1968, by Martin E. Weinstein. New York: Columbia University Press, 1971.

Election Campaigning Japanese Style, by Gerald L. Curtis. New York: Columbia University Press, 1971.

China and Russia: The "Great Game," by O. Edmund Clubb. New York: Columbia University Press, 1971.

Money and Monetary Policy in Communist China, by Katharine Huang Hsiao. New York: Columbia University Press, 1971.

Japanese Culture: A Short History, by H. Paul Varley. New York: Praeger Publishers, 1973.

Law and Policy in China's Foreign Relations: A Study of Attitudes and Practices, by James C. Hsiung. New York: Columbia University Press, 1972.

The District Magistrate in Late Imperial China, by John R. Watt. New York: Columbia University Press, 1972.

Japan's Foreign Policy, 1868–1941: A Research Guide, edited by James W. Morley. New York: Columbia University Press, forthcoming.

Pearl Harbor as History: Japanese-American Relations, 1931–1941, edited by Dorothy Borg and Shumpei Okamoto. New York: Columbia University Press, forthcoming.

Doctors in Politics: The Political Life of the Japan Medical Association, by William E. Steslicke. New York: Praeger Publishers, forthcoming.

Occasional Papers

The Introduction of Socialism into China, by Li Yu-ning. New York: Columbia University Press, 1971.

The Early Chiang Kai-shek: A Study of His Personality and Politics, 1887–1924, by Pichon P. Y. Loh. New York: Columbia University Press, 1971.

Japanese Culture

A Short History

H. PAUL VARLEY

PRAEGER PUBLISHERS
New York · Washington

To Donald Keene

Published in the United States of America in 1973
by Praeger Publishers, Inc.
111 Fourth Avenue, New York, N.Y. 10003

Second printing, 1973

© 1973 by H. Paul Varley

All rights reserved

Library of Congress Catalog Card Number: 76-189926

Printed in the United States of America

Contents

Sections of photographs follow pages 52 and 116.

Preface

This book is intended as a survey, for the general reader, of Japanese higher culture, including religion, the visual arts, literature, the theatre, thought, and those lesser arts, such as the tea ceremony and landscape gardening, that have been uniquely cherished in Japan. I have in particular sought to relate cultural developments to political and institutional trends without burdening the text with an excess of the names, dates, and other details of these trends.

I should like to thank the East Asian Institute of Columbia University for the grant they gave me to go to Japan in the fall of 1971 to work on the latter portion of the book. May I also express my thanks to Professors Donald Keene, Ivan Morris, Burton Watson, and Herschel Webb for reading all or portions of the original manuscript and for making many valuable suggestions.

Finally, I want to extend my warm personal thanks to my good friend Joe Shulman for the many excellent photographs, taken by him when we were in Japan together with our wives last fall, that appear among the illustrations of this book.

New York   H. Paul Varley
June, 1972

Major Periods and Cultural Epochs of Japanese History

Jōmon period	*ca.* 8000–300 B.C.
Yayoi period	*ca.* 300 B.C.–A.D. 300
Tomb period	*ca.* 300–552
Age of Reform	552–710
Asuka epoch (552–645)	
Hakuhō epoch (645–710)	
Nara period	710–784
Tempyō epoch (mid-eighth century)	
Heian period	794–1185
Jōgan epoch (mid- to late ninth century)	
Fujiwara epoch (tenth century to late eleventh century)	
Kamakura period	1185–1333
Kemmu Restoration	1333–1336
Muromachi (Ashikaga) period	1336–1573
Kitayama epoch (late fourteenth and early fifteenth centuries)	
Higashiyama epoch (second half of the fifteenth century)	
Age of Unification	1568–1600
Azuchi-Momoyama epoch (1568–1600 or 1615)	
Namban epoch (late sixteenth and early seventeenth centuries)	
Tokugawa (Edo) period	1600–1867
Genroku epoch (*ca.* 1675–1725)	
Bunka-Bunsei epoch (late eighteenth and early nineteenth centuries)	
Meiji period	1868–1911
Taishō period	1912–1925
Shōwa period	1926–

Chinese Dynasties Since the Time of Unification Under the Han

Han dynasty	206 B.C.–A.D. 220
Period of the six dynasties	220–589
Sui dynasty	589–618
T'ang dynasty	618–907
Period of the five dynasties	907–960
Sung dynasty	960–1279
Southern Sung dynasty (1127–1279)	
Yüan (Mongol) dynasty	1279–1368
Ming dynasty	1368–1644
Ch'ing (Manchu) dynasty)	1644–1911

Author's Notes

Japanese names: The order is family name followed by given name. Thus, Fujiwara Michinaga is Michinaga of the Fujiwara family.

Year-periods: Adopting the Chinese practice, the Japanese of premodern times designated "year-periods" or "calendrical eras" that lasted, as they saw fit, from a few months to several decades. Important events, such as the Taika Reform of 645 and the Ōnin War of 1467–77, came to be known by the year-periods in which they occurred or began. A number of cultural or art epochs, including the Tempyō epoch of the eighth century and the Genroku epoch of the late seventeenth and early eighteenth centuries, also came to be identified by the year-periods with which they roughly coincided. Beginning with the Meiji Restoration of 1868, the year-periods have been made co-terminus with the reigns of emperors.

Use of macrons: The macron is used in the transcribing of Japanese to show when the vowels *o* and *u* should be prolonged in pronunciation. In keeping with a common practice, I have omitted the macrons from such well-known place names as Tokyo, Kyoto, and Honshu, and from historical terms like "daimyo" and "shogun," which appear in most modern English-language dictionaries and which I have used without italicization.

JAPANESE CULTURE

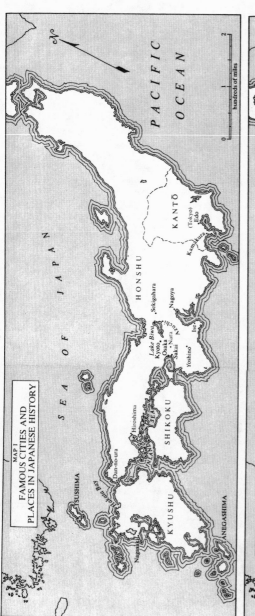

MAP I
FAMOUS CITIES AND
PLACES IN JAPANESE HISTORY

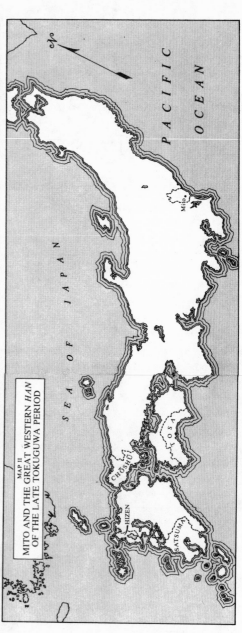

MAP II
MITO AND THE GREAT WESTERN *HAN*
OF THE LATE TOKUGUWA PERIOD

From H. Paul Varley, *A Syllabus of Japanese Civilization.* © 1968 Columbia University Press.
Reprinted by permission of Columbia University Press.

1

The Emergence of Japanese Civilization

MUCH MYSTERY SURROUNDS the origins of the Japanese people. Until very recently, it was believed that the earliest human habitation of Japan dated from only a few thousand years B.C. And although archeological finds since 1949 have revealed human traces from a vastly earlier time, perhaps as long as 500,000 years ago, we still have no sure knowledge of how or whence men first came to Japan.

During the glacial age (about 1,000,000–10,000 B.C.), when much of the water of the earth's North Temperate Zone was drawn into polar ice packs, Japan was connected by land to the continent of Asia. Perhaps the first Japanese came by foot to the islands. Racial affinities with other East Asians and the structural similarity of the Japanese language to Korean and the Ural-Altaic tongues of northern Asia make this land-migration theory plausible. But Japan also has many myths, architectural styles, and customs that suggest influences from Polynesia and Southeast Asia. Hence, we must acknowledge that the Japanese are most likely of diverse racial and cultural origins.

The earliest archeological remains in Japan of artistic interest date from about 8,000 B.C. and are a form of hand-made clay pottery known as Jōmon, or "rope-pattern," from the type of designs with which many were ornamented. Jōmon pottery was made by Neolithic men who hunted and fished for food and who migrated seasonally from settlement to settlement. It was produced over a period of some eight thousand years and varies greatly in shape and decoration according to time and to the region in Japan where it was produced. One of the earliest types of Jōmon pottery was a simple, bullet-shaped cooking vessel that was apparently inserted into sand or soft earth. Later pieces are much more elaborate and have deeply impressed and intricate

Fig. 1
Fig. 2

3

surface designs, widely flared rims, and thick, handle-like appendages. Although there is dispute over the origins of the Jōmon pottery style— certain Jōmon designs, for example, are clearly akin to those found on the Asian continent—there can be little question of the exceptional versatility and imaginativeness of Jōmon craftsmanship, which was exercised with industry and vigor throughout an epoch of many thousands of years.

Fig. 3 The Jōmon Japanese also made earthen figurines, known as *dogū*, that in their distorted representation of half-human, half-beastlike beings seem to be the creation of minds absorbed with superstition and primitive magic. Particularly interesting are the *dogū* that depict female creatures with prominent breasts and pregnant stomachs, physical features that suggest these figurines were used in some sort of fertility rites. Still other *dogū*, whose limbs appear to have been deliberately broken off, were quite possibly employed by medicine men for the purpose of curing ailments of the arms and legs.

About 300 B.C. the development of civilization in Japan was greatly accelerated by the introduction of wet-rice agriculture and the use of metals from the continent. It is possible that the Japanese already practiced rudimentary scratch farming and cultivated products such as nuts and potatoes. But not until they learned how to grow rice in irrigated fields—in the manner of the people of South China—were they transformed into true agriculturalists.

The six hundred years from 300 B.C. until A.D. 300 are known as the Yayoi period, after the site in modern Tokyo where archeological remnants of this phase of Japanese civilization were first discovered. In Yayoi times, the Japanese formed permanent farming communities and became differentiated into social classes. They also gradually began to use metals for their tools and implements, instead of just stone and wood. Since knowledge of bronze and iron entered Japan almost simultaneously, the Yayoi people tended to employ the former for ornamental and the latter for practical purposes.

Fig. 4 Yayoi man used a potter's wheel and, by means of an advanced firing technique, produced vessels of a much greater delicacy than those of Jōmon. The serene and elegant appearance of Yayoi pottery suggests that the civilizing influences that brought new technology to Japan in this age also advanced the mentality of its people. The untamed spirit reflected in the shape and ornamentation of some Jōmon pottery and in the *dogū* figurines was either lost or suppressed by the craftsmen of Yayoi. But perhaps the most striking difference between the two kinds of pottery is that in Jōmon the stress is on decoration, and in Yayoi it is on form. Many Yayoi pieces have no decoration at all, whereas others have bands of thinly incised geometric designs that contrast sharply in their simplicity with the typically florid patterning of Jōmon pottery.

In much the same way that Yayoi pottery seems to be the product of a more civilized or rational mentality, bronze objects found in graves of this period, such as mirrors from China of the Han dynasty (206 B.C.–A.D. 220) and comma-shaped jewels known as *magatama*, were probably treasured for reasons closer to religion than magic.

In addition to the archeological record, knowledge of Japan in the early centuries A.D. may be found in the dynastic histories of China. To the Chinese of this age, the Japanese were one of a number of lesser breeds of people existing beyond the borders of their great Central Kingdom. Accordingly, they relegated the accounts of Japan to the sections in their histories dealing with barbarian affairs.

The Chinese called Japan the land of Wa (which they wrote with a character that means "stunted" or "dwarfed") and described it as consisting of "one hundred"—probably meaning a great many— countries or tribes. They recorded that the people of Wa periodically sent tribute-bearing missions to China during the first and second centuries A.D., and that in the third century there were certain disorders in Wa that led to political consolidation and the establishment of a territorial hegemony under a queen named Pimiko (or Himiko). It is not known where Pimiko had her seat of authority, although quite likely it was in Kyushu and her hegemony did not extend much beyond that westernmost of Japan's major islands. The Chinese observed that

> . . . Pimiko occupied herself with magic and sorcery, bewitching the people. Though mature in age, she remained unmarried. She had a younger brother who assisted her in ruling the country. After she became the ruler, there were few who saw her. She had one thousand women as attendants, but only one man. He served her food and drink and acted as a medium of communication. She resided in a palace surrounded by towers and stockades, with armed guards in a state of constant vigilance.[1]

Pimiko's authority was apparently based on her religious or magical powers and probably derived from the Shamanism of northwestern Asia that is known to have been widely disseminated in early Japan. She is described in the above account as a mediator (shaman) between the people and their gods, and as such may well have been among the first to perform what later became the most sacred function of the Japanese sovereign. According to the mythology, the ruling dynasty of Japan is descended from the Sun Goddess (Amaterasu), the supreme deity or *kami* of the Shinto pantheon, and only a duly selected sovereign from this dynasty is qualified to perform the rites of communion with her that are essential to governing the country.

Some of the descriptions in the Chinese dynastic histories about the customs of Wa are intriguingly similar to the practices or habits of the Japanese today. For example, the Wa people paid deference to their superiors by squatting or kneeling with both hands on the ground; they clapped their hands in worship; and they placed great store in ritual cleansing or purification.

Apart from such observations about worshipful clapping and ritual purification, we know little about the evolution of those religious beliefs of ancient Japan that collectively came to be called Shinto ("the way of the *kami* or gods") to distinguish them from Buddhism, which was introduced to Japan from Korea about the mid-sixth century. In Shinto we can observe a primitive religion of the sort that elsewhere in the world has been absorbed by the universal faiths but that in remote and parochial Japan has been perpetuated into modern times. The central feature of Shinto is its animistic belief in the *kami* spirits that fill the world, inhabiting living things as well as mountains, rocks, streams, and so forth. The *kami* have always been essentially the object of local community and family devotion; indeed, their special character is the intimate association they have with these fundamental entities of Japanese social organization. The very word *kami* has the connotation of "upper" or "above," and not that of "transcendent." In historic times, the Japanese emperor has been revered as the special *kami*-embodiment of Japan and there have been frequent efforts to make Shinto a centralized religion with a hierarchy of deities. Yet this form of Shinto, known as State Shinto, should not be confused with the more basic one, which remains a diffuse worship of *kami* at the local and family levels of society.

The primitive character of Shinto can be seen not only in its *kami* polytheism but also in its lack of an ethical code. Shinto does not hold man basically responsible for his misdeeds. These, along with various physical defilements and natural disasters, are visitations from without and must be handled by means of special rites, such as exorcism and purification. Purification or lustration (of a kind presumably dating back at least to the time of the Chinese observations on the people of Wa) is particularly important in Shinto; in fact, it is the principal act performed at Shinto shrines, usually by the sprinkling of water with a wand.

Although Shinto has an exceptionally rich mythology, with many cycles of tales about *kami*, the Japanese never envisoned their deities in truly anthropomorphic terms, as did the Greeks and other early peoples. Shinto, therefore, has made very little direct contribution to the visual or plastic arts. Not until the introduction of Buddhism in the sixth century did the Japanese begin to produce religious iconography, and then it was the representation in painting and sculpture of the deities of Indian and Chinese Buddhism and not of Japan's native Shinto gods.

Sometime about A.D. 300 Japan entered a new phase in the development of its civilization, called by scholars the tomb age because of the earth and stone grave mounds that were constructed throughout much of the country from about this time until the early seventh century. Many of these grave mounds are simply converted knolls of land, but others are truly stupendous in size and must have required great concentrations of labor. The most characteristic shape of the grave mounds is that of a keyhole, and the largest mounds are in the Kansai region of central Honshu. These giant Kansai mounds appear to be proof that the clan or tribal units of ancient Japan, about which we found references in the dynastic histories of China, were even further unified in this age by chieftains who could warrant such impressive tributes in death.

Among the many different funerary objects found in the tombs are bronze mirrors, swords, and *magatama*. It is quite possible that these three objects, common also in earlier graves, were the special symbols of tribal or clan headship among the ancient Japanese. In historic times, however, they came to be regarded solely as the sacred regalia, or tokens of rulership, of the Japanese imperial family.

From the standpoint of art, the most important objects from the tomb period are clay figurines, usually several feet in height, known as *haniwa*. The *haniwa*, which were implanted on the slopes and tops of the grave mounds, represent a great variety of things: people, animals, houses, and boats, for example. Among the most interesting are armor-clad warriors and horses, which suggests that Japan's rulers at this time may have constituted a professional military élite. Some scholars even theorize that a horse-riding group of nomadic people from northeastern Asia invaded Japan through Korea sometime in the late third or fourth centuries, imposed their rule over the country, and instituted the practice of building grave mounds. This is an intriguing theory and may be true. Although it is unlikely that any single group of people ever invaded en masse and conquered Japan, Chinese, Koreans, and others increasingly migrated to Japan from the fourth and fifth centuries on. These foreigners, who possessed the advanced skills of civilization, including writing and Confucian scholarship, became prominent members, if not the actual leaders, of Japan's emerging aristocracy. By the sixth century, perhaps a third of this aristocracy was of foreign descent.

Fig. 5

Legend has it that an early emperor of Japan was so moved by the agonies of attendants and others buried alive with deceased members of the imperial family that he inaugurated the practice of using clay images in place of people on the occasion of royal funerals. Although often cited to explain the origin of the *haniwa*, this tale seems to have little basis in truth. No evidence has been found that the Japanese actually engaged in this gruesome practice of live burial, even though it was common in ancient China. More important, the images of human beings do not appear until relatively late in the evolution of the *haniwa*. The earlier *haniwa* were, in fact, simply plain cylinders. Perhaps they were employed to reduce erosion or to mark off certain areas on the grave mounds for ritual purposes. On the other hand, the later *haniwa*, which depict living beings and sundry commonplace objects, indicate a new use of these images to reproduce in afterlife a world that was familiar to the deceased.

Apart from certain shamanistic female figurines, most of the *haniwa* are entirely secular in appearance: that is, they have no religious or magical aura about them. This may be a commentary on the simple, naturalistic outlook of the early inhabitants of Japan. A number of Japanese scholars have asserted that the *haniwa* possess a quality they call *heimei*—openness and candor—that reflects the native spirit of Japan before it was altered by Confucian rationalism and the complex religious doctrines of Buddhism. Whether or not this is true, the *haniwa* are aesthetically excellent examples of the Japanese preference, already observable in Yayoi pottery, for plain, uncluttered forms.

Our knowledge of early Japanese architecture comes not only from former building sites uncovered by archeologists but also from the *haniwa* and from pictorial scenes engraved on bronze mirrors and on certain non-functional "bells" known as *dōtaku*, which were apparently used as symbols of community authority in the region of the central provinces before the tomb period. Among the buildings depicted in these clay figurines and scenes in bronze are some whose floors are elevated above the ground by pillars or poles. This type of raised-floor construction, which may come from the South Seas, is a special feature of pre-Buddhist architecture in Japan and has been particularly associated in history with Shinto shrines. Yet it is unlikely that shrine architecture is of great antiquity, inasmuch as *kami* worship and agricultural rites in early times were conducted in the open and participants seem to have felt no need for sacred buildings. Quite likely, it was not until Shinto was influenced by continental Buddhism that it came to employ permanent structures as shrines.

The most venerated shrine in Japan is the Ise Shrine, which is dedicated to the Sun Goddess (Amaterasu), the ancestress of the imperial family. The origins of the imperial family, as set forth in the mythology, may be summarized briefly. In the beginning, there were gods on the "plain of high heaven," and, in the seventh generation, the brother and sister deities of Izanagi and Izanami were instructed to create a "drifting land." Izanagi thereupon thrust his spear into the ocean below, and as he withdrew it brine dripping from the tip formed a small island. Together Izanagi and Izanami proceeded by means of a heavenly bridge to the island and there they begot not only the remainder of the islands of Japan but also a great host of other deities. In the process of giving birth to the fire deity, Izanami was badly burned and descended to the nether world. The ostensibly gallant Izanagi, in a sequence of the mythology strikingly similar to the legend of Orpheus and Eurydice, went to fetch her, but was so repelled by the appearance of Izanami's decaying and maggot-infested body that he beat a hasty retreat. To purify himself (in the finest Shinto tradition), Izanagi went to a stream and, as he disrobed and cleansed his body, he produced a new flock of *kami*. Among these was the Sun Goddess, who sprang into being as Izanagi washed his left eye.

The Sun Goddess, given dominion over the plain of high heaven, directed her grandson, Ninigi, to descend from heaven and establish the rule of his family on earth. At the time of Ninigi's departure, the Sun Goddess bestowed upon him the sacred regalia—mirror, sword, and jewel—as tokens of his mandate to rule. In the Japanese tradition, it is solely on the basis of this mandate that members of the imperial family have legitimately reigned from the founding of the empire in 660 B.C. by Ninigi's grandson, the first emperor Jimmu, to the present day. The reigning emperor, Hirohito, is regarded as the 124th sovereign descended in an unbroken line from Jimmu.

Of the regalia, the mirror was especially treasured because it was believed to represent the *kami*-body of the Sun Goddess herself. It was eventually installed at Ise after the tenth emperor, Sujin, purportedly confessed that he felt uneasy about having it nearby in the palace. The sanctity of the Ise Shrine derives from the fact that since that time (or at least from as early as we know) it has housed the sacred mirror.

One feature of the Ise Shrine, common to all shrines no matter how small, is its entranceway or *torii* (actually the Ise Shrine has several of them). The *torii*, meaning literally "bird perch," is the most familiar *Fig. 6* structure of Shinto and its origin is accounted for in the mythology. It is recorded that on a certain occasion the Sun Goddess, greatly distressed at the unruly conduct of her brother the storm god, who among other things had broken down her field-dividers and weaving looms and had defecated in her palace, secluded herself in a cave and threw the world into darkness. To lure her out, the other deities of heaven prepared a program of riotous entertainment and placed a cock atop a perch, or *torii*, before the cave to signal its commencement. When the Sun Goddess, her curiosity aroused, peeped out, she was seized by a strong-armed deity who pulled her into the open and thereby restored light to the world.

Fig. 7   The buildings at Ise are not of great antiquity; indeed, they are rebuilt every twenty years in adjacent, alternate sites. The records give no explanation for this unusual custom. But since the shrine is made of soft-textured, unpainted cypress, it is possible that one reason was to preserve the freshness of the wood and to avoid the warping and sagging to which this kind of material is susceptible. The severely simple buildings, with their raised floors, thatched roofs, and crossed end rafters, show Shinto architecture at its best. Situated in lovely forest surroundings, they give the feeling of great naturalness and tranquility, of a spirit somehow representative of Japan before the introduction of Buddhism in the sixth century.

2

The Introduction of Buddhism

THE SIXTH CENTURY inaugurated an epoch of great vitality in East Asia. After some three and a half centuries of disunion following the fall of the Han dynasty in 220, China was at length reunited under the Sui dynasty in 589. Although the T'ang replaced the Sui in 618, there was no further disruption of national unity for another three centuries.

The period of disunion in China produced conditions favorable to the spread of Buddhism, which had been introduced from India during the first century A.D., and it was largely as a Buddhist country that China entered its grand age of the T'ang dynasty (618–907). Buddhism had not only secured great numbers of religious converts in China; it had come to be regarded as virtually essential to the institutional centralization of the country, and its themes dominated the world of the visual arts.

Under the T'ang, China enjoyed its greatest national flourishing in history. Its borders were extended to their farthest limits, and Chinese culture radiated outward to neighboring lands. In East Asia, both Korea and Japan were profoundly influenced by T'ang China and underwent broad centralizing reforms on the Chinese model.

At mid-sixth century, Japan (about which the native historical accounts become generally reliable from this time on) was divided into a number of territories controlled by aristocratic clans called *uji*. One clan—the imperial *uji*—had its seat in the central provinces and enjoyed a status approximating that of *primus inter pares* over most of the others, whose lands extended from Kyushu in the west to the eastern provinces of the Kantō. In northern Honshu, conditions were still unruly and barbarous.

Even at this time in Japanese history, there was a pronounced

11

tendency for the heads of the non-imperial *uji* to assume, as ministers at court, much if not all of the emperor's political powers. Although there were a number of forceful sovereigns during the next few centuries, Japan's emperors have in general been noteworthy for the fact that they have reigned but have not ruled.

The imperial institution is a unique feature of Japanese civilization. From at least the sixth century A.D. on, the emperorship has been held by a single family, a dynastic record that makes it by far the most ancient kingly line in the world. Yet, we have no certain or even good knowledge of the origins of the Japanese imperial institution. We have seen that the mythology claims the imperial dynasty was founded in 660 B.C. by a descendant of the Sun Goddess. At present, most scholars believe that, quite apart from its religious association with the august deity of the sun, the dynasty is not nearly of such antiquity but dates from no earlier than about A.D. 300, when Japan (or Yamato, as it was poetically known) entered the tomb age. Still other scholars hypothesize that several "imperial" families successively held suzerainty over the clans of Yamato and that the present dynasty did not come into control of the emperorship until the sixth century.

The word "emperor" is actually misleading when discussing this ancient age, for the emperor we find presiding over the loosely associated clans of the Yamato state in mid-sixth century appears, like a *kami* of primitive Shinto, only to have been relatively superior to or elevated above the leaders of the other clans. Not until the next century did the Japanese, under the influence of Chinese monarchic ideas, transform their sovereign into a transcendentally divine ruler, giving him the Chinese-sounding title of *tennō* that is always translated into English as emperor.

Although the Japanese thus created an exalted emperor figure on the Chinese model, they did not adopt the key Chinese Confucian theory of the emperor ruling through a mandate from heaven. A corollary to this theory was that a mandate granted by heaven to a virtuous ruler could be withdrawn from an unvirtuous one, and it was on the basis of this rationale that the Chinese justified or explained the periodic changes of dynasty in their history. In Japan, on the other hand, the native mythological assertion (noted in the last chapter) that the Sun Goddess had granted a mandate to the imperial family to rule eternally was retained, and the imperial dynasty was thus enabled to achieve its extraordinary line of unbroken rulership throughout historic times until the present day.

Tradition has it that Buddhism was officially introduced to Japan from the Korean kingdom of Paekche in 552. Since about a third of Japan's aristocracy was by that time of foreign descent, the Japanese undoubtedly already knew about Buddhism as well as the other major features of continental civilization. Nevertheless, it was over the issue of whether or not to accept Buddhism that a larger debate concerning national reform arose at the Japanese court in the second half of the sixth century.

Buddhism was at least a thousand years old when it entered Japan. It had emerged in northern India with the teachings of Gautama (*ca.* 563–483 B.C.), the historic Buddha, and had spread throughout the Indian subcontinent and into Southeast and East Asia. But it had become a complex, universalistic religion that embraced doctrines far removed from the basic tenets of its founder. Gautama had taught that the world was a place of suffering; that suffering was caused by man's desires and acquisitiveness; and that release from suffering—enlightenment or buddhahood—could be achieved by a prescribed program known as the eightfold path (right views, right intention, right speech, right action, right livelihood, right effort, right mindfulness, and right concentration). For most people, such release probably would not come easily. The doctrine of karma, or cause and effect, held that acts in previous existences were likely to have enmeshed one tightly in the web of desire and suffering and to have predestined one to at least several more cycles of death and rebirth.

These fundamental teachings of Buddhism, which the contemporary West has found appealing as a psychology, were greatly augmented some five centuries after Gautama's death with the advent of Mahayana, the Buddhism of the "Greater Vehicle." The believers in Mahayana deprecatingly called the earlier form of Buddhism Hinayana, or the "Lesser Vehicle," since it was essentially a body of doctrine designed to instruct individuals in how to achieve release from the cycle of life and death. This, the Mahayanists asserted, implied that buddhahood was really open only to those with a special capacity to follow correctly the eightfold path. They claimed—and indeed produced ancient scriptures to "prove"—that just before his death Gautama had revealed the ultimate truth that all living things have the potentiality for buddhahood. The Mahayanists, moreover, came increasingly to regard Gautama as a transcendent, rather than simply a mortal, being and gave reverence to a new figure, the bodhisattva or "buddha-to-be," who has met all the requirements for buddahood but in his great compassion has postponed his entry into that state in order to assist others in their quest for release from the cycle of life and death.

The Mahayana school of Buddhism, which had its greatest flourishing in East Asia, also accumulated a vast and bewildering pantheon of buddhas and other exalted beings, some of whom were taken from Hinduism and even from the religions of the Near East. In an effort to categorize and account for the roles of these myriad deities, the Mahayanists formulated the theory of the "three forms" of the buddha: his all-embracing, universal, or cosmic form; his transcendent form, in which he might appear as any one of many heavenly figures, such as the healing buddha (in Japanese, Yakushi), the buddha of the future (Miroku), and the buddha of the boundless light (Amida); and his transformation form, or the body he assumed when he existed on earth as Gautama. Without knowledge of this theory of the three forms, one cannot understand the interrelationship among the various Buddhist sects that appeared successively in Japanese history.

It is difficult to gauge the precise impact of Buddhism in Japan during the first century or so after its introduction. In China, it had already proliferated into a number of abstruse metaphysical sects, within both the Hinayana and Mahayana schools, that could scarcely have appealed to the Japanese beyond a small circle of intellectuals at court. As others outside this circle gradually became aware of Buddhism, they apparently regarded it at first as a new and potent form of magic for ensuring more abundant harvests and for warding off calamities. They also responded directly and intuitively to the wonders of Buddhist art as these were displayed in the sculpture, painting, and temple architecture brought to Japan. Moreover, the Japanese probably accepted with little difficulty the validity of Buddhism's most fundamental premises: that all things are impermanent, suffering is universal, and man is the helpless victim of his fate. People in many ages have held these or similar propositions to be true, and we should not be surprised to find the Japanese of this period accepting them in the persuasive language of Buddhism.

Possibly the strongest feeling the Japanese of the seventh and eighth centuries came to have about Buddhism was that it was an essential quality of higher civilization. It is ironic that this religion, which in its origins viewed the world with extreme pessimism and gave no thought to social or political reform, should enter Japan from China as the carrier of such multifarious aspects of civilization, including the ideal of state centralization.

It is impossible to explain in a few words, or perhaps even in many, how primitive Shinto managed to survive the influx of Buddhism. Part of the answer lies in the unusual tolerance of Eastern religious thought in general for "partial" or "alternative" truths and its capacity to synthesize seemingly disparate beliefs and manifestations of the divine. In Japan, for example, the principal *kami* of Shinto came to be regarded as Buddhist deities in different forms, and Shinto shrines were even amalgamated with Buddhist temples. Another reason why the Japanese throughout the ages have with little or no difficulty considered themselves to be both Shintoists and Buddhists is that the doctrines of the two religions complement each other so neatly. Shinto expresses a simple and direct love of nature and its vital reproductive forces, and regards death simply as one of many kinds of defilement. Buddhism, on the other hand, is concerned with life's interminable suffering and seeks to guide living beings on the path to enlightenment. It is fitting that even today in Japan the ceremonies employed to celebrate such events as birth and marriage are Shinto, whereas funerals and communion with the dead are within the purview of Buddhism.

The dispute in Japan in the mid-sixth century over whether or not to accept Buddhism, and at the same time to undertake national reforms, divided the Japanese court into two opposing camps. One consisted of families which, as Shinto ritualists and élite imperial guards, felt most threatened by the changes Buddhism portended; the other camp, including the Soga family, took a progressive position in favor of Buddhism and reform. In the late 580's, the Soga prevailed militarily over their opponents and, further strengthened by marriage ties to the imperial family, inaugurated an epoch of great renovation in Japan.

The most important leader of the early years of reform was Prince Shōtoku (574–622), who with Soga blessing became crown prince and regent for an undistinguished empress. Shōtoku has been greatly idealized in history and it is difficult to judge how much credit he truly deserves for the measures and policies attributed to him. Yet, he seems ardently to have loved learning and probably he was instrumental in expanding the relations with Sui China that were critical at this time to the advancement of Japanese civilization. Quite likely it was also Shōtoku who wrote the note to the Sui court in 607 that began: "From the sovereign of the land of the rising sun to the sovereign of the land of the setting sun." The Sui emperor did not appreciate this lack of respect and refused to reply; but the note made the important point that Japan intended to uphold its independence and would not accept the status of humble subordination usually expected of countries that sent tribute to mighty China.

Formerly, the Japanese had called their country Yamato, but from about the early seventh century on they adapted the designation of Nihon (or Nippon), written with the Chinese characters for "sun" and "source." Apparently they hoped that this designation, derived from the fact that Japan's location in the sea to the east made it the "source of the sun," would give them greater prestige in the eyes of the Chinese. Whether or not it did, eventually it was the Chinese pronunciation for Nihon—Jihpen—that was transmitted back to Europe by Marco Polo in the thirteenth century and incorporated into the European tongues in forms like the English "Japan."

The Japanese dispatched a total of four missions to Sui China during the period 600–614 and fifteen to T'ang between 630 and 838. The larger missions usually consisted of groups of about four ships that transported more than five hundred people, including official envoys, students, Buddhist monks, and translators. Some of these visitors remained abroad for long periods of time—up to thirty or more years— and some never returned. The trip was exceedingly dangerous, and the fact that so many risked it attests to the avidity with which the Japanese of this age sought to acquire the learning and culture of China.

Although there are no replicas or contemporary drawings of the ships used in the missions to Sui and T'ang, we know that their sail and rudder systems were primitive and that they were obliged to rely on the seasonal winds. They usually left in the spring, when the prevailing winds were westward, and returned in the winter, when the winds blew to the east. The shortest route to the continent was across the 115-mile channel that separates Kyushu from southern Korea. But sometimes the Japanese ships were blown off course and drifted far down the Chinese coast. During most of the seventh century, when relations with Korea were poor, the Japanese set sail directly for South China, although the passage was longer and more difficult. The return trip, which almost always began from the mouth of the Yangtze River, was the most treacherous of all. A miscalculation or an accidental alteration in course could carry the ships into the vastness of the Pacific Ocean. Often they landed on islands in the Ryukyu chain and were obliged to make their way home as best they could.

Dangerous as they were, the missions to China from the seventh through the mid-ninth centuries were essential to the establishment of Japan's first centralized state. The Japanese borrowed freely from a civilization that, at least in material and technological terms, was vastly superior to their own. Yet Japan's cultural borrowing was sufficiently selective to bring about the evolution of a society which, although it owed much to China, became unique in its own right.

The influence of Korea in this transmission of Chinese civilization to Japan has not yet received adequate attention among scholars. During the first century or so A.D., Japan's relations with Korea had been close, and various Japanese tribal states had dispatched missions to China via the Han Chinese military commanderies in Korea. Sometime in the late fourth century—after formation of the Yamato hegemony in the central provinces—Japan established either a colony or a military outpost known as Mimana on the southern tip of the Korean peninsula. For the next 200 years, Japanese armies were involved in the endless struggles for supremacy among Korea's three kingdoms: Koguryŏ, Paekche, and Silla. By the sixth century, Japan had come in general to support Paekche—which is credited with officially introducing Buddhism to the Yamato court in 552—against the rising might of Silla. But Japan's efforts were not sufficient to alter the trend of events in Korea. Silla destroyed Mimana in 562, Paekche in 663, and Koguryŏ in 668; it thereby unified Korea as a centralized state on the lines of T'ang China, much like the newly reformed state that was emerging in Japan during the same period.

Koreans and Chinese had migrated to Japan from at least the beginning of the fifth century. But during Silla's rise to power the number of immigrants from the continent—especially refugees from Paekche and Koguryŏ—increased substantially, as we can tell from accounts of how they were given land and allowed to settle in different parts of the country. Throughout the seventh century, which was of course the great age of reform, these Korean immigrants played a vital role as scribes, craftsmen, and artists in the advancement of culture and civilization in Japan.

Prince Shōtoku and other Japanese intellectuals of the early reform period studied not only Buddhism, but also the teachings of Chinese Confucianism. Like Buddhism, Confucianism was about a millennium old when it entered Japan and it had expanded greatly beyond the simple humanism of Confucius (551–479 B.C.) and his followers. The early Confucianists were concerned with man in society, and not with metaphysical speculation: they preached the cultivation of virtue and its application to public service. In his famous seventeen-article "Constitution" of 604, Prince Shōtoku, in addition to calling for the reverence of Buddhism, sought to propagate Confucian principles among the Japanese. Although this document may appear to be merely a collection of simplistic maxims—for example, that harmony should be prized and that ministers should obey imperial commands, behave decorously, reject their covetous desires, and attend court early in the morning—it constitutes the first statement in Japanese history of the need for ethical government.

Despite Prince Shōtoku's efforts to stimulate central reform, very little of real significance could be achieved so long as the aristocratic clans continued to exercise almost complete autonomy over their lands and the people on them. After Shōtoku's death in 622, the Soga, who had been the progressive advocates of Buddhism and the adoption of Chinese culture a half-century earlier, became the chief obstacles to reform of the decentralized *uji* system. In the early 640's, there formed at court an anti-Soga faction that included an imperial prince, leaders of various ministerial houses, and men who had studied in China. In 645, this group forcibly overthrew the Soga, reasserted the supremacy of the throne (the Soga were accused of having plotted to supplant the imperial family), and instituted the reform of Taika ("Great Change").

The Taika Reform was essentially a land reform patterned on the institutions of T'ang China. Although a paucity of records makes it impossible to determine just how extensively it was carried out, the intent of the Reform was to nationalize all agricultural land—that is, to make it the emperor's land—and to render all the people of the country direct subjects of the throne. Land was then to be parceled out in equal plots to farmers to work during their lifetimes. Upon the death of a farmer, his plot would revert back to the state for redistribution.

This is a gross oversimplification of the provisions of the Taika Reform, but it will suffice to show the idealistic concept of land equalization upon which the Reform rested. This concept had evolved from Confucian egalitarianism, which held that the equal division of land would render the people content and harmonious. Equality, however, was to apply only to the lower, peasant class of society. Members of the aristocracy were to receive special emoluments of land based on considerations such as rank, office, and meritorious service. In this way, the aristocracy was enabled to remain about as privileged economically as it had been before the Reform.

In practice, then, the equal-field system of the Taika Reform was only equal for some people. Moreover, its conscientious implementation would have required an administrative organization far more elaborate than Japan possessed in this age. Perhaps we should marvel that the system worked as effectively as it did; yet within a century it had begun to decay. The aristocratic families, along with Buddhist temples and Shinto shrines, started to accumulate private estates that were in many ways similar to the territorial holdings of the pre-Taika *uji*.

Another major act of reform was the promulgation by the court in 702 of the Taihō ("Great Treasure") Code, which specified the central and provincial offices of the new government (some of which were already functioning) and set forth general laws of conduct for the Japanese people. Also modeled on T'ang, the Taihō Code provided Japan with an elaborate and symmetrical bureaucratic structure of the sort that had evolved over a millennium or more in China. Although it functioned smoothly enough through most of the eighth century, it ultimately proved too weighty and inflexible for Japan in this early stage of its historical development. Beginning in the ninth century, new offices opened outside the provisions of the Taihō Code successively became the real centers of national power in Japan.

In 710, the court moved to the newly constructed city of Nara, which remained the capital of Japan until 784. Before this move, the site of the court had often been shifted, usually in and around the central provinces. Some claim that the Shinto view of death as a defilement—and the death of a sovereign as the defilement of an entire community—was the main reason for this constant moving about.

But another likely reason is that the loose control of the Yamato court over the territorial *uji* in earlier centuries necessitated its frequent transfer from place to place for strategic purposes. When the Soga became politically dominant in the late sixth century, they established the court at Asuka to the south of present-day Nara, where their seat of territorial power was located.

The epoch from the introduction of Buddhism in 552 until the Taika Reform of 645 is generally known in art history as the Asuka period. Most, if not all, of the Buddhist statuary, painting, and temple architecture of the Asuka period was produced by Chinese and Korean craftsmen. It is therefore not until a later age that we can speak of the true beginnings of Japanese Buddhist art. Nevertheless, the treasures of the Asuka period, which are in the manner of China's Six Dynasties era (220–589), are of inestimable value not only because of their individual merits but also because they constitute the largest body of Six Dynasties-style art extant. Owing to warfare and other vicissitudes, few examples remain in China or Korea.

Although the first Buddhist temples in Japan were constructed by the Soga in the late sixth century, none has survived. Of the buildings still standing, by far the oldest—and indeed the oldest wooden buildings in the world—are at the Hōryūji Temple, located to the southwest of Nara. Originally constructed in 607 under the patronage of Prince Shōtoku, the Hōryūji may have been partly or entirely destroyed by fire in 670 and rebuilt shortly after the turn of the century. Even so, it contains buildings that clearly antedate those of any other temple in Japan.

Buddhist temples of this age were arranged in patterns known as *garan*. Although the *garan* varied in the number and arrangement of their structures, they usually had certain common features: a roofed gallery in the form of a square or rectangle, with an entrance gate in the center of its southern side that enclosed the main compound of the temple; a so-called golden hall to house the temple's principal images of devotion; a lecture hall; and at least one pagoda, a type of building derived from the Indian stupa and originally intended to contain the relic of a Buddhist saint. At the Hōryūji, the golden hall *Figs. 8-9* and a single, five-storied pagoda are located to the right and left inside the entrance gate, and the lecture hall is to the rear of the compound, actually integrated into the northern side of the gallery. The chief characteristics of the golden hall—probably the oldest of the Hōryūji buildings and especially representative of the Buddhist architectural style of the Six Dynasties period—are its raised stone base and its hipped and gabled upper roof.

Among the statuary in the golden hall is a trinity of figures in bronze, set in relief against flaming body halos. According to an in-

Fig. 10 scription, this was cast in 623 to commemorate the death two years earlier of Prince Shōtoku. It shows the historical Buddha, Gautama (in Japanese, Shaka), flanked by two attendant bodhisattvas. The Buddha is seated cross-legged on a dais with his clothing draped in the stylized waterfall pattern of the Six Dynasties period. He also strikes one of the many mudras or special hand positions of Buddhist iconography (the upraised hand here gives assurance against fear and the open palm is a sign of charity); and he has a protuberance on his head and a third eye that indicate extraordinary knowledge and vision and are among some twenty-three bodily signs introduced by the Mahayana Buddhists to indicate Gautama's superhuman qualities. The expression on the faces of all three figures of the trinity is that known as the "archaic smile," whose impersonality and vague mysteriousness contrast strikingly with the unabashed frankness we noted in the countenances of many of the early native *haniwa* figurines of human beings.

The bodhisattvas, both of whom stand on pedestals of lotus blossoms, are attired in the sort of princely garb that Gautama wore before he renounced the world. In the Buddhist tradition, the lotus, which may be found floating on the surface of the murkiest water, stands for purity. It can also symbolize the universe, with each of its petals representing a separate, constituent world.

Two excellent examples of wooden sculpture from the Asuka period are the figure in the Hōryūji of the bodhisattva Kannon, known as the *Figs. 11–12* Kudara Kannon, and the seated image in a nearby nunnery of Miroku, the buddha of the future. Both statues have features of the Six Dynasties style—for example, the stiff, saw-toothed drapery of the Kannon and the waterfall pattern in the lower folds of the Miroku's clothing. Yet, there is also a suggestion in both of the voluptuousness and earthly sensuality that were to appear later in the sculpture of the T'ang. The Miroku, whose surface appears like metal after centuries of rubbing with incense, has been particularly admired for its tender, dreamlike expression and for the gentle manner in which the hand is raised to the face. It strikes a mudra characteristic of Miroku statues.

The art epoch from the Taika Reform of 645 until the founding of the great capital city of Nara in 710 is usually called the Hakuhō period after one of the calendrical designations of the age. It was a time of vigorous reforming effort in Japan, directed by the imperial family itself; and some of the more powerful sovereigns in Japanese history ruled during the Hakuhō period. Of these, it was the emperor Temmu (reigned 673–86) who first advanced Buddhism as the great protector of the country and of the imperial family. Buddhism had previously been patronized by individuals, such as Prince Shōtoku and certain chieftains of the Soga family. Under Temmu and his successors, Buddhism received the official patronage of the court, which sponsored the construction of a series of great temples during the late seventh and eighth centuries.

In both sculpture and painting, the Hakuhō period marked the transition in Japan, after a time lag of about a half-century, from the Buddhist art style of China's Six Dynasties era to that of the T'ang. A bronze trinity (now situated in the Yakushiji Temple in *Fig. 13* Nara) of Yakushi, the healing buddha, and two attendant bodhisattvas exemplifies the great T'ang style of sculpture as it was produced in Japan. The main elements of this style can perhaps best be seen in the figures of the bodhisattvas: for example, in their sensuously curved and fleshy bodies, their raised hair-styling, and their more naturally hanging draperies.

The finest examples of painting from the Hakuhō period are the frescoes that adorn the interior of the golden hall at the Hōryūji. Although a fire in 1949 badly damaged these frescoes, photographs show how they formerly appeared. An attendant bodhisattva in one *Fig. 14* of the trinities depicted was especially well preserved and has been widely admired as one of the best examples of T'ang painting. Quite similar in appearance to the bodhisattvas in the Yakushi trinity of bronze statues, it shows the great skill in linear technique of the artist of this age. Its even lines have been called wirelike in contrast to the alternately thick and thin lines, derived from the brushwork of calligraphy, that were later so favored by painters in China and Japan.

The site for Nara was chosen by Chinese geomancy, the art of selecting suitable terrain on the basis of the favorable arrangement of its surrounding hills and the auspicious character of its "wind and water." Modeled after the T'ang capital of Ch'ang-an, although on a smaller scale, Nara was laid out in orderly fashion with the palace enclosure in the north-center, a grand boulevard running down its middle to the city's main gate of entrance in the south, and evenly intersecting north-south and east-west avenues. Unlike the Chinese, the Japanese never constructed walled cities; and although the population of Nara probably reached 200,000 in the eighth century, making it Japan's first truly urban center, contemporary accounts describe it as a city of open spaces with many fields interspersed among the buildings.

The orderliness of the original plan for Nara paralleled the balanced arrangement of the governmental offices and boards elaborated in the Taihō Code, and reflected the fundamental Chinese taste for symmetry in such matters. Some have speculated that the Japanese, on the other hand, inherently prefer asymmetry. In any case, just as they ultimately deviated from China's form of a balanced bureaucracy, the Japanese also failed to develop Nara as planned. The present city lies almost entirely in the northeastern suburbs of the eighth-century plan, and only recently placed markers enable us to see where the palace enclosure and other important sites of the original Nara were located. Kyoto, which became the seat of the court in 794 after its move from Nara, was also laid out symmetrically like Ch'ang-an; and it too spread erratically into the northeastern suburbs. But, whereas Kyoto was often devastated by warfare and other disasters during the medieval period and has few buildings within its city limits that predate the sixteenth century, Nara has retained substantially intact a number of splendid edifices and their contents dating from the eighth century.

Even today, the visitor to Nara can recapture much of the splendor of the brilliant youth of Japanese civilization. Nevertheless, it is difficult, in view of the later introversion of Japanese society, to envision how extraordinarily cosmopolitan Nara must have been in the eighth century. The Japanese of the Nara period were the eager pupils of Chinese civilization, and T'ang China was then the greatest empire in the world. The Buddhist art of China, which the Japanese fervently emulated, was an amalgam of many influences, not only from India but also from regions as remote as Persia, Greece, and the Byzantine empire, all of which were in contact with China by means of the overland caravan route known as the Silk Road. *Objets d'art*, many still preserved in Nara, were imported from these exotic places; and the Japanese court of the eighth century welcomed visitors from India and other parts of Asia outside China, visitors of a variety that would not appear in Japan again until modern times.

One unusual aspect of Nara civilization was the degree of dependence of the Japanese on the Chinese written language. There is no archeological or other evidence to indicate that the Japanese ever independently attempted to devise a script of their own. The apparent reason is simply that, in remote times, they became aware of the sophisticated writing system of China and, as they advanced in the ways of civilization, were content to use Chinese for purposes other than speech, much as Latin was employed in Europe during the Middle Ages.

This could not, however, be a permanently satisfactory arrangement, since structurally the Chinese and Japanese languages are vastly different. Chinese is monosyllabic, terse, and has no grammatical inflections. Tense and mood are either ignored or expressed by means of syntax and word position within a sentence. Japanese, on the other hand, is polysyllabic, diffuse and, like the Indo-European tongues, highly inflected.

After some fumbling starts in the Nara period, the Japanese in the ninth century finally evolved a syllabary of approximately fifty symbols (derived from Chinese characters) called *kana*. Although they could thenceforth theoretically write their language exclusively in *kana*, they had by this time also imported a great number of Chinese words into their vocabulary, words that were most appropriately written with Chinese characters (even though they were pronounced differently in Japanese).

Ultimately, the Japanese came to write in a mixture of Chinese characters and *kana*. In the modern language, the characters are used mainly for substantives, adjectives, and verbal stems, and the *kana* symbols are employed as grammatical markers and for the writing (among other things) of adverbs and foreign names. There is little question that Japanese is the most complex written language in the world today, and the modern man who holds utility to be the ultimate value must sorely lament that the Japanese ever became burdened with the Chinese writing system. Yet, from the aesthetic standpoint, the Chinese characters have been infinitely enriching, and through the centuries have provided an intimate cultural bond between the Chinese and Japanese (as well as the Koreans, who have also utilized Chinese ideographs) that is one of the most significant features of East Asian civilization.

The oldest extant books of the Japanese are two mythico-historical works entitled *Kojiki* (*Record of Ancient Matters*) and *Nihon Shoki* (*Chronicles of Japan*), completed in 712 and 720, respectively. Prince Shōtoku supposedly wrote texts a century earlier on both Buddhism and history, but these were destroyed in the burning of the Soga family's library at the time of the 645 Taika coup.

It is fitting that Japan's earliest remaining works, composed at a time when the country was so strongly under the civilizing influence of China, should be of a historical character. In the Confucian tradition, the writing of history has always been held in the highest esteem, since Confucianists believe that the lessons of the past provide the best guide for ethical rule in the present and future. In contrast to the Indians, who have always been absorbed with metaphysical and religious speculation and scarcely at all with history, the Chinese are among the world's greatest record-keepers. They revere the written word, no doubt even more so because of the evocative nature of their ideographic script, and they transmitted this reverence for writing to the Japanese at an early date.

The *Kojiki* consists of an account of Japan from its creation to approximately the year A.D. 500, plus additional genealogical data about the imperial family for the next century and a quarter. Unreliable as history, it is written in a complex style that employs Chinese ideographs both in the conventional manner and to represent phonetically the sounds of the Japanese language of the eighth century. Because of its difficulty, the *Kojiki* received scant attention for more than a thousand years; not until the great scholar Motoori Norinaga (1730–1801) devoted more than three decades to its decipherment did its contents become widely known even among the Japanese.

The *Kojiki* and *Nihon Shoki* (whose first part covers much the same ground) are the principal repositories of Japan's extraordinarily rich mythology, a mythology derived from a variety of materials including ancient songs and legends, word etymologies, professed genealogies, and religious rites. Although the two works contain numerous variant tales, they give essentially the same account of the course of Japan up to the eve of recorded history in the sixth century. Japanese scholars of the twentieth century have proved conclusively that this central narrative of myths, which tells of the descent of the imperial family from the omnipotent Sun Goddess and of its assumption of eternal rule on earth, was entirely contrived sometime during the reform period of the late sixth and seventh centuries to justify the claim to sovereignty of the reigning imperial dynasty. Moreover, both books, but particularly the *Kojiki*, have been shaped to give antiquity and luster to the genealogies of the leading courtier families of the same period.

In contrast to the *Kojiki*, the *Nihon Shoki* is written in Chinese and has been read and studied throughout the ages. It is also a much longer work and contains, in addition to the mythology, a generally reliable history of the sixth and seventh centuries. Indeed, it is virtually the only written source for affairs in Japan during this age and became the first of six "national histories" that cover events up to 887.

Nara civilization reached its apogee in the Tempyō epoch of Emperor Shōmu (reigned 724–49). Shōmu is remembered as perhaps the most devoutly Buddhist emperor in Japanese history, and certainly Buddhism enjoyed unprecedented favor during his reign. Yet, this favor seems to have been based more on adoration than understanding. The so-called six sects of Nara Buddhism were highly complex metaphysical systems imported from China that, doctrinally, provided little more than intellectual exercise for a handful of priestly devotees in Japan. Some were never established as independent sects, and none acquired a significant following among the Japanese people.

Judged by the great rage at Nara for the copying of sutras to obtain health and prosperity, Buddhism still held its appeal as potent magic. The particular favor enjoyed by the healing buddha, Yakushi, suggests that the primitive faith-healing instincts of the Japanese were widely aroused by this popular Mahayanist deity.

But by far the most significant role of Buddhism in the Tempyō epoch was as the great protector of the state. Shōmu, who founded a national Buddhist center at the Tōdaiji Temple in Nara and caused branch temples and nunneries to be constructed in the provinces, carried to its climax the policy of state sponsorship of Buddhism inaugurated by Temmu half a century earlier. Ironically, Shōmu's great undertaking so taxed the public resources of the Nara court that, far from strengthening central rule as he wished, it was probably the single most important factor in stimulating a decline in national administration over the next century and a half.

Whatever the long-range effects of its construction on the course of political events, the Tōdaiji became one of the greatest Buddhist establishments in Japan and the focal point for the brilliant age of Tempyō art. Compared to the Hōryūji, the Tōdaiji was laid out on a   *Fig. 15* mammoth scale. It was spread over an extensive tract of land and its central image, housed in the largest wooden structure in the world, was a bronze statue 53 feet tall of the cosmic buddha Vairochana (called in Japanese *daibutsu* or "great buddha") that required eight   *Fig. 16* attempts before it was successfully cast. At the *daibutsu's* "eye-opening" ceremony in 752, when a cleric from India painted in the pupils of its eyes to give it symbolic life, there were some 10,000 Buddhist priests in attendance and many visitors from distant lands. It was by all accounts one of the grandest occasions in early Japanese history.

Shortly before the eye-opening ceremony, Shōmu, who in 749 had abdicated the throne in favor of his daughter, appeared before the *daibutsu* and humbly declared himself a servant to the three Buddhist treasures (the buddha, the law, and the priesthood). This act was the high point in the Nara court's public infatuation with Buddhism. Although many later sovereigns were personally devout Buddhists, none after Shōmu ever made this sort of official gesture of submission to Buddhism or to any religion other than Shinto.

Among the many excellent examples of Tempyō art at the Tōdaiji are statues in two new mediums, clay and dry lacquer. In the unusual technique of dry lacquer sculpture, the artist began with either a clay base or a wooden frame and built up a shell consisting of alternate layers of fabric—mainly hemp—and lacquer. The very nature of the material made a certain stiffness in the trunks and limbs of the finished figures inevitable. Nevertheless, as can clearly be seen in one of the fierce guardian deities at the Tōdaiji, the sculptors in dry lacquer were   *Fig. 17* able to achieve much of the realistic detailing that was so characteristic of the T'ang-inspired art of the Tempyō period.

Possibly the most famous work in dry lacquer is the image at the Tōshōdaiji in Nara of the blind Chinese priest Ganjin (688–763),   *Fig. 18* who after several unsuccessful attempts made the perilous crossing to Japan in 754 to found one of the six Nara sects. This is the oldest surviving portrait of· an actual person in Japanese history. There is a painting from the late seventh century of Prince Shōtoku and two of his sons, but it was done many years after the prince's death and was drawn in such a stylized Chinese fashion that the artist obviously made no attempt to portray the features of real individuals. The Ganjin statue, on the other hand, is extraordinarily lifelike and shows the priest in an attitude of intense concentration. It was this kind of emotionally moving realism that so greatly impressed Japanese sculptors of later centuries when they looked back for inspiration to the classical art of the Tempyō period.

Fig. 19 Near the Tōdaiji and originally part of the temple complex is a remarkable building called the Shōsōin. It has the appearance of a gigantic, elongated log cabin with its floor raised some 9 feet off the ground on massive wooden pillars. Actually, the Shōsōin consists of three separate units that are joined together, each with its own entranceway, and it is a storehouse of world art from the eighth century. It has stood intact for more than eleven centuries and before modern times was opened only infrequently, sometimes remaining sealed for periods of up to a century or more. Because of its special construction—in addition to a raised floor, it has sides made of logs that expand and contract to maintain the temperature and humidity inside at a more even level—the Shōsōin has preserved its contents in near perfect condition.

Of the 10,000 or so items contained in the Shōsōin, more than 600 were the personal belongings of Emperor Shōmu; they include books, clothing, swords and other weapons, Buddhist rosaries, musical instruments, mirrors, screens, and gaming boards. There are also the ritual objects used in the eye-opening ceremony for the *daibutsu*, as well as many maps, administrative documents, medicines, and masks of wood and dry lacquer used in *gigaku*, a form of dance learned from China that was popular at Buddhist temples during the Nara period.

The imported objects come from virtually every part of the known world of Asia and Europe—including China, Southeast and Central Asia, India, Arabia, Persia, Assyria, Egypt, Greece, and Rome—and include a vast variety of fabrics, household belongings, blown and cut glass, ceramicware, paintings, and statuary.

The outpouring of visual art in the Tempyō period was accompanied by the first great blossoming of Japanese poetry. Although there are a number of simple and artless songs in both the *Kojiki* and *Nihon Shoki* and although efforts to poetize are very ancient in Japan, the compilation about mid-eighth century of the *Man'yōshū* (*Collection of a Myriad Leaves*) marked the true beginning of the Japanese poetic tradition. A lengthy collection of some 4,500 poems, the *Man'yōshū* is not only Japan's first anthology but in the minds of many the finest, astonishing as this may seem for so early a work. Some of the *Man'yōshū* poems are spuriously attributed to emperors and other lofty individuals of the fourth and fifth centuries, an age shrouded in myth, and a great many more are anonymous. Its poems appear in fact to constitute a sampling of composition from about the middle of the seventh century to the middle of the eighth, although we cannot know how representative this sampling is of all the poems that must have been written in Japan during that period.

Several features of the *Man'yōshū* set it apart from later anthologies. First, it possesses a kind of native freshness and youthful vigor in its verses that was lost in later centuries after Japanese culture had been more fully transformed by the influence of continental civilization. Secondly, its poems appear to have been written by people from many classes of society, including peasants, frontier guards, and even beggars, as well as the aristocrats who through much of the premodern era completely monopolized poetic composition. Some modern scholars believe that those *Man'yōshū* poems whose authors appear to have been non-aristocratic were, in reality, composed by courtiers who "went primitive." Nevertheless, the poems were at least written from the standpoint of the non-aristocrat, a fact that distinguishes them from virtually all the other poetry composed in Japan for many centuries to come.

A third feature of the *Man'yōshū* is the variety (by Japanese standards) of its poetic forms. Included in it are a number of so-called long poems (*chōka*) that possess a considerable grandeur and sweep. Yet, even at this time the Japanese showed a marked preference for shorter verse, and the great majority of poems in the *Man'yōshū* are in the *tanka* ("short poem")[2] form of thirty-one syllables—consisting of five lines of 5, 7, 5, 7, and 7 syllables—that was employed almost exclusively by poets for the next 500 years or more. Even when poets once again turned to other forms, they usually selected those that were variants of the *tanka*. For example, the linked verse that became popular from about the fourteenth century on was composed by two or more poets who divided the *tanka* into two "links" (one made up of the first three lines of 5, 7, and 5 syllables and the other of the last two lines of 7 and 7 syllables), which could be joined together endlessly. And the famous seventeen-syllable *haiku* that came into fashion in the seventeenth century consisted simply of the first link of the *tanka*.

No complete explanation can be given of the Japanese predilection for brief poetry, but it is certainly due in large part to the nature of the Japanese language. Japanese has very few vowel sounds and is constructed almost solely of independent vowels (*a, i, u, e, o*) and short, "open" syllables that consist of a consonant and a vowel (for example, *ka, su, mo*). The language therefore lacks the variety of sound necessary for true poetic rhyme: indeed, it rhymes too readily. Moreover, it has little stress, another element often used in prosody. Without recourse to rhyme or stress, Japanese poets have generally found it difficult to write lengthy pieces. The longer the poem, the greater the risk that it will become indistinguishable from prose. Instead, poets have since earliest times preferred shorter poetic forms, usually written in combinations of five- and seven-syllable lines. No one has been able to say with certainty why the five- and seven-syllable line units have been so preferred, although one interesting conjecture is that they are another reflection of the Japanese taste for the asymmetrical.

Precluded by the scope of the *tanka* from writing extended narratives or developing complex ideas, poets have concentrated on imagery to elicit direct emotional responses from their audiences. They have also fully exploited the exceptional capacity of the Japanese language for subtle shadings and nuance, and have utilized certain devices such as the "pivot word" (*kakekotoba*) to enrich the texture of their lines and to make possible the expression of double and even triple meanings. Use of the pivot word can be illustrated by the line *Senkata naku*, "There is nothing to be done." *Naku* renders the phrase negative, but at the same time it has the independent meaning of "to cry." Thus, an expression of despair may simultaneously convey the idea of weeping.

During the Heian period (794–1185), when poetry became the exclusive property of the courtier class, strict rules were evolved that severely limited the range of poetic topics and the moods under which poets could compose. Poetry was intended to be moving but not overpowering. As an eminent critic of the early tenth century said, poets should be inspired to verse

> when they looked at the scattered blossoms of a spring morning; when they listened of an autumn evening to the falling of the leaves; when they sighed over the snow and waves reflected with each passing year by their looking glasses; when they were startled into thoughts on the brevity of life by seeing the dew on the grass or the foam on the water; when, yesterday all proud and splendid, they have fallen from fortune into loneliness; or when, having been dearly loved, are neglected.[3]

By contrast, the *Man'yōshū* contains poems dealing with many of the subjects that later poets came to regard as unfitting or excessively harsh for their elegant poeticizing, such as inconsolable grief upon the death of a loved one, poverty, and stark human suffering. A "long poem" from the anthology expresses one poet's feelings after the loss of his wife:

Since in Karu lived my wife,
I wished to be with her to my heart's content;
But I could not visit her constantly
Because of the many watching eyes—
Men would know of our troth,
Had I sought her too often.
So our love remained secret like a rock-pent pool;
I cherished her in my heart,
Looking to aftertime when we should be together,
And lived secure in my trust
As one riding a great ship.
Suddenly there came a messenger
Who told me she was dead—
Was gone like a yellow leaf of autumn,
Dead as the day dies with the setting sun,
Lost as the bright moon is lost behind the cloud,
Alas, she is no more, whose soul
Was bent to mine like bending seaweed!

When the word was brought to me
I knew not what to do nor what to say;
But restless at the mere news,
And hoping to heal my grief
Even a thousandth part,
I journeyed to Karu and searched the market place
Where my wife was wont to go!

There I stood and listened
But no voice of her I heard,
Though the birds sang in the Unebi Mountains;
None passed by who even looked like my wife.
I could only call her name and wave my sleeve.[4]

One of the most famous of the *Man'yōshū* poems is the "Dialogue on Poverty," which begins with these lines:

On the night when the rain beats,
Driven by the wind,
On the night when the snowflakes mingle
With the sleety rain,
I feel so helplessly cold.
I nibble at a lump of salt,
Sip the hot, oft-diluted dregs of sake;
And coughing, snuffling,

And stroking my scanty beard,
I say in my pride,
"There's none worthy, save I!"
But I shiver still with cold.
I pull up my hempen bedclothes,
Wear what few sleeveless clothes I have,
But cold and bitter is the night!
As for those poorer than myself,
Their parents must be cold and hungry,
Their wives and children beg and cry.
Then, how do you struggle through life? [5]

The poem cited above on the death of a wife is by Kakinomoto Hitomaro, the finest poet represented in the *Man'yōshū* and perhaps the greatest in all Japanese literature. Few details remain about Kakinomoto's life, although it is known that he was of low courtier rank, held some provincial posts, and served as court poet during the late seventh and early eighth centuries. The function of court poet in Kakinomoto's time entailed the composition of commemorative poems or encomiums on occasions such as courtly journeys or imperial hunts and of eulogies upon the deaths of members of the imperial family. This use of poetry for the expression of lofty sentiment in response to prominent public events or ceremonies was no doubt influenced by the Chinese practice, but it was not perpetuated in Japan much beyond Kakinomoto's time. Japanese poets have always been powerfully drawn to personal lyricism rather than the pronouncement of what may be regarded as more socially elevated, if not precisely moralistic, feelings. The early Japanese language was particularly suited to lyrical expression, and the extent to which Japanese poets went to retain that quality can be seen in how carefully they protected their native poetic vocabulary, consisting mostly of concrete, descriptive terms, from the intrusion of more abstract and complex Chinese loan words. Kakinomoto Hitomaro was fully capable of writing lyrical poetry, as his deeply felt lament on the death of his wife reveals; but he also composed sustained verse, particularly in the "long poem" form, on topics of public and stately relevance that were not regarded as the proper concern of later poets.

In addition to composing poetry in their own language, the early Japanese also wrote verse in Chinese. The difficulties of writing in a foreign tongue are obviously enormous; yet, Chinese culture was held in the highest esteem by the Japanese, and for a time, especially during the early ninth century, it appeared that the courtiers might cease entirely their literary efforts in the Japanese language and devote themselves exclusively to composition in Chinese. Fortunately for the evolution of a native culture, this did not occur. But Chinese nevertheless continued to hold much attraction for the Japanese, both as a classical language and, in the realm of poetry, as a means to express those ideas of a complex or abstract nature for which the *tanka* was totally inadequate. The earliest anthology of Chinese poetry by Japanese, the *Kaifūsō (Fond Recollections of Poetry)*, was compiled in the mid-Nara period, about the same time as the *Man'yōshū*. An example taken from this anthology is the following piece, "Composed at a Party for the Korean Envoy":

Mountain windows scan the deep valley;
Groves of pine line the evening streams.
We have asked to our feast the distant envoy;
At this table of parting we try the pleasures of poetry.
The crickets are hushed, the cold night wind blows;
Geese fly beneath the clear autumn moon.
We offer this flower-spiced wine in hopes
To beguile the cares of your long return.[6]

3

The Court at Its Zenith

IN 794, THE COURT MOVED to the newly constructed city of Heian or Kyoto, about 28 miles north of Nara. The decision to leave Nara was apparently made for several reasons. Many people at court had become alarmed over the degree of official favor accorded to Buddhism and the manifold opportunities presented to Buddhist priests to interfere in the business of state. Their fears were particularly aroused when an empress (Shōmu's daughter) became romantically involved with a faith-healing priest named Dōkyō. Before the loss of his patroness, who died in 770, Dōkyō rose to the highest ecclesiastical and ministerial positions in the land and even sought, through the pronouncement of an oracle, to ascend the throne itself. Dōkyō thus achieved notoriety in Japanese history as a commoner who blatantly challenged the imperial family's sacrosanct claim to reign exclusively over Japan. The Dōkyō affair appears to have convinced the court of two things: that Nara, with its many Buddhist establishments and its ubiquitous priesthood, was no longer satisfactory for the conduct of secular affairs; and that henceforth the line of succession to the throne should be confined solely to male members of the imperial family.

Another reason for the move to Kyoto was that Nara, situated in the mountainous southern region of the central provinces, had become too cramped as a location for the court. Kyoto provided much freer access, both by land and water, to the rest of the country. In particular, the court could more readily undertake from Kyoto the expansion and consolidation of its control over the eastern and northern provinces, a region that had until this time been occupied chiefly by recalcitrant tribesmen known as Emishi.

The Emishi, referred to in early accounts as "hairy people," have

32

often been identified with the Ainu, a race of Caucasians who live in Hokkaido, the northernmost of Japan's major islands, and number today only a few thousand. It was long believed that the Ainu once occupied all of Japan and, driven steadily eastward and northward by the advance of Yamato civilization, suffered a fate similar to that of the American Indians. Since the Ainu, as Caucasians, have considerably more body hair than the Japanese, it appeared obvious that they were the very "hairy Emishi" mentioned in the pages of the *Nihon Shoki* and other historical accounts. Yet, there are several reasons to doubt this linking of Ainu and Emishi. For one thing, the expression "hairy people" was loosely and pejoratively applied in both China and Japan to uncivilized people in general—people who were regarded as unkempt, dirty, and uncouth—and did not necessarily imply that such people were racially endowed with a greater quantity of hair. Also, mummified bodies of Japanese warrior chieftains of later centuries in the north, who reportedly had Emishi mothers, have been examined and found to possess none of the bodily characteristics of the Ainu.

There is, then, a strong possibility that the Ainu, whose precise origins remain a mystery, never settled extensively south of Hokkaido; and that the Emishi were in fact ethnically the same as the Japanese, but were not incorporated into the Yamato state when it was established in the central and western provinces during the fourth through the sixth centuries. In any event, after several failures, armies dispatched by the Heian court finally inflicted decisive defeat on the Emishi in the early years of the ninth century and thus permanently eliminated the threat posed by these ferocious tribesmen on the eastern frontier.

After the move to Kyoto, the court attempted to encourage the activities of Buddhist prelates who would devote their attention to spiritual rather than worldly matters. Among the first to receive court patronage was Saichō (767–822), who journeyed to China in 804 and returned to found the Tendai Sect of Buddhism at the Enryakuji, a temple he had earlier opened on Mount Hiei northeast of Kyoto. The Enryakuji was in a particularly favorable spot, since it was believed that evil spirits invaded from the northeast and it could serve as guardian of the capital.

Tendai was broadly founded on the teachings of the Mahayana or Greater Vehicle school of Buddhism. Its basic scripture, the *Lotus Sutra*, purportedly contained Gautama's last sermon in which he revealed to his disciples the universality of the buddha potential. The Buddha asserted that until this time he had allowed individuals to practice Hinayana, the Lesser Vehicle, and to seek their own enlightenments. Now mankind was prepared for the final truth that everyone could attain buddhahood. We noted that this universalistic concept of Mahayana was accompanied both by a tendency to regard the Buddha as a transcendent, rather than earthly, being and by adulation for the bodhisattva, or buddha-to-be, who would assist others on the path to buddhahood.

The Tendai center at the Enryakuji played an extremely prominent role in premodern Japanese history. It became a vast complex of more than 3,000 buildings, where priests engaged in a wide range of both spiritual and secular studies. In the best Far Eastern tradition, the Tendai priests sought to synthesize all known religious truths and practices; and ultimately it was Tendai that, beginning in the late Heian period, spawned the various popular sects that finally spread Buddhism to the common people throughout Japan.

Another, and less edifying, way in which the Enryakuji attained distinction in premodern times was as a center for *akusō* or "rowdy monks." During the Nara period, the court had strictly limited the entry of people other than members of the aristocracy into the Buddhist priesthood. But after the move of the capital to Kyoto, entry restrictions were relaxed and the more important Buddhist temples, which were already in the process of acquiring great wealth in landed estates, hired increasing numbers of peasants to serve in their private armies. By the tenth and eleventh centuries, these hordes of *akusō* had become regularly engaged not only in fighting among themselves but also in intimidating Kyoto into meeting their demands for such things as ecclesiastical positions at court and titles to desirable pieces of estate land.

The manner in which the Enryakuji monks commonly made their demands upon the court reveals something of the ties that had evolved by this time between Buddhist temples and Shinto shrines. Obtaining the sacred *kami* emblems of the Hie Shrine located at the foot of Mount Hiei, the monks placed them in a portable car and transported the car to the capital, where they deposited it at a busy intersection near the palace. Since no one dared touch the car, activities simply ceased in that part of the city until the monks, their demands met, condescended to remove it and carry it back to the mountain.

Although the Tendai Sect's Enryakuji Temple became a great national center for Buddhist studies in Japan, the particular kind of Buddhism that exerted the strongest influence at court during the early Heian period was Tantrism. Tantrism was a branch of Mahayana Buddhism established independently in India about A.D. 600 and subsequently transmitted to China and Japan. Because of its stress on incantations, spells, and primitive magic, Tantrism has been viewed by many outsiders as a corrupt and decadent phase of Buddhism after the period of its greatest historical flourishing. Insofar as one part of Tantrism became associated with Indian Shakti practices dealing with death, destruction, and living sacrifices, there may be some justification for this view. But the form of Tantrism that spread to the Far East did not embrace such grotesque practices. Known also as esoteric Buddhism because of its insistence on the secret transmission of its teachings, Tantrism came to hold a unique appeal for the aristocracy of the Heian court and to provide a powerful stimulus to the arts in Japan during the ninth and tenth centuries.

Tantrism was introduced to Japan as the Shingon ("true word") Sect by the priest Kūkai (774–835; also familiarly known by his posthumous canonical name of Kōbō Daishi, or Great Teacher Kōbō), who traveled to China in 804 on the same mission as Saichō. Kūkai, who founded a Shingon center atop Mount Kōya near modern Osaka, was without question one of the most outstanding figures in Japanese history. The distinguished Western scholar of Japan, Sir George Sansom, has said of him:

> His memory lives all over the country, his name is a household word in the remotest places, not only as a saint, but as a preacher, a scholar, a painter, an inventor, an explorer and—sure passport to fame—a great calligrapher.[7]

Among other things, Kūkai is credited with inventing the *kana* syllabary. Most likely *kana* was more the product of evolution than invention. But it is also believed that knowledge of Sanskrit provided at least some of the inspiration that led to *kana*, and Kūkai is known to have become an avid student of Sanskrit during his three-year stay in China.

Kūkai's scholarly accomplishments were imposing. In a tract entitled *The Ten Stages of Religious Consciousness*, he made perhaps the most famous attempt in Japanese history to synthesize and evaluate various religious beliefs according to their higher or lower "stages of consciousness." At the bottom, Kūkai placed the animal passions, where no religious consciousness at all existed; he then proceeded upward by stages through Confucianism, Taoism, various Hinayana and quasi-Mahayana sects, fully developed Mahayana and, finally, to the ultimate religious consciousness of Shingon itself.

Shingon is centered on belief in the cosmic buddha Vairochana (in Japanese, Dainichi). All things—including the historical Buddha, Gautama, and such transcendent beings as Yakushi (the healing buddha) and Amida (the buddha of the boundless light)—are merely manifestations of this universal entity. In order to enter into communion with Dainichi and to realize the essential oneness of all existence, the supplicant must utilize the Three Mysteries of speech, body, and mind. Proper ritual performance requires the coordinated practice of all three mysteries; but perhaps the most important is that of speech, which calls for the recitation of spells or "true words" (mantras in Sanskrit; *shingon* in Japanese). The use of words as spells has fascinated man throughout his existence, and the mantras of esoteric Buddhism derive from an ancient tradition. Probably the most famous mantra is the Tibetan phrase *Om mani padme hum* ("The jewel is in the lotus!"), but there are a great many others also employed in the religious supplications of esotericism.

The mysteries of the body are based primarily on the hand poses known as mudras. We have seen the use of mudras for iconographic purposes in sculpture and in pictorial representations of buddhas and bodhisattvas. In Shingon ritual, on the other hand, mudras are struck by the *believer* as he addresses himself to these superior beings.

Fig. 20   A device used in Shingon as an aid to meditation is the mandala, or cosmic diagram. Mandalas may simply be sketched on the ground and expunged after the completion of a rite; or they may be permanently produced as carvings and paintings. In Japan, the most common type of mandala is the hanging scroll, although there are also a number of mandalas carved in relief and painted on temple walls. These diagrams, which usually depict Dainichi surrounded by the myriad lesser figures of the Shingon pantheon, are often superior works of art. And indeed in the Heian period the exceptional visual attraction of the mandalas and other Shingon icons greatly helped to endear esotericism to the Kyoto courtiers, who were finely sensitive to beauty in all its forms.

It was by no means simply the visual delights of Shingon that made it so popular at the Heian court. Despite efforts during the Taika or Great Reform era to create a Confucian-type meritocracy under the throne, Japan's ruling class had remained preponderantly aristocratic: that is, birth almost invariably took precedence over ability or achievement. In the Nara period, there was some opportunity for men of modest backgrounds to advance by entering the Buddhist priesthood or by specializing in Chinese studies; but in Heian times the court reverted to a rigid hierarchical ordering of society determined solely by family origins. It is not surprising, therefore, that the Heian courtiers found congenial a sect like Shingon, which similarly asserted a fixed hierarchy among its pantheon of deities headed by Dainichi. Interestingly, Dainichi is written with the characters for "great sun"; and the Japanese were not slow to identify him with the supreme Shinto deity, the Sun Goddess. Going a step further, they were able to liken the gods of Shingon collectively to the community of *kami* from whom all the great courtier families claimed descent.

The exclusive, esoteric character of Shingon also appealed greatly to the Heian courtiers. Although Shingon, like Mahayana Buddhism in general, preached the universality of the buddha potential, in practice it confronted its would-be followers with such complex and time-consuming practices that only priests or leisured aristocrats could hope to master them. And in any case Shingon gave the general populace little chance even to attempt the practices by keeping them secret from all but a favored few. The mysteries of Shingon were theoretically transmitted solely by the teacher, or guru, to his direct disciples. Outsiders might derive some satisfaction from contemplating with awe the dark wonders of Shingon, but as the uninitiated they would forever be denied the highest rewards it promised.

So strongly did the courtiers favor Shingon that, in order to meet the competition, the Tendai Sect also evolved a form of esotericism. It is scarcely an exaggeration to say that esoteric Buddhism, particularly during the ninth and tenth centuries, permeated every aspect of the lives of the Heian aristocracy. Its aestheticism, exclusivity, and promise of realizing through arcane practices the buddha nature in this life were irresistible to the courtiers. Yet, esoteric Buddhism, although it may have been established on a high plane by Kūkai and his immediate successors, was particularly susceptible to corruption; and in the late Heian period, it degenerated to the point where its clergy engaged in base practices, accepting fees from the laity to secure direct benefits in health, fame, and prosperity.

An important trend among the new sects of Heian Buddhism was their move away from the busy centers of temporal life and political activity to mountainous, remote regions. Kyoto soon became as clustered with temples as Nara, but at least the example was set for some temples to locate where the temptations of worldly pleasures were minimal and where monks could truly lead the disciplined and meditative religious life.

Buddhism had entered Japan as part of a great reforming process aimed at centralization, and it was surely a sign of maturity that, after some two centuries, an increasing number of both secular and religious leaders saw the importance of drawing a distinction between the proper spheres of activity of the court (as an administrative body) and the Buddhist church. The Heian sects sought to sustain the idea of Buddhism as the guardian of the nation, and rowdy monks engaged in ugly quarrels over quite mundane issues; but still there was general recognition of the need henceforth to keep church and state separate.

The founding of temples in mountainous regions also brought significant changes in Buddhist architecture. Only two buildings remain from the early Heian period—the golden hall and pagoda of a Shingon temple, the Murōji, situated in a dense forest of towering cryptomeria about 40 miles from Kyoto—but we can tell from these, as well as from various reconstructions, what the new trends in architecture were. The orderly, *garan*-type layouts were abandoned by the mountain temples in favor of adapting the shapes and placement of their buildings to the special features of rough, uneven terrain. This kind of architectural integration with the natural environment seems to have been particularly to the liking of the Japanese. It was reminiscent of earlier Shinto architecture and, at the same time, revealed the Far Eastern impulse to merge with—rather than seek to overcome—nature. A keen sensitivity to nature and a desire to find human identity with it in all its manifestations are among the strongest themes in the Japanese cultural tradition.

Other features of Shinto architecture incorporated into both temple and secular buildings in the early Heian (or, to art historians, Jōgan) period were the elevation of floors above ground level and the thatching of roofs with cyprus bark instead of clay tiles. These features can *Fig. 21*   plainly be seen in the old imperial palace (Shishinden) in Kyoto. The buildings of the palace compound were frequently destroyed by fire, and the present structures, most of them erected in the nineteenth century, are not even situated in the same part of the city as the original compound. Nevertheless, they are faithful reproductions and, in the absence of other buildings, give us at least some idea of what the capital looked like in early Heian times.

Buddhist sculpture of the Jōgan period showed a marked change from the realistic, often grandly imposing works of the Tempyō epoch. The court had withdrawn its direct patronage of Buddhism and, although many temples became privately affluent through the acquisition of landed estates, there was no further urge to undertake such vast artistic projects as the casting of the *daibutsu*, which had required the concerted effort of many craftsmen. Jōgan statues were generally much smaller than those of Tempyō and were most likely carved by individual sculptors, who made very little use of the materials favored during Tempyō—bronze, clay, and dry lacquer—but preferred, instead, to work chiefly in wood. One reason for the new preference for wood was the interest aroused by the sandalwood statues imported from China about this time and in vogue at court.

Many Jōgan statues were carved out of single blocks of wood, a fact that helps account for their general smallness. They were also left either entirely unpainted or with only the lips and eyes tinted in order not to seal off the natural fragrance of the wood.

An excellent example of Jōgan sculpture in wood is the statue of the healing buddha, Yakushi, at the Jingoji in Kyoto. The rigid stance and stylized clothing of the buddha may appear to signify a reversion to an earlier, less sophisticated method of sculpture. But in fact they reflect the wish, in line with esoteric tastes, to produce figures that were unearthly and mysterious. The statue's facial expression is grim and forbidding, and its body is much heavier and more gross-looking than the typical Tempyō image. The "wave" pattern of its draperies is characteristic of Jōgan sculpture and can be seen even more sharply delineated in the seated image of the historical buddha at the Murōji.

Apart from the mandalas, virtually the only paintings extant from the Jōgan epoch are representations of ferocious and hideous creatures such as Fudō, "the immovable." These creatures, some of which have multiple heads and arms, were in reality the cosmic buddha, Dainichi, in altered forms, and their job was to frighten and destroy the enemies of Buddhism. Fudō is usually shown with a flaming body halo, a sword in one hand and a rope in the other.

Esoteric iconography inspired some Jōgan artists to attempt the first plastic representations of the deities of Shinto. Several of these *kami* figures still remain, but there is little to indicate that any real impetus was given at this time to evolve a new form of Shinto art.

The court of the early ninth century was outwardly perhaps even more enamored of Chinese civilization than its predecessor at Nara a century earlier. Chinese poetry was in particular the rage among Emperor Saga (reigned 809–23) and his intimates, who held competitions in Chinese versemanship, compiled anthologies in the manner of the *Kaifūsō*, and virtually ignored the *tanka*. It was also during Saga's reign that Kūkai was first received at court. A brilliant scholar, litterateur, and gifted writer in Chinese, Kūkai has been ranked along with Saga and Tachibana Hayanari, who headed the mission that Saichō and Kūkai accompanied to the continent in 804, as one of the three "great brushes" or calligraphers of the age. Kūkai had visited Ch'ang-an, the wondrous capital of T'ang, and had returned not only with many books and works of art but also with knowledge of the latest Chinese fashions, including the vogue for esoteric Buddhism. A contemporary observer might well have judged, from the preferences of such luminaries at court as Saga and Kūkai, that Japan of the early ninth century had indeed become a miniature model of China.

We can see in retrospect that the Japanese did not slavishly copy Chinese civilization; some important institutions never took root in Japanese soil and others were considerably remolded to suit the native setting. In addition to abandoning the fundamental Confucian principle of government by merit, the Japanese also ultimately rejected the T'ang "equal-field" system of land distribution. Within a few centuries, nearly all agricultural land in the country had fallen into the hands of the aristocracy as private estates. Along with a parallel deterioration of the court's provincial administration, this process created conditions (as we shall see in the next chapter) that gave rise to a warrior class in the provinces in mid- and late Heian times.

The most significant political development at court in the ninth century was the rise of a single clan—the Fujiwara—which was descended from one of the chief architects of the Great Reform and came to dominate the imperial family through marriage even more completely and for a much longer time than the Soga. Insinuating themselves ever closer to the throne, the Fujiwara in 858 assumed the office of imperial regent (held previously only by members of royalty, such as Prince Shōtoku) and within a century became the undisputed wielders of absolute power at court.

Fujiwara mastery over the imperial family was to a great extent made possible by the peculiarities of Heian marriage customs. Usually, although not invariably, courtiers of this age established formal residence in the homes of their wives. From the contemporary literature it appears that the typical courtier kept one or more secondary wives and mistresses and frequently was lax in visiting his principal wife, perhaps not calling upon her more than once or twice a month. Yet, the principal wife's home remained their joint residence and it was there that the children were raised. Although emperors did not actually move in with their Fujiwara wives, the offspring of such unions also were reared in the mansions of the maternal relatives. Between the late ninth and late eleventh centuries, emperors without exception were the sons of Fujiwara mothers, and in view of their upbringing no doubt identified themselves as closely with the Fujiwara as with the imperial family.

Even as the Fujiwara began their rise to power, the court reached the decision to terminate official relations with China. One reason for this decision, made sometime after the last mission of 838, was that the T'ang dynasty had fallen into decline and China was no longer a safe place for travel; but perhaps more fundamental was the fact that the Japanese did not feel the same need as before to look to China for guidance and inspiration. The long period of cultural borrowing, begun some two and a half centuries earlier, had at last come to an end.

The Japanese court of the late ninth century not only severed official relations with China; it also gradually withdrew from all but the most necessary dealings with the provinces of Japan itself. In contrast to its cosmopolitanism in the Nara period, the court in the tenth century became isolated to an extraordinary degree from the rest of Japanese society. Of the various causes for this isolation, one of the most decisive was the court's system of ministerial ranking by which infinitely greater luster and prestige was bestowed upon officials in the capital than upon those in the provinces. To accept and occupy a provincial post, the courtier was obliged not only to foresake the comforts and cultural attractions of the Heian capital, but also to suffer diminished status and even risk social opprobrium. For want of opportunity in Kyoto, some courtiers had no alternative; moreover, the possibility of acquiring new wealth in the provinces was tempting. But for a member of the upper nobility, life away from the capital was almost unthinkable. Even if given an important governorship, he would be apt either to send a deputy in his place or simply direct the vice-governor, usually a local magnate, to look after the administrative affairs of the province.

The epoch of the tenth century and most of the eleventh was one of "power and glory" for the Fujiwara regents. It was also an age when the Japanese brought to maturity their classical culture. Although it owed much to its Chinese antecedents, this culture was nevertheless genuinely unique and a true product of the native genius.

Of all the arts that flourished at court during the Fujiwara epoch, the one that most embodied its creative spirit was literature and, in particular, poetry. The ninth-century craze for Chinese verse waned with the trailing off of relations with the continent, and the courtiers turned their attention once again to the *tanka*. Before long, their passion for this traditional form of poetic expression was revived to the point of near insatiability and they devoted themselves endlessly to composition both in private and in the company of others at poetry contests, where teams of the right and left were called upon to compose on given themes. The ability to recognize a *tanka* allusion and to extemporize at least passable lines became absolutely essential, not only in the more formal tests of poetic competence to which the courtier was put, but also in everyday social intercourse. Probably no other society in history has placed so great a premium on versification.

Inseparable from the revival of interest in the *tanka*, and indeed the development of Fujiwara literature in general, was the evolution of the *kana* syllabary. Even at the height of enthusiasm for Chinese poetry at the court of Emperor Saga earlier in the ninth century, this means for writing in the vernacular was being perfected. Kūkai himself, as we have seen, was closely associated with the "invention" of *kana*.

During the time of Saga, three imperially authorized or official anthologies of Chinese poetry were compiled, and in 905 the first official anthology of *tanka*, the *Kokinshū* (*Collection of Ancient and Modern Poems*) was produced at court. Although the earlier, unofficial *Man'yōshū* had been a superb collection, it was the *Kokinshū* that truly set the standards for classical Japanese poetry. The *Man'yōshū* had been written by means of a complex use of Chinese ideographs to represent Japanese phonetics, and the Heian courtiers found it obscure and difficult to read. Moreover, the *Man'yōshū* set forth the sentiments of a quite different age. In the new world of the *Kokinshū*, refinement, taste, and decorum took absolute precedence over candor and vigorous emotional expression. The Heian poet, as we can observe in the following poems from the *Kokinshū*, was expected to versify at the proper time and in the proper mood:

> This perfectly still
> Spring day bathed in the soft light
> From the spread-out sky,
> Why do the cherry blossoms
> So restlessly scatter down?

> Although I am sure
> That he will not be coming,
> In the evening light
> When the locusts shrilly call
> I go to the door and wait.[8]

It was eminently proper to respond sensitively to the charm of a spring day and to reflect wistfully upon the brevity of life as called to mind by the scattering of the cherry blossoms; it was also most fitting for the poet to express loneliness and yearning for a lover, so long as he did not carry his feelings to the point of uncontrollable anger or anguish at being neglected.

The author of the first poem above was Ki no Tsurayuki (868?–946), a leading poet of the day and one of the compilers of the *Kokinshū*. Ki also wrote the preface to this anthology and thereby produced not only the first important piece of literary criticism in Japanese history but also an excellent statement of the standards that guided the courtly taste in versification. In the opening lines to the preface, Ki expressed the deep psychological, social, and aesthetic significance that he, as a representative of the Heian courtier class of the early tenth century, attached to poetry:

The poetry of Japan has its roots in the human heart and flourishes in the countless leaves of words. Because human beings possess interests of so many kinds, it is in poetry that they give expression to the meditations of their hearts in terms of the sights appearing before their eyes and the sounds coming to their ears. Hearing the warbler sing among the blossoms and the frog in his fresh waters—is there any living being not given to song? It is poetry which, without exertion, moves heaven and earth, stirs the feelings of gods and spirits invisible to the eye, softens the relations between men and women, calms the hearts of fierce warriors.[9]

In all his actions the Heian courtier aspired to *miyabi*—courtly refinement—and it was this quality that became the most enduring aesthetic legacy of Japan's classical age. Even after rough provincial warriors rose to become the new rulers of the land in the late twelfth century, they instinctively responded to and sought to perpetuate the courtly tradition as epitomized in *miyabi*. The turbulent centuries of the medieval age produced many new cultural pursuits that catered to the tastes of various classes of society, including warriors, merchants, and even peasants. Yet, coloring nearly all these pursuits was *miyabi*, reflected in a fundamental preference on the part of the Japanese for the elegant, the restrained, and the subtly suggestive. There is indeed a strong temptation to assert that *miyabi*—as first codified, so to speak, in the poems of the *Kokinshū*—has constituted the most basic theme in Japanese aesthetics. As one Western authority has observed, "Nothing in the West can compare with the role which aesthetics has played in Japanese life and history since the Heian period"; and "the miyabi spirit of refined sensibility is still very much in evidence" in modern aesthetic criticism.[10]

In addition to reviving interest in Japanese poetry, the use of *kana* also made possible the evolution of a native prose literature. The origins of the mature prose of the Fujiwara epoch can only be roughly identified, although they seem to lie primarily in two early kinds of works, the so-called tale (*monogatari*) and the private diary (*nikki*). The term "*monogatari*" has been used loosely through much of Japanese history for a wide variety of writings, from purely fictional prose to quasi-historical chronicles. In its earliest usage, however, *monogatari* meant certain supernatural or fantastic tales that derived both from oral folk legends and from Buddhist miracle stories written in Chinese. The oldest extant *monogatari* of this type is *The Tale of the Bamboo Cutter* (*Taketori Monogatari*), dating from the late ninth or tenth century. It is the story of an old man who finds a princess in a piece of bamboo. The princess, upon growing into comely maidenhood, tantalizes various suitors by refusing to marry them unless they perform hopelessly difficult deeds. Finally, when she is embarrassingly faced with the amorous advances of the emperor himself, the princess flies away to the moon.

The second kind of incipient Heian prose writing was the private diary. Public diaries or journals, written in Chinese, had been kept in Japan since at least Nara times; but the private diary, if we think of it as an accounting of daily events expressed in an intimate and personal mode, could not truly be undertaken until the development of *kana* enabled would-be diarists to write in the vernacular of their age. The earliest private diary that we have is the *Tosa Diary* (*Tosa Nikki*) of Ki no Tsurayuki. Written about 935, it recounts Ki's journey by boat to the capital from the province of Tosa, where he had just concluded a term as governor. The most distinctive feature of this work, as of all literary or artistic diaries of the Heian period, is the inclusion of a large number of poems. Many entries in the *Tosa Diary*, in fact, consist merely of a poem or two with some brief comments about the circumstances that inspired composition. For example:

> *Eleventh day:* After a little rain the skies cleared. Continuing upriver, we noticed a line of hills converging on the eastern bank. When we learned that this is the Yawata Hachiman Shrine, there was great rejoicing and we humbly abased ourselves in thanks. The bridge of Yamazaki came in sight at last, and our feelings of joy could no longer be restrained. Here, close by the Ōōji Temple, our boat came to anchor; and here we waited, while various matters were negotiated for the remainder of our journey. By the riverside, near the temple, there were many willow trees, and one of our company, admiring their reflection in the water, made the poem:
>
> > A pattern of wave ripples, woven—it seems—
> > On a loom of green willows reflected in the stream.[11]

One stimulus, then, to the evolution of Japanese prose seems to have been the need to elucidate the reasons for writing poetry, a need that can be traced back to certain explanatory notes appended to poems in the *Man'yōshū*. In any event, prose has from this earliest time been closely linked to poetry in the history of Japanese literature. In the diaries of the Heian period, poems are presented as the distinct compositions of one person to another and usually serve as a means for the expression of their most strongly felt emotions. On the other hand, in such later literary forms as the *nō* theatre of the medieval age and the bourgeois novels and puppet plays of the seventeenth and eighteenth centuries, metrical lines of seven and five syllables were generally employed for poetically toned renderings of the heightened, climatic passages of otherwise prose narratives.

The opening lines of the *Tosa Diary* state: "It is said that diaries are kept by men, but I shall see if a woman cannot also keep one."[12] Although it is generally agreed that Ki no Tsurayuki wrote this earliest of private diaries, he chose to use the subterfuge that it was kept by his wife. An obvious reason for this was that men regarded Chinese as the only proper and dignified medium for writing. Women, who had far less opportunity to learn Chinese, were the ones who turned most readily to *kana* to express themselves in the vernacular, and it was they who became the greatest writers of prose literature in the Heian period.

The first truly feminine diary was the late tenth century record known as *The Gossamer Years* (*Kagerō Nikki*), written by a woman identified only as the "mother of (Fujiwara) Michitsuna." Unlike the *Tosa Diary*, which was kept on a day-to-day basis and seems to present events as a fairly consistent and balanced chronology, *The Gossamer Years* is a sporadic and uneven account spread over some twenty-one years, from 954 to 974. The entries for some days are exceedingly detailed, but there are also long periods of time during which nothing at all is reported. This loose handling of the diary form (in fact, much of this diary was probably written toward the end of or even after the period it covers), combined with the intensely personal and subjective character of the writing, makes *The Gossamer Years* very much like a kind of autobiography or even an "I-novel"; and indeed the distinction between the diary and the fictional tale was often quite vague in Heian literature.

Whereas the *Tosa Diary* is centered on a journey (a common theme in diaries and other personal accounts), *The Gossamer Years* deals with an equally popular theme, the romance. The mother of Michitsuna was married to Fujiwara Kaneie (929–90), who eventually became imperial regent at court. Like most high-ranking Heian courtiers, Kaneie was not a faithful husband, and after an affectionate beginning with his wife (who bore him the boy Michitsuna), he began to neglect her for other women. Most of *The Gossamer Years* deals with the author's distress and fretful resentment over the fact that her husband comes to call upon her with less and less frequency. Left alone with little to break the tedium of her sequestered existence (a fate all too common among Heian court ladies), the mother of Michitsuna is driven to a neurotic outpouring of self-pity and absorption with her own grievances to the exclusion of any consideration for the feelings of others.

Another type of contemporary literature very similar to the private diary was the poem-tale (*uta-monogatari*), the most celebrated of which is *The Tales of Ise* (*Ise Monogatari*), compiled sometime in the early tenth century. *The Tales of Ise* consists of 125 passages or episodes of varying length, loosely grouped together, and each containing one or more poems. Most of the poems deal with love, and particularly with the romantic adventures of a great court lover and poet of the previous century, Ariwara no Narihira (825–80). Quite likely *The Tales of Ise* was compiled by one or more persons who gathered a collection of poems, most of them by Narihira, and then placed them in narrative contexts by drawing on biographical information concerning Narihira's life. To the foreigner, *The Tales of Ise* is apt to seem like a light and even insignificant work, but it has been venerated by the Japanese through the centuries as one of the greatest masterpieces in their literature. A typical passage from *The Tales of Ise* goes like this:

> In former times there lived a young nobleman named Narihira. Upon receiving the ceremony of initiation into manhood, he set forth upon a ceremonial falconry excursion, to review his estates at the village of Kasuga, near the former capital of Nara.

> In the village there dwelt alone two young sisters possessed of a disturbing beauty. The young nobleman gazed at the two secretly from the shade of the enclosure around their house. It filled his heart with longing that in this rustic village he should have found so unexpectedly such lovely maidens. Removing the wide sleeve from the silk cloak he was wearing, Narihira inscribed a verse upon it and sent it to the girls. The cloak he was wearing bore a bold pattern of passionflowers:

> Young maiden-flowers
> Of Kasuga, you dye my cloak;
> And wildly like them grows
> This passion in my heart,
> Abundantly, without end.

> The maidens must have thought this eminently suited to the occasion, for it was composed in the same mood as the well-known

> For whom has my heart
> Like the passionflower patterns
> Of Michinoku
> Been thrown into disarray?
> All on account of you.

This is the kind of facile elegance in which the men of old excelled.[13]

The crowning achievement in the development of prose in the early and middle Heian period was the completion shortly after 1000 of *The Tale of Genji (Genji Monogatari)*, a massive novel by Murasaki Shikibu, a lady-in-waiting at court. In spite of the excellence of much other Heian literature, it is Murasaki's incomparable masterpiece that recreates the age for us, or at least the age as seen through the eyes of the privileged Heian courtiers. The leading character of this novel, Genji, "The Shining Prince," was the son of an emperor by a low-ranking concubine and a paragon of all the Heian virtues: he was dazzlingly handsome, a great lover, poet, calligrapher, musician and dancer, and the possessor of impeccable taste in a society that was in a very real sense ruled by taste.

Like most of his peers, Genji had little official business to occupy him at court, where affairs were controlled by a few leading Fujiwara ministers. Instead, he devoted himself mostly to the gentle arts and especially to the pursuit of love, an endeavor that involved him in a seemingly endless string of romantic entanglements. In Genji's circle, the typical love affair was conducted according to exacting dictates of taste. Lovers delighted each other by exchanging poems written on fans or on carefully selected and scented stationery, which they adorned with delicate sprays of flowers. A faulty handwriting, a missed allusion, or a poor matching of colors could quickly dampen a courtier's ardor. On the other hand, the scent of a delicately mixed perfume or the haunting notes of a zithern on a soft summer night could excite his greatest passion and launch him recklessly on a romantic escapade whose outcome was more than likely to have embarrassing and even disastrous results both for the lovers and for others among the intimately associated members of Heian courtier society.

In a famous scene that takes place one rainy night, when Genji and his friends informally assess the merits of womanhood, there is this exchange between To no Chujo, a young Fujiwara, and Genji:

To no Chujo: "I have at last discovered that there exists no woman of whom one can say 'Here is perfection. This is indeed she.' There are many who have the superficial art of writing a good running hand, or if occasion requires of making a quick repartee. But there are few who will stand the ordeal of any further test. Usually their minds are entirely occupied by admiration for their own accomplishments, and their abuse of all rivals creates a most unpleasant impression. Some again are adored by over-fond parents. These have since childhood been guarded behind lattice windows and no knowledge of them is allowed to reach the outer-world, save that of their excellence in some accomplishment or art; and this may indeed sometimes arouse our interest. She is pretty and graceful and has not yet mixed at all with the world. Such a girl by closely copying some model and applying herself with great industry will often succeed in really mastering one of the minor and ephemeral arts. Her friends are careful to say nothing of her defects and to exaggerate her accomplishments, and while we cannot altogether trust their praise we cannot believe that their judgement is entirely astray. But when we take steps to test their statements we are invariably disappointed."

He paused, seeming to be slightly ashamed of the cynical tone which he had adopted, and added "I know my experience is not large, but that is the conclusion I have come to so far." Then Genji, smiling: "And are there any who lack even one accomplishment?" "No doubt, but in such a case it is unlikely that anyone would be successfully decoyed. The number of those who have nothing to recommend them and of those in whom nothing but good can be found is probably equal. I divide women into three classes. Those of high rank and birth are made such a fuss of and their weak points are so completely concealed that we are certain to be told that they are paragons. About those of the middle class everyone is allowed to express his own opinion, and we shall have much conflicting evidence to sift. As for the lower classes, they do not concern us." [14]

The Tale of Genji has long been held by Japanese critics to exemplify the aesthetic quality of *mono no aware*, a "sensitivity to things." Originally, the adjective *aware*, which was used with great frequency by Lady Murasaki and other contemporary writers, seems simply to have meant the kind of emotional response to the beauties of nature or the more gentle of human relations that was likely to elicit such an expression of spontaneous feeling as "Ah!" Hence, many people have defined *mono no aware* as the "ahness of things." But the term in Murasaki's day also had the sense of sadness or melancholy that permeates so much of Heian literature, and could even connote "pathos" or "wretchedness," the chief meaning or meanings it was to acquire in later centuries.

If *mono no aware* is the predominant mood of Heian literature, there is at least one work—*The Pillow Book* (*Makura no Sōshi*) of Sei Shōnagon—that exudes a quality quite the opposite, that of *okashi*: "lightness" or "wit." Like her near contemporary, Lady Murasaki, Sei Shōnagon also served as a lady-in-waiting at court. Her book (the title presumably taken from the fact that she kept it close at hand— that is, near or even *in* her wooden pillow) is a miscellany of jottings, anecdotes, aphorisms, and personal opinions. Sei had a keenly observant eye, especially for human foibles, which she delighted in exploiting; and indeed, with her assertiveness and biting tongue, she may be regarded as a kind of forerunner of the militant women's liberationist in her behavior toward men. She records, for example, the following account of what occurred when a courtier named Narimasa, whom she held in low esteem, attempted to visit her secretly one night:

"May I presume to come in?" he said several times in a strangely husky and excited voice. I looked up in amazement, and by the light of the lamp that had been placed behind the curtain of state I could see that Narimasa was standing outside the door, which he had now opened about half a foot. The situation amused me. As a rule he would not have dreamt of indulging in such lecherous behavior; as the Empress was staying in his house, he evidently felt he could do as he pleased. Waking up the young woman next to me, I exclaimed, "Look who is here! What an unlikely sight!" They all sat up and, seeing Narimasa by the door, burst into laughter. "Who are you?" I said. "Don't try to hide!" "Oh no," he replied. "It's simply that the master of the house has something to discuss with the lady-in-waiting in charge."

"It was your gate I was speaking about," I said. "I don't remember asking you to open the sliding-door."

"Yes indeed," he answered. "It is precisely the matter of the gate that I wanted to discuss with you. May I not presume to come in for a moment?"

"Really!" said one of the young women. "How unpleasant! No, he certainly cannot come in."

"Oh, I see," said Narimasa. "There are other young ladies in the room." Closing the door behind him, he left, followed by our loud laughter.[15]

The Pillow Book is the earliest example of still another type of literature—the miscellany or "running brush" (*zuihitsu*)—that has enjoyed much popularity in Japanese history. Along with the diary and the poem-tale, the miscellany, like horizontal picture scrolls and linked verse, reflects the Japanese preference for the episodic and loosely joined, rather than the long and unified, artistic form. *The Tale of Genji*, as a great, sustained work, was exceptional. In literature, the Japanese have concentrated on polishing short passages, phrases, words, and even syllables—no better proof of this exists than their consuming love for the *tanka*—and have been little inclined to think in terms of plot development or the carefully constructed narrative line.

Although written in fifty-four chapters, *The Tale of Genji* is actually divided into two major parts. The first centers on the life and loves of Genji, and the second deals with the generation at court after Genji's death. The Genji chapters, despite their prevailing mood of sadness and melancholy, portray a truly ideal society, a society whose members little doubted that theirs was the best of worlds possible in this life. Genji and his companions were not much given to philosophical speculation but seem instinctively to have accepted the implications of esoteric Buddhism that ultimate truth or reality lay in the very splendor of their own existence. Genji in particular represented the perfection of the Heian courtier, and upon his death, as the opening lines of the book's second part lament, there was no one to take his place.

Among Genji's successors, we find new doubts and psychological uncertainties that alter the tone of the novel: there is almost a presentiment in the book's latter part of the momentous changes that within a century or so were to bring about the decline of courtier society and the rise of a provincial warrior class. Some historians have suggested that Heian aristocratic society, even at its peak, was unbearably stultifying to all but the privileged few—mostly members of the Fujiwara and imperial families—who could aspire to advancement at court;

that, despite the idealization of court life in the earlier volumes of *The Tale of Genji*, there was discontent among many courtiers over their lot. No doubt the rumblings of the military in the provinces, which mounted steadily during the eleventh century, were also disquieting to the courtiers in spite of their outward show of aloofness toward provincial affairs.

While the term *monogatari* was applied during the Fujiwara epoch to such differing literary works as poem-tales and novels, it was also used for a new type of historical writing. The *Nihon Shoki* had been produced by the Nara court as the first of what was intended to be an ongoing series of official histories of Japan, much like the dynastic histories of China. As it turned out, six such national histories, covering up to the year 887, were actually compiled. All were written in Chinese and, with the exception of the *Nihon Shoki*, were notably dull, consisting as they did of a dry recitation of the facts and events of courtier government.

One reason for abandonment of the practice of compiling national histories was the general turning away from Chinese-derived institutions and patterns of behavior that accompanied the cessation of official missions to the continent in the latter part of the ninth century. Also, in the same way that the newly acquired capacity to write in Japanese with the use of *kana* encouraged the keeping of private diaries, people at court were inspired to record the historical events of their age in a more colorful, personally interpretive fashion. Although not precisely the same in structure, the national histories had been patterned on the highly formal dynastic records of the great bureaucratic state of China. Yet, Heian Japan had not become a bureaucratic state on the order of China; and the Heian courtiers, far from taxing their minds with lofty matters of national administration and imperial record-keeping, had become ever more introspectively absorbed with their own ceremonially oriented life in the capital. It was only natural that, in history as in literature, they should develop new mediums of composition more suitable to the expression of their sentiments concerning the public and private affairs of Kyoto courtier society.

Much as the fictional tale appears to have colored the factual diary, the historical accounts (commonly called *rekishi monogatari* or historical tales) that evolved in the Fujiwara epoch and after were greatly influenced by the novelistic style of *The Tale of Genji*. The first history of this kind was *The Tales of Glory* (*Eiga Monogatari*) that deals with the rise and flourishing of the Fujiwara during the period 897–1092. As Genji was the hero of Murasaki's book, so the great Fujiwara regent Michinaga (966–1027) was the main personage in *The*

Tales of Glory (a comparison that is not altogether far-fetched, since it has been speculated that Lady Murasaki had Michinaga at least partly in mind when she created the fictional character of Genji). In sharp contrast to the detached and official tone of most of the six national histories, *The Tales of Glory* expresses open interest in and warm admiration for the success of the Fujiwara, and particularly the prepotent Michinaga. The literarily styled historical tale thus created in *The Tales of Glory* was to evolve, with the rise of the samurai class in ensuing centuries, into the war tale, one of the major forms of writing in Japan's medieval age.

Whereas formerly they had scarcely questioned that spiritual fulfillment could be found in this world, the courtiers of the eleventh century increasingly cherished the thought of attaining salvation in the next. Such salvationism was not new to Japan but had been introduced to it as early as the seventh century in the teachings of Pure Land Buddhism. Pure Land Buddhism was based on adoration of the transcendent buddha Amida, who an eternity earlier had vowed to save all beings, provided only that they placed their faith wholly in him. By simply reciting the *nembutsu* (an invocation in praise of Amida),[16] an individual could ensure that upon death he would be transported to the blissful "pure land" of Amida in the western realm of the universe.

Amidism was made particularly appealing to the courtiers of the late Heian period by the popular doctrine of *mappō*, "the latter days of the Buddhist law." This doctrine held that after the death of Gautama, some five centuries B.C., Buddhism would pass through three great ages: an age of the flourishing of the law, of its decline, and finally of its disappearance in the degenerate days of *mappō*. Once the age of *mappō* commenced—and by Japanese calculations that would be in the year 1052—individuals could no longer hope to achieve Buddhist enlightenment by their own efforts, as had the followers of Hinayana and even of the Mahayanist sects of Shingon and Tendai esotericism. There would be no alternative during *mappō* but to throw oneself on the saving grace of another, such as Amida, in the hope of attaining rebirth in paradise.

Eventually, it was the Pure Land Sect, with its simple message of universal salvation, that provided the practical means for the spread of Buddhism to all classes of Japanese in the medieval era. But in its first phase of development in Japan, Amidism was embraced by and interpreted in characteristically aesthetic terms by the Heian courtiers. In the *Ōjō Yōshū* (*Essentials of Salvation*), for example, the Tendai priest Genshin (942–1017) urged the practice of the *nembutsu* and vividly pictured the attractions of the pure land.

After the believer is born into this land and when he experiences the pleasures of the first opening of the lotus, his joy becomes a hundred times greater than before. It is comparable to a blind man gaining sight for the first time, or to entering a royal palace directly after leaving some rural region. Looking at his own body, it becomes purplish gold in color. He is gowned naturally in jeweled garments. Rings, bracelets, a crown of jewels, and other ornaments in countless profusion adorn his body. And when he looks upon the light radiating from the Buddha, he obtains pure vision, and because of his experiences in former lives, he hears the sounds of all things. And no matter what color he may see or what sound he may hear, it is a thing of marvel. Such is the ornamentation of space above that the eye becomes lost in the traces of clouds. The melody of the wheel of the wonderful Law as it turns, flows throughout this land of jeweled sound. Palaces, halls, forests, and ponds shine and glitter everywhere. Flocks of wild ducks, geese, and mandarin ducks fly about in the distance and near at hand. One may see multitudes from all the worlds being born into this land like sudden showers of rain.[17]

One of the favorite themes in Fujiwara art was the *raigō*, a pictorial representation of the coming of Amida at the time of death to lead the way to the pure land; and among the most famous *raigō* paintings is a triptych traditionally attributed to Genshin, who was a fine artist as well as a scholar (even though this work was obviously done by someone else a century or more after Genshin's death). Amida is shown descending to earth on a great swirl of clouds in the company of twenty-five bodhisattvas, some playing musical instruments, some clasping their hands in prayer, and still others holding forth votive offerings. The formal way in which the figure of Amida, facing directly frontward, has been inserted into the center of the picture gives it a stiffly iconographic appearance; yet the gentle and even smiling expressions of all the figures—Amida as well as the host of bodhisattvas —are strikingly different from the fierce, unearthly visages of Jōgan art. The Fujiwara epoch, in literature as well as the visual arts, was soft, approachable, and "feminine." By contrast, the earlier Jōgan epoch had been forbidding, secretive (esoteric), and "masculine."

The favor that Amidism came to enjoy among the courtiers in the eleventh century is significantly revealed in the conduct of the regent Michinaga, who in his heyday had joyfully exclaimed in verse his contentment with the world:

> The full moon makes me feel
> That the world is mine indeed;
> Like the moon I shine
> Unveiled by clouds.

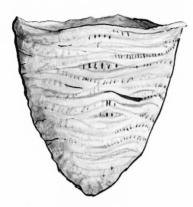

Fig. 1   Early Jōmon pottery (*drawing by Arthur Fleisher*)

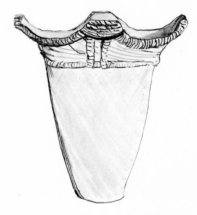

Fig. 2   Later Jōmon pottery (*drawing by Arthur Fleisher*)

Fig. 3   Dogū figurine (*drawing by Arthur Fleisher*)

Fig. 4   Yayoi pottery (*drawing by Arthur Fleisher*)

Fig. 5 *Haniwa* (*Consulate General of Japan, New York*)

Fig. 6 *Torii* at Miyajima in the Inland Sea (*Consulate General of Japan, New York*)

Fig. 7 Ise Shrine (*Consulate General of Japan, New York*)

Fig. 8 *Garan* of the Hōryūji Temple (*Consulate General of Japan, New York*)

Fig. 9 Golden Hall of the Hōryūji Temple (*photograph by Joseph Shulman*)

Fig. 10 Shaka trinity at the Hōryūji Temple (*Asuka-en*)

Fig. 11 Kudara Kannon at the Hōryūji Temple (*Asuka-en*)

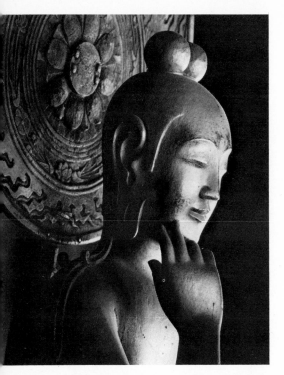

Fig. 12 Miroku Buddha (*Asuka-en*)

Fig. 13 From the Yakushi trinity at the Yakushiji Temple (*Asuka-en*)

Fig. 14 Attendant bodhisattva: detail of fresco in the Golden Hall at the Hōryūji Temple (*Asuka-en*)

Fig. 15 Tōdaiji Temple (*Consulate General of Japan, New York*)

Fig. 16 *Daibutsu* at the Tōdaiji Temple (*Consulate General of Japan, New York*)

Fig. 17 Guardian deity in dry lacquer at the Tōdaiji Temple (*Charles E. Tuttle Publishing* Co.)

Fig. 19 Shōsōin (*Asuka-en*)

Fig. 18 ◀ Statue of Ganjin at the Tōshōdaiji
Temple (*Asuka-en*)

Fig. 20 Mandala (*courtesy of the Brooklyn Museum*)

Fig. 21 Shishinden of the imperial palace in Kyoto (*photograph by Joseph Shulman*)

Fig. 22   Byōdōin Temple (*photograph by Joseph Shulman*)

Fig. 23   Statue of Amida Buddha by Jōchō at the Byōdōin Temple
(*Consulate General of Japan, New York*)

Fig. 24 *Shinden-style mansion of the Heian period* (*drawing by Arthur Fleisher*)

Fig. 25 Scene from the Genji Scrolls: Yamato paintings on sliding doors in background; "screen of state" in foreground (*Tokugawa Art Museum, Nagoya, Japan*)

Fig. 26 Scene from the Animal Scrolls (*Benrido Company*)

Fig. 27   Scene from the Animal Scrolls (*Benrido Company*)

Fig. 28 "Burning of the Sanjō Palace": a scene from the Heiji Scroll depicting fighting between the Minamoto and Taira in 1159 (Museum of Fine Arts, Boston)

Yet, as death approached, Michinaga turned his thoughts ever more to Amida and the hereafter. Following a practice that became common in Japan, he sought in his final moments to facilitate Amida's descent to lead him to the pure land by facing his bed toward the west and holding in his hand a colored string attached to Amida in a *raigō* painting. Later artists, in their desire to emphasize the rapidity with which true believers could expect to be transported to the pure land, painted *raigō* that showed Amida and the heavenly host coming down toward the viewer in great haste (rather than in the gentle, floating manner of the work described above). The *raigō* scene was even re-enacted dramatically, and there is at least one recorded case of a man who, on his deathbed, engaged a group of priests to visit him dressed as Amida and the twenty-five attendant bodhisattvas.

The temple where Michinaga died, the *Hōjōji*, is no longer in existence, but we are told that he had it built with the intent of reproducing on earth the beauties and delights of the pure land. Michinaga's son, the regent Yorimichi (992–1074), also sought to recreate the pure land in the Byōdōin, a temple at Uji, several miles to the south of Kyoto. Opened in 1052, the first year of *mappō*, the Byōdōin has the finest remaining examples of Fujiwara period architecture, including the much admired Phoenix Hall, a light, elegantly designed structure that was apparently given its name in later times because it is shaped like a phoenix (or, at least, like a bird), with wings extended in flight. Inside the hall is a sculptural representation of the *raigō*, with a central image of Amida and, attached to the upper parts of the walls, small, gracefully shaped figures of the bodhisattvas, adorned with halos and riding wisps of clouds. The Amida image, which is made of wood and has the characteristic gentleness and courtly air of Fujiwara art, is the work of Jōchō (d. 1057), the most celebrated sculptor of his age and one of the first persons in Japanese history to receive distinction and honor from the court as an artist of individuality and not merely a craftsman.

Fig. 22

Fig. 23

Although no examples of domestic architecture remain from the Heian period, we know from written accounts and picture scrolls what sort of mansions the courtiers built for themselves during the age of Fujiwara ascendancy. The chief architectural style for aristocratic homes, known as *shinden* construction, consisted in fact of a collection of one-story structures laid out very much like the Byōdōin Temple.

Fig. 24

Inasmuch as the courtiers preferred to live within the city limits of Kyoto, they were obliged for want of space to build their homes on fairly small plots of land, usually not more than two and a half acres or so in size. The typical *shinden* mansion consisted of a main building facing southward—the *shinden* or "living quarters" of the master of the family—and three secondary buildings to the east, west, and north. All four structures were raised about a foot above the ground and were connected by covered corridors. There were also two additional corridors leading southward to miniature fishing pavilions that bordered on a small lake with an artificial island in its center. The lake was usually fed by a stream flowing from the northeast, often under the mansion itself, and it was by the stream's banks that the courtiers enjoyed gathering for poetry parties. At such parties, a cup of rice wine was floated downstream and, as it came to each guest, he was obliged to take it from the water, drink, and recite a verse.

Like modern Japanese homes, those of the Heian courtiers had partitions, sliding doors, and shutters that could readily be removed to make smaller rooms into larger ones and to open the whole interior of a building to the out-of-doors. Also, like most homes in Japan today, the *shinden* were sparsely furnished. Although chairs were coming into general use in China about this time, they were not adopted by the Heian Japanese except for certain ceremonial purposes. A few chests, braziers, and small tables were the only objects likely to be left out in the open in *shinden* rooms and not stored away after use.

One item of furniture that was unique to courtier society was the so-called screen of state, behind which ladies ensconsed themselves when receiving visitors. Conspicuously depicted in the twelfth-century picture scrolls based on *The Tale of Genji*, the screens of state were wooden frames, several feet in height, with draperies hung loosely from their crosspieces. They could be easily moved about, and often came to represent the final fragile barrier to the Heian gallant in his quest to consummate a romantic liaison.

4

The Advent of a New Age

THE *haniwa* FIGURINES of armor-clad warriors and their mounts and the numerous military accoutrements dating from the proto-historic tomb period are plain evidence that the fighting traditions of the Japanese go back to remote antiquity. There is, moreover, the strong likelihood that these traditions were nourished uninterruptedly in the provinces even during the centuries when an elegant and refined cultural life was evolving under continental influence in the central region of Japan.

Although court administration of the provinces was ostensibly vigorous following the Great Reform of 645, it gradually declined during the eighth and ninth centuries; and in the tenth, as courtier society reached its apex of brilliance in Kyoto, control of affairs outside the central region devolved almost entirely into the hands of provincial families. Impelled to deal on their own with the maintenance of local order, these families increasingly resorted to arms; and from about mid-Heian times they came to form a distinct warrior class.

The process by which a provincial warrior class emerged in Japan was complex and differed from region to region: yet one area in particular—the eastern provinces of the Kantō—became its true spawning ground. The Kantō was still rugged frontier country, with vast tracts of open fields to draw adventuresome settlers, and the records give accounts from an early date of feuding there over land and power. From at least the early tenth century, chieftains arose in the Kantō to form fighting bands, consisting at first chiefly of members of their own families, but with the passage of time incorporating also outsiders as feudal, vassal-like retainers. These bands engaged in struggles, formed leagues, and established hegemonies; and gradually certain

55

great leaders appeared to contend for military control over ever larger territories, up to one or more provinces.

Even though the provincial warriors never lost their awe and admiration for the culture of the imperial court, their fundamental values were the antithesis of those of the Heian courtiers. They were samurai—men who "served"—and they behaved in accordance with an unwritten code that stressed manly arrogance, fighting prowess, unswerving loyalty to one's overlord, and a truculent pride in family lineage.

Paradoxical though it may sound, the greatest samurai leaders came from a background of courtier society itself. The rise of the Fujiwara to absolute power in Kyoto stifled opportunity for others at court, including those from the less privileged branches of the Fujiwara and even members of the imperial family. Many of these individuals left Kyoto to accept appointments to offices in the provincial governments. Settling permanently in the provinces after expiration of their terms of office, they took up warrior ways, became the leaders of bands, and attracted members of lesser samurai families as their supporters and vassals. Ultimately, two great clans descended from princely forebears—the Taira and Minamoto—emerged to the forefront of samurai society and became the principal contenders for warrior supremacy of the land.

Although at first there was no clear territorial division of influence, by the late eleventh and early twelfth centuries, the Minamoto came to exert their sway mainly over the Kantō, whereas the Taira steadily acquired land and influence in the central and western provinces. Control of the fertile Kantō—the birthplace of the samurai and a region some ten times greater than the plain of the central provinces —eventually proved decisive in enabling the Minamoto to found the first truly warrior form of government in Japan at Kamakura in 1185. But proximity to the court in Kyoto gave the Taira an early advantage over the Minamoto in the epic struggle that ensued between these two great samurai houses about the middle of the twelfth century.

The Taira benefited especially by an important political development at court in the late eleventh century. During the last years of the regent Yorimichi, founder of the Byōdōin Temple at Uji, Fujiwara power in Kyoto began to wane, and the first of a series of abdicated sovereigns arose to reassert the traditional claim of the imperial family to rule in fact as well as in name. The abdicated sovereigns, known also as "cloistered emperors," sought further to weaken the Fujiwara monopoly of courtier government by engaging as their aides and officials members of other houses, including samurai of the Taira clan. Under the patronage of the cloistered emperors, the Taira became the first non-courtiers to gain ceremonial admittance to the imperial palace. They also received extensive grants in estate lands and appointments to various provincial governorships in the western provinces of Honshu and in Kyushu.

Despite the assertiveness of the cloistered emperors, political conditions in Kyoto steadily deteriorated during the twelfth century. By mid-century, serious divisions had appeared within the Fujiwara and imperial families, and quarrelsome samurai of both the Taira and Minamoto clans were gathering in ever greater numbers in Kyoto. In the 1150's, the tranquility of the "flowery capital" was rudely shattered by two fierce clashes of arms. The first of these, in 1156, found the Taira and Minamoto intermingled on both sides, but the second in 1159 resulted in a resounding victory of the Taira over their archrivals and the inauguration of some twenty years of Taira dominance at court under the leadership of Kiyomori (1118–81).

The age of Taira ascendancy was a transitional period in Japanese history. Although samurai warriors, the Taira attempted to follow in the footsteps of the Fujiwara courtiers by marrying into the imperial family and by assuming many of the highest ministerial positions at court. In thus devoting their attention to traditional court politics and ignoring the pressing need for new administrative controls in the provinces, the Taira directly contributed to their own downfall, which occurred in a climactic renewal of struggle with the Minamoto in 1180–85.

Our chief source of information about the rise and fall of the Taira is a work entitled *The Tale of the Heike* (another name for the Taira), the best of the genre of quasi-historical literature known as war tales. As their designation implies, the war tales deal with the attitudes and conduct of the newly emergent samurai class. Linguistically, whereas *The Tale of Genji* had been written almost entirely in *kana* and with few Chinese loan words, the war tales were by and large composed in the mixed style of ideographs and *kana*—with a liberal dosage of Chinese vocabulary (pronounced, of course, in the Japanese fashion)—that eventually led to modern written Japanese.

Some of the war tales were composed shortly after the events they describe, while others were put into writing on the basis of an earlier oral tradition. *The Tale of the Heike* was probably first compiled as a book in the mid-thirteenth century, nearly a hundred years after the epoch of Taira glory that it recounts. By that time, its most exciting episodes had already been widely disseminated by itinerant storytellers, usually Buddhist monks, who chanted their narratives on journeys around the country to the accompaniment of a kind of lute known as the *biwa*. From the body of war tales that spans the medieval centuries, those dealing with the twelfth-century Taira and Minamoto have in particular remained immensely popular among the Japanese throughout the ages and have been the stuff from which countless plays, dramatic dances, and the like have been fashioned.

The later war tales degenerated into mere recitations of the interminable battles of the middle ages, one often indistinguishable from another. But in *The Tale of the Heike* and a few others we have a priceless repository of the ethos of the medieval samurai. Despite the apparent lust of the samurai for armed combat and martial renown, much romanticized in later centuries, the underlying tone of the medieval age in Japan was from the beginning somber, pessimistic, and despairing. In *The Tale of Genji* the mood shifted from satisfaction with the perfections of Heian courtier society to uncertainty about this life and a craving for salvation in the next. Yet, the very fact that the courtiers came to conceive of Amida's western paradise as an idealization of their own world, and tried to recreate it in architecture and landscape, reveals that they were far from prepared to discard the temporal values they had long cherished. How different are the sentiments expressed in the opening lines of *The Tale of the Heike*, a work that in many ways served to announce the advent of the medieval age:

> In the sound of the bell of the Gion Temple echoes the impermanence of all things. The pale hue of the flowers of the teak-tree shows the truth that they who prosper must fall. The proud ones do not last long, but vanish like a spring-night's dream. And the mighty ones too will perish in the end, like dust before the wind.[18]

In their brief period of ascendancy the Taira did little to improve rulership in Japan, and their name has come down in history as synonymous with the proud and the mighty who "will perish in the end, like dust before the wind." But in one of their major pursuits— overseas trade and intercourse—they opened the door to a new flow of influence from China that significantly affected both the direction and tempo of cultural development in medieval Japan.

Although official relations with the tottering T'ang dynasty had been terminated in the late ninth century, contacts with the continent were never completely severed, and throughout the tenth and eleventh centuries private traders continued to operate out of Kyushu, particularly the ancient port of Hakata. Moreover, the Heian court, even though it steadfastly refused to dispatch its own missions again to China, kept officials permanently stationed at a commandery near Hakata to oversee the import trade and to requisition choice luxury goods for sale and distribution among the Kyoto aristocrats. When the Taira, with the backing of the cloistered emperors at court, became influential in the western provinces in the twelfth century, they naturally took a keen interest in and eventually came to monopolize the highly profitable maritime trade with China.

China of the Sung dynasty (960-1279) was a changed country from the expansionist, cosmopolitan land of T'ang times that the Japanese had so assiduously copied in their Great Reform several centuries earlier. China could no longer serve as a giant conduit for the flow of world art and culture to remote Japan. From its founding, the Sung dynasty was harassed by barbarian tribes pressing in from the north and northwest. And indeed, just as the Taira assumed a commanding position in Japan's burgeoning overseas trade in the early twelfth century, North China fell to foreign invaders. The Sung—known henceforth as the Southern Sung (1127–1279)—moved its capital from Kaifeng in the north to Hangchow south of the Yangtze delta, where it remained until overthrown by the Mongols of Khubilai Khan in 1279.

Despite political woes and territorial losses, the Sung was a time of great advancement in Chinese civilization. Some scholars, impressed by the extensive growth in cities, commerce, maritime trade, and governmental bureaucratization in the late T'ang and Sung, have even asserted that this was the age when China entered its "early modern" phase. The Sung was also a brilliant period culturally. No doubt most of the major developments of the Sung in art, religion, and philosophy would in time have been transmitted to Japan. But the fortuitous combination of desire on the part of the Sung to increase its foreign trade with Japan and the vigorous initiative taken in maritime activity by the Taira greatly speeded the process of transmission.

One of the earliest and most important results of this new wave of cultural transmission from the continent was a revival of interest in Japan in pure scholarship. The Nara court, following the Chinese model, had founded a central college in the capital and had directed that branch colleges be established in the various provinces. The ostensible purpose of this system of colleges, which by the mid-Nara period had evolved a fourfold curriculum of Confucian classics, literature, law, and mathematics, was to provide a channel of advancement in the court bureaucracy for sons of the lower (including the provincial) aristocracy. But in actual practice very little opportunity to advance was provided, and the bestowal of courtier ranks and offices continued to be made almost entirely on grounds of birth. Before long, the college system languished, and the great courtier families assumed responsibility through private academies for the education of their own children. Moreover, as the courtiers of the early Heian period became increasingly infatuated with literature (that is, belles-lettres), they almost totally neglected the other fields of academic or scholarly pursuit. Courtier society came to offer scant reward to the individual who, say, patiently acquired a profound knowledge of the *Analects of Confucius*; yet it liberally heaped laurels upon and promised literary immortality to the author of superior poems.

The Sung period in China, on the other hand, was an exceptional age for scholarship, most notably perhaps in history and in the compilation of encyclopedias and catalogs of art works. This scholarly activity was greatly facilitated by the development of printing, invented by the Chinese several centuries earlier.

Japanese visitors to Sung China were much impressed by the general availability of printed books on a great variety of subjects, including history, Buddhism, Confucianism, literature, medicine, and geography, and carried them in ever greater numbers back to Japan. By the time of the Taira supremacy, collections of Chinese books had become important status symbols among upper-class Japanese. Kiyomori is said, for example, to have gone to extravagant lengths to obtain a 1,000-volume encyclopedia whose export was prohibited by the Sung. Some courtiers confided in their diaries that they had little or no personal interest in these books but nevertheless felt constrained to acquire them for the sake of appearances. Yet, the Chinese books brought to Japan about this time in the thousands and even in the tens of thousands not only provided the nuclei for many new libraries but motivated the Japanese to print their own books and to a very great extent stimulated and made possible the varied and energetic scholarly activities of the coming medieval age.

One of the finest artistic achievements of the middle and late Heian period was the evolution of a native style of essentially secular painting that reached its apex in the narrative picture scrolls of the twelfth century. The products of this style of painting are called "Yamato [that is, Japanese] pictures" to distinguish them from works categorized as "Chinese pictures."

Painting in Japan from the seventh to the ninth centuries, like art in general, had been done almost entirely in the Chinese manner. Portraits of people, for example, showed Chinese-looking features, and even landscapes were mere imitations of noted places in China. The evolution of Yamato pictures from the ninth century on constituted a transition from this kind of copying to more original painting that dealt with Japanese people in Japanese settings.

Nearly all of the early Yamato pictures were painted either on folding screens or sliding doors. Regrettably, like the *shinden* mansions in which they were kept, none has survived. Yet there are abundant descriptions in the records of what they looked like; and in the background scenes of some of the later narrative scrolls—for example, the twelfth-century works based on *The Tale of Genji*—we can glimpse screens and doors pictorially decorated in the Yamato style.

These early Yamato pictures, which reached their peak of popularity in the Fujiwara epoch, depicted either pure landscapes or landscapes in which courtiers were shown at their leisure: viewing the moon, gathering the first blossoms of spring, or simply standing amid the tranquil beauties of nature. The two major themes were the seasons and famous places of Japan.

It is doubtful that any other people in history has ever been as absorbed as the Japanese in their literature and art with the seasons and the varying moods they bring. In works of prose, such as *The Tale of Genji*, there is a constant awareness of the seasons and their intimate association with the life cycle of the Heian courtier; and in *tanka* poetry, we find numerous words and phrases that stereotypically identify the time of year, such as the "morning mists" of spring or the "cry of the deer" in autumn. Yamato pictures, as well, came to have many associative subjects linked with each of the seasons: for example, the morning glories, lotus ponds, and Kamo festival of summer and winter's mountain villages, waterfowl, and the sacred *kagura* dance.

A unique feature of the Yamato pictures of famous places was that they were painted for the most part by people who had never seen these places, except possibly the ones closest to Kyoto. In other words, the Yamato artists produced provincial scenes either as they were traditionally supposed to appear or as the artists imagined them to appear. There could be no more telling proof than this of the extent to which the Heian courtiers had come to conceive of the world outside Kyoto and its environs in almost purely abstract, aesthetic terms.

With development of the *kana* syllabary and the use of *kana* for the writing of *tanka*, Yamato artists began to add poems to their pictures appropriate to the particular seasons and settings they were depicting. They thus joined together three forms of art: poetry, calligraphy, and painting. And in the process they contributed a narrative or descriptive element to their works that led from the painting of individual scenes on screens and doors to the use of Yamato pictures as illustrations in books, and finally, about the turn of the twelfth century, to the development of narrative scrolls (perhaps most conveniently referred to henceforth as *emaki* to avoid confusion with the earlier types of Yamato pictures).

Although horizontal handscrolls had long been used for pictorial purposes in China, it was the Japanese who in the late Heian period came to employ them in the creation of a major art form. The oldest, and in many ways the most splendid, of the *emaki* extant from Heian times are the Genji Scrolls, probably painted sometime around the mid-twelfth century. There may originally have been as many as twenty

Fig. 25

of these scrolls but only four have come down to us. Strictly speaking, the Genji Scrolls are not fully narrative pictures, since they do not possess the horizontal flow of movement and the blending of scenes one into another that became the dominant characteristic of subsequent *emaki*. Rather, the Genji Scrolls consist of separate scenes with sections of text interspersed among them.

A distinctive technical convention utilized in the Genji Scrolls is the removal of roofs from buildings to provide oblique views into their interiors from above. Another is the drawing of faces with stylized "straight lines for eyes and hooks for noses." This elimination of facial expression seems particularly fitting for the portrayal of members of a society that so admired fixed, ideal types. Like the authors of much of Heian literature, the artists of the Genji Scrolls sought more to create a series of moods than to depict particular individuals and particular situations (although of course we know from the novel who the people are and what they are doing).

Another fine *emaki* of the twelfth century is the Ban Dainagon Scroll, which relates a complex political intrigue of 866 in which a certain Great Councilor Ban was alleged to have caused the destruction by fire of one of the principal gateways leading into the palace compound in Kyoto. Completed about 1175, this work is of a different character from that of the Genji Scrolls. In contrast to the static, stylized beauty of the latter, it is full of action. Moreover, although set chiefly in Kyoto, the Ban Dainagon Scroll is crowded with people from both the upper and lower classes. As we run our eyes from right to left, we see animated figures enacting the continuous flow of narrative: the conspiracy that led to the burning of the palace gateway, the chance discovery that Ban was involved in it, and finally his banishment from the capital.

A particularly unusual set of early *emaki* are the "Animal Scrolls" traditionally attributed to a Buddhist priest named Toba (1053–1140), although stylistic analysis by scholars suggests that the Scrolls were not all painted by the same person and were in fact probably done over a period of some hundred years from Toba's time until the early *Fig. 26* thirteenth century. The most artistically admirable sections of the Scrolls show animals, including rabbits, monkeys, frogs, and foxes, frolicking and gamboling about. The animals are drawn with a marvelously sure and skillful brush stroke and are the product of a technique of playful or caricature-like artwork that can be traced back to certain charcoal sketches done on the walls of the Hōryūji Temple in the late seventh century and to pictures found in the Shōsōin storehouse of the Nara period. The Animal Scrolls are also interesting from the standpoint of social history, for they contain a number of scenes in which animals, representing people, are shown satirizing contem-

porary life, particularly the corrupt ways of some members of the
Buddhist priesthood. One especially blasphemous scene shows a monkey, garbed like a priest, paying ceremonial homage to a giant frog of
a buddha who is seated on a temporary outdoor altar. *Fig. 27*

Emaki were produced during the next few centuries on a variety of
themes, including battles, the lives of famous priests, and the histories
of noted temples; and there will be occasion in the next chapter to
comment on one or two of the more important of these as they appear
in the development of medieval culture. *Fig. 28*

5

The Canons of Medieval Taste

ENCOURAGED BY MANIFOLD SIGNS of discontent with the arbitrary and dictatorial rule of the Taira in Kyoto, the Minamoto rose in revolt in the provinces in 1180 and provoked a five-year war that ended in total victory over the Taira at the great naval battle of Dannoura in the Straits of Shimonoseki in 1185. The commander-in-chief of the Minamoto was Yoritomo (1147–99), who established his base at Kamakura in the Kantō. Unlike Kiyomori, the former Taira leader who died in 1181, Yoritomo deliberately avoided entanglement in courtier politics at Kyoto. Instead, he remained in Kamakura even after the war and retained direct control over the eastern heartland of samurai society.

The government that Yoritomo founded at Kamakura is known in English as the Shogunate, after the title of shogun ("generalissimo") that the Minamoto chieftain received from the imperial court. Creation of this exclusively military organization marked the beginning of the medieval era of Japanese history, an era that lasted until the commencement of early modern times at the end of the sixteenth century.

There is no question that the Kamakura Shogunate represented a radically new form of government in Japan, situated far from the traditional seat of courtier authority in the central provinces and staffed by warriors who were related by feudal ties of personal loyalties. Yet the Shogunate was in no sense a rebel regime; on the contrary, it was founded and operated in an entirely "legitimate" fashion. Yoritomo, who remained ever deferential in his formal dealings with the court, was careful to secure imperial sanctification both for his own position and for the important administrative acts of the new Shogunate, such as the expansion of its power to the national level through the appointment in 1185 of Minamoto vassals as land stewards and constables to estates and provinces throughout the country.

The fighting between Taira and Minamoto that led to defeat of the former and ushered in the medieval era (the first part of which, 1185–1333, is also designated the Kamakura period) is most vividly retold in *The Tale of the Heike.* But there is another book, written in the early thirteenth century by Kamo no Chōmei (1153–1216), a former courtier turned religious recluse, that is also an important literary account of this pivotal epoch in Japanese history. Chōmei's work, the *Hōjōki (An Account of a Ten-foot-square Hut)*, is a brief miscellany written in essentially the same style of classical Japanese as *The Tale of the Heike.* Quite unlike the latter, however, it makes no direct mention of the titanic struggle between Taira and Minamoto waged in the early 1180's but instead describes the series of disasters—some natural, others induced by the war—that struck the capital during these years. The *Hōjōki* also presents in Buddhist terms a pessimistic view of this world as a place of foulness and suffering that is perhaps even more emphatic than the one given in *The Tale of the Heike.* The phrase "ten-foot-square hut" refers to the exceedingly modest dwelling on a mountain outside the capital that Chōmei selected as his home in the effort to renounce all worldly attachments. In the end, he sadly admits that he has failed to find complete release from earthly things and, in fact, has become attached even to his little hut.

An event during the war that was especially shocking to contemporaries was the wanton destruction by the Taira of the Tōdaiji Temple in Nara. The Tōdaiji, it will be recalled, had been constructed under imperial auspices in the mid-eighth century to serve as one of the principal symbols of centralized court rule in Japan. Its loss must have struck many as an irrefutable sign that the country had come to final disaster in the age of *mappō*. Yet, tragic though it was, the burning of the Tōdaiji actually stimulated a minor renaissance in the art of the Nara period.

This renaissance came about when, shortly after the end of hostilities between the Taira and Minamoto in 1185, a drive was undertaken to raise funds for rebuilding the Tōdaiji. Generous contributions were acquired from members of both the courtier and warrior élites, including the new shogun, Yoritomo. Before long, Nara was bustling with activity, as work was begun at the sites of both the Tōdaiji and the Kōfukuji, another major temple devastated by the Taira. Jobs were made available to artists and craftsmen, and new attention was focused on the former seat of imperial rule and its art treasures.

The Nara renaissance of the late twelfth century gave particular opportunity for fame to a group of sculptors known as the "kei" school (from the fact that its members all used "kei" in their assumed names).

The most distinguished member of this school was Unkei, whose familiarity with the Tempyō art of his native Nara is evident in such realistic pieces as the statues in wood at the Kōfukuji of two historical personages of Indian Buddhism. Stylistically, the statues are reminiscent of the dry lacquer image noted in an earlier chapter of the blind priest, Ganjin, who emigrated from China in the eighth century to found one of the "six sects" of Nara Buddhism.

Although not a member of the warrior class, Unkei has been called a samurai sculptor, because most of his surviving works seem to be imbued with the vigor and strength of the new military age. No doubt these general qualities of vigor and strength, so different from the softness and even femininity of Fujiwara art, derived at least in part from Unkei's familiarity with the styles of other, earlier art epochs, including Jōgan (early Heian) as well as Tempyō. Yet, in the minds of many critics, Unkei was also deeply influenced as an artist by his exposure to warrior life in Kamakura, which he visited to do work on commission for high officers of the Shogunate. Hence, one may well choose to regard as "samurai pieces" such realistically detailed and dynamically postured statues as the two guardian deities at the Tōdaiji (attributed to Unkei and another member of his school, Kaikei).

Despite the achievements of Unkei, his colleagues, and some of his successors, sculpture—and especially religious sculpture—declined steadily during the Kamakura period and never again became a major art in Japan. Probably the chief reason for this was that the medieval sects of Buddhism strongly de-emphasized iconography and the use of art for strictly religious purposes.

Like Buddhist sculpture, Buddhist painting also steadily gave ground to secular art in medieval times. One of the most significant developments in painting was in the field of realistic portraiture. So far as we know, Heian artists had made no attempt to depict the actual likenesses of real people. Some scholars suggest that this was largely because the deeply superstitious courtiers feared that portraits might be used for the casting of evil spells. In any case, it was not until about the time of the struggles between the Taira and the Minamoto that the earliest portraits were done. Among the best known is one of Yoritomo by an artist of the Fujiwara clan.

The founding of the Kamakura Shogunate did not cause the immediate fossilization of the imperial court as a governing body. Indeed, the court retained certain residual powers for at least another century and a half (for example, it continued to appoint governors who operated side by side in the provinces with the military constables), and when the Shogunate was overthrown in 1333 an emperor even attempted to restore the throne to a position of absolute rulership in the country.

But the trend during the medieval age was inexorably toward the imposition of feudal control at every level of society. And from the outset of the age we find a despairing awareness among the courtiers that their days of splendor as a ruling élite could never be revived. Increasingly deprived of political power, the courtiers became ever more covetous of their role as the custodians of traditional culture. This can perhaps best be seen in the realm of poetry, long one of the most esteemed of the gentle pursuits. Some skill in *tanka* versification had of course been mandatory for members of the courtier class throughout most of the Heian period. In the medieval age, it became a way of life for its chief practitioners, who formed exclusive cliques and entered into fierce rivalries over issues involving minute differences in style, choice of words, and appropriate poetic topics.

Needless to say, medieval poets never used *tanka* to describe the fighting and disorder that accompanied the rise of the samurai to power. But the sentiments they sought to express were nevertheless far darker and more deeply moving than those of their predecessors a century or so earlier. Here, for example, are two poems from the *Shinkokinshū* (*New Kokinshū*), compiled about 1205 and usually regarded as the last of the great imperially authorized anthologies:

> In a tree standing
> Beside a desolate field,
> The voice of a dove
> Calling to its companions—
> Lonely, terrible evening.

> Living all alone
> In this space between the rocks
> Far from the city,
> Here, where no one can see me,
> I shall give myself to grief.[19]

As implied in the title *New Kokinshū*, the poets of the Kamakura period were inclined more and more to look to the past for inspiration. They admired particularly the poems of the tenth-century anthology, *Kokinshū*, but were also influenced to a greater degree than before by the monumental *Man'yōshū* of the Nara period. We observed that the *Man'yōshū*, written by means of a complex use of Chinese ideographs to reproduce the sounds of Japanese, was excessively recondite for the Heian period courtiers. It is estimated that before the medieval age only a few hundred of its more than 4,500 poems could be fully understood. But with the renewal of scholarship in Japan in late Heian times, there was a revival of interest in and study of the *Man'yōshū*; and during the thirteenth century, a Tendai priest named Senkaku produced the first complete *Man'yōshū* commentary.

One of the compilers of the *Shinkokinshū*, and the most distinguished poet of his day, was Fujiwara Teika (1162–1241). Of all the courtiers of the early Kamakura period, Teika is the best known for his desire to escape from reality into the realm of art. Upon hearing of Minamoto Yoritomo's rising against the Taira in 1180, for example, Teika noted in his diary that, although his ears were assailed by news of military rebellion and chastisement, such events were of no concern to him. The only thing he wished to do was to compose supremely beautiful *tanka*.

In at least one respect, Teika was a product of his age, since he was an outstanding scholar as well as poet. Moreover, he was instrumental in setting forth and applying the aesthetic principles that were largely to dictate the tastes of the medieval era. We noted that the most important aesthetic quality of the age of the *Kokinshū* was *miyabi* or courtly refinement, a quality that has indeed run through Japanese culture to the present day. In medieval times the fashionable elegance connoted by Heian period *miyabi* was transmuted into *yūgen*, mystery or profundity. In striving for *yūgen*, the artist, whether a writer of *tanka* or a performer of the *nō* theatre in later centuries, sought in an almost mystical way to suggest, with only a few words or gestures, the absolute or eternal. This poem by Teika possesses the kind of symbolism that is associated in medieval Japanese poetry with *yūgen*:

> When the floating bridge
> Of the dream of a spring night
> Was snapped, I woke:
> In the sky a bank of clouds
> Was drawing away from the peak.[20]

While certain courtiers like Teika attempted to evade the realities of the new age by devoting themselves singlemindedly to the traditional arts, other individuals were drawn into the great movements of religious conversion that occurred in the late twelfth and thirteenth centuries. There had been a scattering of evangelists from at least the eighth century in Japan who had traveled into the provinces bearing the gospel and helping with the building of bridges, the digging of wells, and other public works. In the Heian period, the priest Kūya (903–72) became especially famous as a popularizer of Amidism. He danced through the streets and sang songs such as this:

He never fails
To reach the Lotus Land of Bliss
Who calls,
If only once,
The name of Amida.[21]

But not until the Kamakura period was Buddhism finally carried to all corners of the country.

Amidism had appealed to the Heian courtiers in part because of the opportunity it gave them to reproduce in literature and art the blisses of the pure land and the joy of Amida's descent to greet those about to enter it. Yet the *nembutsu*, or invocation of Amida's name, had simply been one of a number of practices followed by the doctrinally catholic adherents of Tendai Buddhism, and Amidism was not established as a separate sect until the time of the evangelist Hōnen (1133–1212).

Like all the great religious leaders of the Kamakura period, Hōnen received his early priestly training at the Tendai center on Mount Hiei. He found himself, however, increasingly dissatisfied with the older Buddhist methods of seeking enlightenment or salvation through individual, merit-producing acts, and came to stress utter reliance upon and faith in Amida as the only one able to save men in the corrupt age of *mappō*. Yet, in actual practice, Hōnen did not insist upon *absolute faith* in Amida's saving grace.

One of the most fundamental doctrinal problems in Pure Land Buddhism was whether the *nembutsu*—the calling upon Amida to be saved—should be recited once or many times. Since, theoretically, Amida had vowed to save all those who acknowledged their own helplessness and who threw themselves upon his infinite mercy, one recitation should have sufficed. But there was an apparently natural tendency for some people to believe that they could make their salvation more certain or even achieve a "better salvation" if they repeated the *nembutsu* over and over. The individual who was thus motivated to recite the *nembutsu* continuously was, of course, either consciously or unconsciously guilty of a certain lack of trust in Amida, since he felt the need to bolster his faith through added personal effort. Moreover, if repetition of the *nembutsu* was indeed helpful in the quest for salvation, then those with the greater leisure to practice it would have the best chance to be saved.

It was Hōnen's disciple, Shinran (1173–1262), who finally resolved this problem by asserting that Amida promised salvation unconditionally to all who sincerely called upon him once, whether or not they actually pronounced the *nembutsu* aloud. With salvation assured by this single act, the individual was free to recite the *nembutsu* as often as he wished, but such recitation would then be simply an expression of thanksgiving to Amida, and would in no way modify the already given promise of rebirth in the pure land.

Shinran spent many years in the provinces, especially the Kantō, where he preached his message of salvation through unquestioning faith in Amida. He had particular success as a proselytizer among the peasantry, who formed the nucleus of what came to be known as the True Sect of Pure Land Buddhism. Through the centuries, this sect has attracted one of the largest followings among the Japanese, and its founder, Shinran, has been canonized as one of his country's most original religious thinkers.

Another evangelist of Pure Land Buddhism, active in the late thirteenth century, was Ippen (1239–89), who urged the practice of the "circulating *nembutsu*" or chanting of praise to Amida with and among people everywhere. Although Ippen cannot be ranked in importance with Hōnen and Shinran in the history of Pure Land Buddhism in Japan, he has been immortalized in one of the finest of all medieval *emaki*: the Scroll of Saint Ippen, painted approximately ten years after the evangelist's death.

This scroll is a narrative record of Ippen's travels throughout the country, during the course of which he purportedly gathered the astounding total of some 2.5 million converts to his sect of Amidism. The Ippen Scroll is not only a work of art, it is also an invaluable document of thirteenth-century social history. Artistically, the scroll is perhaps most admired for its landscape background, which, although purely Japanese in subject matter, is executed in a style that shows the strong influence of Sung China. In the fifteenth and sixteenth centuries, as we shall see, Sung painting served as the inspiration for a distinguished line of landscape artists in Japan.

As a social document, the Ippen Scroll contains scenes of virtually every major aspect of life and social activity in the Kamakura period, including people at work and play in the countryside and towns and gathered to meet Ippen at Shinto shrines, Buddhist temples, and the private homes of the well-to-do. In one particularly lively scene from the scroll, Ippen is shown leading a group of followers in the ecstatic practice of the "dancing *nembutsu*": that is, the singing of praise to Amida while dancing and tapping small hand-drums. The dancers are tightly crowded into a small frame structure, elegant carriages are clustered about on the street outside, and high-born ladies can be seen mingling with the townspeople.

Apart from the proponents of Pure Land Buddhism, the person who most forcefully propagated the idea of universal salvation through faith was Nichiren (1222–82). One of the most exceptional and interesting figures in Japanese history, Nichiren founded the only major sect of Buddhism in Japan that did not derive directly from a religious institution already established in China. The chief factor in determining the nature of Nichiren Buddhism was Nichiren's own extraordinary personality. But, in order to understand how and why the sect arose in the mid-thirteenth century, it is essential also to note the particular political and social conditions under which Nichiren grew to maturity.

When the great founder of the Kamakura Shogunate, Minamoto Yoritomo, died in 1199, he was succeeded as shogun by a young and ineffectual son. A power struggle soon arose among the leading vassals of the Minamoto, and in the early years of the thirteenth century the Hōjō family emerged as the new de facto rulers of the Shogunate. But the Hōjō chieftain, in characteristic Japanese fashion, sought to avoid being stigmatized as a mere power seeker by assuming the rather modest-sounding title of shogunal regent and by designating an infant of the courtier clan of Fujiwara to occupy the prestigious, but now politically impotent, office of shogun.[22]

While the Hōjō were consolidating their position at Kamakura, a certain former (cloistered) emperor in Kyoto organized a plot to overthrow the Shogunate, which seemed so torn with internal strife after Yoritomo's death. In 1221, the cloistered emperor branded the Hōjō regent a rebel and called upon people everywhere to rise and destroy the Shogunate. But the Hōjō, acting decisively, sent an army to Kyoto that swiftly overran the cloistered emperor's poorly organized troops.

This brief clash of arms was a great blow to the *ancien régime* in Kyoto, even though many members of the courtier class had refused to join the cloistered emperor's cause. As victors, the Hōjō were able to confiscate thousands of additional estate holdings for distribution among their samurai followers and to appoint many new military officials throughout the country. Moreover, the Hōjō from this time on not only dictated to a far greater degree than before the conduct of affairs at court, they even assumed the right to decide the line of succession to the throne.

Nichiren was born in a fishing village in the Kantō the year after the cloistered emperor's disastrously unsuccessful attempt to overthrow the Hōjō. He went through his formative years in an age when the fortunes of the imperial court and those institutions that supported it, including the Tendai and Shingon churches, were far lower than they had been during the youth of Hōnen or even of Shinran. Nichiren appears, moreover, to have been more profoundly affected by the concept of *mappō* than probably any other religious leader of the Kamakura period. After a number of years of study at the Tendai center on Mount Hiei and elsewhere, he formed an apocalyptic view of the deterioration of Japan from within and its destruction from without. An exceptionally large number of natural disasters appeared during the mid-thirteenth century to confirm his prediction of internal deterioration; and the two attempts of the Mongols to invade Japan in 1274 and 1281, although unsuccessful, seemed to be chilling portents that the country might indeed be overwhelmed by forces from outside its borders.

Nichiren asserted in loudly militant terms that Japan was suffering such agonies because of the propagation of false Buddhist doctrines. He held that ultimate religious truth lay solely in the *Lotus Sutra*, the basic text of the Greater Vehicle of Buddhism in which Gautama had revealed that all beings possess the potentiality for buddhahood. At the time of its founding in Japan by Saichō in the early ninth century, the Tendai Sect had been based primarily on the *Lotus Sutra*; but, in the intervening centuries, Tendai had deviated from the *Sutra*'s teachings and had even spawned new sects, like those of Pure Land Buddhism, that encouraged practices entirely at variance with these teachings.

As a result of his virulent attacks on the other sects of Buddhism and his criticism of the conduct of national affairs, Nichiren was often in trouble with the Shogunate authorities, was in fact twice exiled from Kamakura, and was even sentenced to death. Still, he continued to insist that salvation for mankind and for Japan could only be achieved through absolute faith in the *Lotus Sutra*. He preached that, for the individual, there was no need to attempt to read and understand the *Sutra*; buddhahood was attainable simply through recitation of the formula, reminiscent of the *nembutsu*, of "Praise to the Wonderful Law of the *Lotus Sutra*."

Nichiren's name is written with the characters for "sun" and "lotus." Lotus, of course, represents the *Lotus Sutra*, whereas sun stands for Japan. Nichiren came to envision that, when the age of *mappō* reached its cataclysmic end (which he believed was very near), a great new Buddhist era would commence in which Japan would become the central Buddhist see in the world and in which he, Nichiren, would play a founding role in religious history similar to that of Gautama.

This kind of Japan-centered millennial thinking has led a number of commentators to claim that Nichiren was the first nationalist in Japanese history. Although "nationalist" is probably too modern a term to apply to a person of the thirteenth century, Nichiren certainly had a consciousness of country that set him apart from the other Buddhist leaders of the age.

The last of the so-called new sects of Kamakura Buddhism was Zen, which like Amidism had long been known to the Japanese but was not established independently in Japan until the early medieval age. First organized as a sect in China in the sixth century by a semi-legendary Indian priest named Bodhidharma, Zen appears in many ways to be closer to original Buddhism than any of the sects we have examined thus far.

Zen literally means "meditation," and meditation—particularly in the cross-legged Yogic position—is one of the most fundamental practices in Buddhism. Gautama, in fact, is purported to have achieved his own enlightenment while in a deep meditative state. In Zen, enlightenment (*satori*) may be interpreted as the final realization that man's suffering stems from his striving for such things as wealth and power that appear to be real, but actually are illusory. Unlike the salvationist sects of Pure Land and Nichiren Buddhism, which called upon the individual to escape from suffering by placing his faith completely in some other being or thing (Amida or the *Lotus Sutra*), Zen encouraged him to seek personal enlightenment—that is, to realize his buddha nature— through discipline and effort.

The main doctrinal difference between the two major sects of Zen established in Japan during the Kamakura period—Rinzai and Sōtō— is whether enlightenment or *satori* can be achieved "suddenly" (Rinzai) or is attainable only "gradually" by means of a long process of seated meditation (Sōtō). The problem of *satori* in Zen has been made especially hard for outsiders to understand because Zen masters in both China and Japan have either refused to discuss it at all or have commented on it only in terms that seem to be nonsensical. A master of old, for example, was likely to reply to a query about *satori* with a phrase such as "Three pounds of flax!" The apparent implication was that Zen enlightenment could not be "explained," but could only be experienced directly.

Because of its stress on self-discipline and control, Zen seemed particularly appropriate as a creed for the warriors of medieval Japan, and no doubt it exerted a strong influence on the molding of the samurai way of life. But there is danger in overestimating the degree to which Zen was embraced as a religion by the medieval samurai. For all its anti-intellectual claims to simplicity and directness of communica- tion, Zen was more attractive to the sophisticated than to the un- cultivated mind. The vast majority of medieval samurai were rough, unlettered men engaged in a brutal profession, and they sought their religious solace chiefly in the salvationist sects. The reason for Zen's success in the medieval age lay in large part in its strong appeal to the ruling members of samurai society.

Although they could not easily reconcile it with the basic premises of their religion, the Zen priests of medieval Japan had a lively interest in all sorts of intellectual and cultural matters. They journeyed fre- quently to China and indeed became the principal agents for the transmission of Chinese ideas and fashions back to Japan. In short, they carried on the new phase of cultural borrowing from the continent that had commenced after the founding of the Sung dynasty in the late tenth century and was accelerated during the expansion of overseas trade under the Taira in the twelfth. The leaders of the Shogunate welcomed Zen priests (both Japanese and Chinese) to Kamakura not only because of their interest in Zen, but also because these priests could serve to elevate the cultural life of the new military capital.

On the whole, the Hōjō regents exercised firm and just rule over samurai society through most of the thirteenth century. Unlike Minamoto Yoritomo, who had governed in a highly autocratic way, the Hōjō opened a Council of State to enable chieftains of the other great samurai families of the east to participate in the decision-making of the Shogunate. Moreover, the Hōjō based their rule on an epochal formulary, the Jōei Code of 1232, which contained detailed provisions dealing with those matters that were of most concern to the members of a warrior class, including the duties of land stewards and constables, the distribution of fiefs, and the settlement of armed disputes.

Even while the Hōjō were thus placing the Shogunate on a firm institutional basis, events were occurring on the continent that were to present Japan with its only major foreign threat in premodern historical times. In the early thirteenth century, the Mongols under Chingghis Khan assembled one of the greatest empires in the history of the world, conquering North China and extending their territorial control across Asia and into Eastern Europe. After Chingghis's death, the Chinese portion of his empire was inherited by his son Khubilai Khan. It took Khubilai until 1279 to destroy the Southern Sung and to unite all of China under the Yüan or "Original" dynasty (1270–1368). But even before this final achievement, Khubilai sought to bring Japan into a subservient, tributary relationship. The other countries of East Asia had long accepted as a matter of course such a relationship with the mighty Middle Kingdom of China, but the Japanese from at least the time of Prince Shōtoku in the early seventh century had steadfastly resisted being drawn into it.

When the Japanese now refused to submit to Khubilai's imperious and threatening demands, he launched two great armadas against them in 1274 and 1281. In the first invasion, the Mongol force numbered some 40,000 men, and in the second nearly 100,000. Both took place at Hakata Bay in northern Kyushu, and both ultimately failed because of typhoons that drove the Mongol fleets back out to sea. Apart from the sheer desire to force the submission of all those who had the temerity to oppose him, it is difficult to discern any reason sufficient to explain Khubilai's willingness to expend such effort in the attempt to invade remote, and in the Chinese scheme of things, insignificant Japan.

Unlike the samurai of Japan, who were accustomed to single, man-to-man combat, the Mongols fought in organized units and used weapons such as catapults and exploding balls that were unfamiliar to the Japanese. With their superior troop coordination and military technology, these foreign invaders might well have prevailed had they not encountered such bad weather. To the Japanese, however, the typhoons were not accidental, but were *kamikaze* or "winds sent by the gods" to save their country in its hour of greatest peril. In later centuries, this *kamikaze* idea exerted a powerful influence on the Japanese myth—finally shattered in World War II—of national invincibility.

The Mongol threat was an important, but not sole, cause for the decline of the Kamakura Shogunate in the late thirteenth and early fourteenth centuries. Another was the emergence in various regions of the country of new warrior bands that the Shogunate, organized originally as a military hegemony over the eastern provinces, found increasingly difficult to control. Still another was a succession dispute that erupted between two branches of the imperial family about the time of the invasions.

This dispute appeared at first to be of little significance, since the Hōjō had stripped the imperial family of nearly all political power a half-century earlier; and an agreement by which the so-called senior and junior branches of the family alternately provided candidates for the emperorship worked tolerably well for a number of years. Then, in 1318, Godaigo (1288–1339), a most forceful and headstrong member of the junior branch, ascended the throne and determined not only to transmit the line of succession exclusively to his own descendants but also to restore the throne to real power.

Godaigo's restorationist or loyalist movement was successful in 1333 when the forces that rallied to him, including both courtiers and samurai, overthrew the Kamakura Shogunate and gave the emperor the opportunity to rule, as well as reign, that he had long sought. But the Restoration of Godaigo lasted a scant three years and was a generally reactionary and impractical attempt to turn the course of history back to the early Heian period, before power was first taken from the throne by the Fujiwara regents.

Totally unable to meet the real governing needs of the medieval age, the Restoration regime was overthrown in 1336 by Ashikaga Takauji (1305–58), the chieftain of a main branch of the great Minamoto clan. After driving Godaigo and his remnant supporters to refuge in the mountainous region of Yoshino to the south, Takauji placed a member of the senior branch of the imperial family on the throne and established a new military administration in Kyoto, known in history as the Ashikaga or Muromachi Shogunate (1336–1573). The first half-century of Muromachi times, 1336–92, is also designated the epoch of the Northern and Southern Courts, inasmuch as Godaigo and his successors maintained an opposition Southern Court at Yoshino during this period that challenged the legitimacy of what it regarded as the puppet Northern Court of the Ashikaga in Kyoto.

The era of the Restoration and of fighting between the Northern and Southern Courts was one of great confusion and deeply divided loyalties. It also marked the last time in premodern history that either the throne or the courtier class played an active role in the rulership of Japan. In 1392, the Ashikaga, promising a return to the earlier practice of alternate succession, persuaded the Southern emperor (Godaigo's grandson) to return to Kyoto and thus brought to an end the great dynastic schism. In fact, the Ashikaga never kept their promise about returning to alternate succession and the southern branch of the imperial family slipped into oblivion. Even the northern branch, although left in possession of the throne, retained no governing authority whatever, and from this time on the emperorship was little more than a legitimating talisman for the rule of successive military houses.

Probably the single most important historical record of the fourteenth century is a lengthy war tale, covering the period from about 1318 until 1368, with the incongruous-sounding title of *Taiheiki* or *Chronicle of Great Peace*. Although unquestionably inferior in literary quality to *The Tale of the Heike*, the *Taiheiki* has in some respects had a more profound influence on the way in which the Japanese have viewed their premodern age of the samurai. Like *The Tale of the Heike*, the *Taiheiki* has also been a rich source for itinerant story-tellers and chanters, and in subsequent centuries its most exciting episodes became just as familiar to Japanese everywhere. But whereas *The Tale of the Heike* has been enjoyed purely as a military epic, the *Taiheiki* has become a kind of sourcebook for modern imperial loyalism.

Although the Southern Court lost in its struggle with the Ashikaga-dominated Northern Court, later generations (after the end of the medieval age) came increasingly to feel that Godaigo, for all his ineptitude in governing during the Restoration, had been wrongfully deprived of his imperial prerogatives by the Ashikaga. These later generations were also deeply stirred by the accounts in the *Taiheiki* of the selfless devotion and sacrifice of the courtiers and samurai who fought for the ill-fated Southern cause. And in the modern era, the Japanese have revered the more prominent of these Southern supporters as the finest examples in their history of unswerving loyalty to the throne.

(At the same time, they have regarded Ashikaga Takauji and his chief lieutenants as the most unpardonable of national traitors.)

Another important literary work of the mid-fourteenth century is the *Essays in Idleness* (*Tsurezuregusa*), a collection of notes, anecdotes, and personal observations by Yoshida Kenkō (1283–1350), a court poet who took Buddhist vows in his later years. Written about the time of Godaigo's Restoration (although without a word concerning the momentous political and military events of the day), the *Essays in Idleness* is structurally very much like the Heian period miscellany, *The Pillow Book*. In content, however, the two books clearly reflect the differences between the ages in which they were written. Whereas *The Pillow Book* is biting, witty, and "up-to-date," Kenkō's work is an elegant expression of the tastes and feelings of a medieval man who possessed both a fine sensitivity for the poignancy of life and the perishability of all things and a profound nostalgia for the customs and ways of the past.

Unlike the author of *Hōjōki* in early Kamakura times, Kenkō was not overcome with anguish by the suffering that accompanies the ceaseless flow and change of life. Indeed, he felt that "The most precious thing in life is its uncertainty," and delighted in something precisely because its beauty promised to be brief or because it already showed signs of fading. Moreover, Kenkō never expressed his love for former times in cloyingly sentimental terms, but with such simple eloquence as:

In all things I yearn for the past. Modern fashions seem to keep on growing more and more debased. I find that even among the splendid pieces of furniture built by our master cabinetmakers, those in the old forms are the most pleasing. And as for writing letters, surviving scraps from the past reveal how superb the phrasing used to be. The ordinary spoken language has also steadily coarsened. People used to say "raise the carriage shafts" or "trim the lamp wick," but people today say "raise it" or "trim it." 23

The *Essays in Idleness* has long been revered by the Japanese as a veritable bible of traditional etiquette and aesthetic tastes. Many of Kenkō's preferences—for the asymmetrical instead of the regular, for the subtly suggestive rather than the boldly asserted—can be traced to much earlier times in the development of Japanese culture. But one important criterion of his aesthetic taste, expressed most concisely in the term *sabi* (aged or antique), was distinctly a product of the medieval era. Along with *yūgen*, it is a quality that touched nearly all the cultural pursuits of the medieval centuries of Japanese history. The Heian courtiers had particularly loved what was new and fresh, but the medieval Japanese developed a strong liking also for things that showed signs of wear and decay, for the withered, the rusted, the broken, and imperfect. Kenkō, for example, states that:

> Somebody once remarked that thin silk was not satisfactory as a scroll wrapping because it was so easily torn. Ton'a replied, "It is only after the silk wrapper has frayed at top and bottom, and the mother-of-pearl has fallen from the roller that a scroll looks beautiful." This opinion demonstrated the excellent taste of the man. People often say that a set of books looks ugly if all volumes are not in the same format, but I was impressed to hear the Abbot Kōyū say, "It is typical of the unintelligent man to insist on assembling complete sets of everything. Imperfect sets are better." [24]

The Muromachi period was the most tumultuous age in Japanese history. During its two and a half centuries, there was almost continuous warfare in one part of the country or another. The third Ashikaga shogun, Yoshimitsu (1358–1408), brought order to much of Japan in the late fourteenth and early fifteenth centuries by skillfully imposing his control over a group of semi-autonomous regional barons or daimyos that emerged out of the fighting between adherents of the Northern and Southern Courts. But after Yoshimitsu's death, the Shogunate steadily declined; and for its last hundred years or so it was almost completely powerless as a central government.

Yoshimitsu was not only an outstanding military leader but also a generous and discerning patron of the arts. Presiding in nearly regal fashion over both courtier and warrior élites in Kyoto, he was to a great extent personally responsible for the exceptional flourishing of culture that occurred in his age (known as the Kitayama epoch after *Fig. 29* the location of his monastic retreat, the Golden Pavilion, in the Northern Hills outside Kyoto).

An important stimulus to Kitayama culture was the renewal by Yoshimitsu of formal contacts with China. Trade and exchange between Japan and China had been minimized during and after the Mongol invasions. But, by the early fourteenth century, animosities had subsided on both sides to the point where Japan's military rulers felt secure in dispatching two trading missions to China (in 1325 and 1341) to acquire funds for the repair of one Zen temple and the construction of another.

In 1368, the same year that Yoshimitsu became shogun, the alien Mongol dynasty of China was overthrown and was replaced by the Ming (1368–1644). Shortly after its founding, the Ming made overtures to Japan requesting aid in the suppression of Japanese-led pirates or *wakō*, who had been marauding the coasts of Korea and China in the century following the Mongol invasions. It was ostensibly in response to these overtures for assistance that Yoshimitsu entered into official relations with the Ming, although privately he was no doubt more strongly motivated to establish such relations from his desire to develop a profitable overseas trade.

Later nationalist historians have roundly denounced Yoshimitsu for accepting a tributary relationship with China of the kind that the Japanese had for some 800 years steadfastly rejected, even to the point of precipitating the Mongol invasions a century earlier. Viewed impartially, the missions that were sent periodically to China from Yoshimitsu's time until the end of the Muromachi era were not only commercially profitable, they also provided a steady and highly significant flow of culture from the Ming to medieval Japan.

The Zen temples of Kyoto took the lead in the first phase of intercourse with Ming China. These institutions were excellently suited, owing both to their intimate ties with ruling circles of the Shogunate and the general interests and training of their priesthoods, to serve as traders and cultural emissaries to China. One important result of their cultural involvement with China about this time was the production of a large body of literature and scholarship that is rather loosely termed Gozan (Five Zen Temples) literature.[25] Composed entirely in Chinese, the poetry and prose of the leading Gozan writers has been judged by many critics as excessively imitative and pedantic (and far removed from the proper activities of a branch of Buddhism that theoretically eschewed intellectualism and the written word). There can be no question, on the other hand, of the great value of the research and pure scholarship undertaken by the Gozan temples. In addition to exegetical studies on Buddhism and Confucianism, they compiled dictionaries, encyclopedias, and other reference-type materials that provided the groundwork for nearly all subsequent scholarly activity in premodern Japan.

By far the most splendid cultural achievement of the Kitayama epoch was the *nō* ("talent" or "ability") theatre. The precise origins of *nō*, a form of drama based on the dance, are unknown; but it is certain that they were highly diverse, and that *nō* derived from influences both foreign and native, aristocratic and plebeian. Among the earliest of such influences were various types of dance, music, and theatrical entertainment—including juggling, acrobatics, and magic—imported from China during the seventh and eighth centuries. One of these Chinese imports was converted and ossified by the Japanese into a solemn and stately court dance called *bugaku* (done to the accompaniment of *gagaku* or "elegant music"), while others enjoyed only a temporary vogue and declined. Still others, merging with miscellaneous native entertainments and ceremonials, ultimately contributed to the development of *nō*.

The two most popular theatrical forms of the early medieval age were "monkey music" (*sarugaku*) and "field music" (*dengaku*). Nobody knows the exact meaning of the term "monkey music," although possibly it comes from the comic-like acrobatics and mimicry practiced by *sarugaku* actors. *Dengaku*, on the other hand, was a type of entertainment based originally on the singing and dancing of peasants "in the fields" at harvest festivals.

By the Kitayama epoch, *sarugaku* and *dengaku*, though rivals with their own schools of performers, appear to have influenced each other to the point where they were probably quite similar in actual presentation. We know from the records that both were immensely popular with people in the capital and elsewhere. The last of the Hōjō regents, for example, is reputed to have loved *dengaku* and other diversions so much that he completely neglected his duties at Kamakura; and, in 1349, so many people crowded in to see a *dengaku* performance in Kyoto that the stands collapsed and scores were killed.

The fact that *sarugaku*, rather than *dengaku*, was transformed during the Kitayama epoch into *nō* was partially fortuitous. In 1374, Yoshimitsu attended his first performance of *sarugaku* and was so captivated by two of its actors, Kan'ami (1333–84) and his son Zeami (1363–1443), that henceforth he lavishly patronized their art. This was a most significant event in Japanese cultural history, since without Yoshimitsu's backing the geniuses of Kan'ami and Zeami, who were instrumental in the creation and perfection of *nō*, might have been dissipated on a theatrical form that still catered to rather low and earthy tastes. Given entree to the highest social circles in Kyoto, these two men elevated and refined *sarugaku* to a dramatic art of great beauty and sublimity that could appeal to the most aristocratic of sensibilities.

Kan'ami and Zeami were not only actors, they were also playwrights; and many of the finest plays in the *nō* repertory can either positively or with reasonable assurance be attributed to their brushes. Zeami, moreover, was an outstanding critic of his day and has left invaluable commentaries on medieval aesthetic and dramatic tastes, tastes which he himself was so influential in molding.

When Zeami first met Yoshimitsu in 1374 he had been a mere child of eleven, and quite likely it was his physical beauty as much as anything that first attracted the shogun, who had a particular fondness for pretty boys. After Yoshimitsu's death in 1408, Zeami and his school of *nō* were temporarily forced into eclipse by those in the Shogunate who resented the extraordinary privileges he had previously received. But the popularity of *nō* was by this time too firmly established to be readily destroyed. Before long, it was once again in favor with the Ashikaga shoguns and enjoyed their patronage for the remainder of the medieval age.

Donald Keene has defined *nō* as "a dramatic poem concerned with remote or supernatural events, performed by a dancer, often masked, who shares with lesser personages and a chorus the singing and declamation of the poetry." [26] The main dancer or actor is known as the *shite*, and the lesser personages include the *waki* or "side person," who usually introduces the play and asks the questions that induce the *shite* to tell his story, and one or more *tsure* (companions).

To the uninitiated, *nō* can seem painfully slow and its plots so thin as to be almost nonexistent. Moreover, there is little if any attempt made in *nō* to be realistic. It is a theatre of symbolism, employing highly stylized, even ritualistic manners of speech and movement. The very suggestion of realism is often deliberately avoided by having, for example, an old man play the role of a young girl or a little boy that of a great general (all performers in *nō*, incidentally, are males). The *nō* actor is in particular expected to cultivate two qualities: *monomane* or the "imitation of things"; and *yūgen*. *Monomane* does not of course mean the capacity to act realistically, but to perform the various symbolic movements demanded by the roles of the five categories of *nō* plays—god plays, warrior plays, women plays, miscellaneous plays, and demon plays. Although he regarded mastery of *monomane* as essential, Zeami stressed that the supreme measure of the *nō* actor was his ability to convey an aura of *yūgen* or dark and mysterious beauty, the most treasured (and difficult to define) aesthetic quality of the medieval age.

Fig. 30

No words can adequately capture the drama and emotional impact of a *nō* play for the reader who has never actually seen one performed; but a brief description of a play—Zeami's haunting *Nonomiya* or *The Shrine in the Fields*—will at least serve to indicate how a work of this form of medieval Japanese theatre is structured and presented.

The *shite* or protagonist in *The Shrine in the Fields* (a woman play) is a fictional figure from *The Tale of Genji*, Lady Rokujō, a proud and jealous lover of Prince Genji. Like so many other plays in the *nō* repertory, it is opened by an intinerant priest (the *waki*), who announces that he has been visiting the famous sites of Kyoto and would like to go to nearby Sagano to see the Shrine in the Fields where each newly appointed vestal virgin of the Great Shrine at Ise temporarily resided before proceeding to Ise. By a mere turn of his body, the priest indicates that he has made the journey to Sagano, and he kneels before the shrine. As he is praying, a girl enters and, upon questioning, tells the story of how, when Lady Rokujō was staying at Nonomiya with her daughter who had been appointed as the Ise virgin, she was visited by Prince Genji. The time of the year was autumn, the season most dearly cherished in the Japanese tradition because of its many reminders of the inevitable passing of all things, and the poetic dialogue of *The Shrine in the Fields* is suffused with autumnal melancholy and loneliness. By the end of the first scene, it has become clear to the priest that the girl is actually the ghost of Lady Rokujō, who is torn between her continuing worldly passion for Genji and her desire to achieve Buddhist salvation. In the second and last scene, the *shite*, who has temporarily exited,[27] reappears in the unmistakable form of Lady Rokujō and dances the *shimai*, an often protracted dance which constitutes the dramatic climax of the play. At the end of her dance, Lady Rokujō steps through the small wooden *torii* or gateway—the only prop used in *The Shrine in the Fields*—and thus symbolically departs the world and achieves salvation.

Perhaps the best-loved *nō* play is *Matsukaze*, also a woman play, which was written by Kan'ami and revised by Zeami. It tells the sad tale of the ghosts of two sisters—Matsukaze ("Wind-in-the-pines") and Murasame ("Autumn rain") [28]—who when alive had spent their days in the lowly occupation of gathering brine to make salt at their native place of Suma on the Inland Sea. Once, many many years earlier, a courtier named Yukihira had spent some time in exile at Suma; and even after his return to the capital and his death shortly thereafter, the girls remained sunk in grief over the love they had both felt for him. In the final scene of the play, as a gale howls and breakers crash at Suma, Matsukaze and Murasame vow that they will continue to await Yukihira's promised return; but, with the aid of prayers by the priest who has visited them, they are finally released from their tormented existence, and in the end all that remains is the memory of their names in the form of "autumn rain" and "wind in the pines":

> *Matsukaze:* So we await him. He will come,
> 　　　　　　Constant ever, green as a pine.
> *Murasame:* Yes, we can trust
> 　　　　　　his poem:
> *Chorus:* "I have gone away
> *Matsukaze:* Into the mountains of Inaba,
> 　　　　　　Covered with pines,
> 　　　　　　But if I hear you pine,
> 　　　　　　I shall come back at once."
> 　　　　　　Those are the mountain pines
> 　　　　　　Of distant Inaba,
> 　　　　　　And these are the pines
> 　　　　　　On the curving Suma shore.
> 　　　　　　Here our dear prince once lived.
> 　　　　　　If Yukihira comes again,
> 　　　　　　I shall go stand under the tree
> 　　　　　　Bent by the sea-wind,

And, tenderly, tell him
I love him still!
Chorus: Madly the gale howls through the pines,
And breakers crash in Suma Bay;
Through the frenzied night
We have come to you
In a dream of deluded passion.
Pray for us! Pray for our rest!
Now we take our leave. The retreating waves
Hiss far away, and a wind sweeps down
From the mountain to Suma Bay.
The cocks are crowing on the barrier road.
Your dream is over. Day has come.
Last night you heard the autumn rain;
This morning all that is left
Is the wind in the pines.
The wind in the pines.[29]

Another type of theatre, which developed in the shadow of $n\bar{o}$, was $ky\bar{o}gen$ ("mad words"). One kind of $ky\bar{o}gen$ served as an interlude between the scenes of a $n\bar{o}$ play, during which a rustic or person of the locality appeared and, in words much more understandable than the frequently difficult language of $n\bar{o}$, gave additional background information about the region and the leading characters of the play.

Other $ky\bar{o}gen$ were written as separate skits of a comical or farcical nature and were often interspersed on the same programs with $n\bar{o}$ plays, partly to provide relief from the unremitting gloom that pervades nearly all of $n\bar{o}$. The humor of these independent $ky\bar{o}gen$ was very broad and slapstick. Many skits were based on situations in which clever servants outwitted their daimyo masters. Some scholars have sought to interpet such $ky\bar{o}gen$ as proof that the lower members of society held strong class antagonisms against their superiors in medieval times. There were indeed many instances of social unrest in the medieval age, but it is doubtful that the antics of $ky\bar{o}gen$ reflected true "class antagonisms." $Ky\bar{o}gen$ were produced to entertain and, although occasionally attacked by puritans as irreverent in tone, they were appreciated by audiences from all stations of life, including the daimyos and other people derided in them.

Other artistic pursuits of the Kitayama epoch included linked verse, the tea ceremony, and monochrome painting. But these are more appropriately discussed in the context of the second great cultural phase of the Muromachi era, which occurred during the time of Yoshimitsu's grandson, the eighth Ashikaga shogun Yoshimasa (1436-90).

Yoshimasa became shogun in 1443 at the age of seven and at a time when great forces of upheaval, from peasant uprisings to quarrels among unruly daimyos, were at work throughout Japanese society. Even the strongest of shoguns would have been hard-pressed to hold together the delicately balanced Ashikaga hegemony at mid-fifteenth century; and Yoshimasa—young, pampered, and effete—gave no promise whatever of becoming such as shogun. Yoshimasa was an almost inevitable product of the gradual merger of courtier and warrior élites that had occurred in Kyoto since the time of Yoshimitsu. Although the samurai leaders of the Shogunate controlled the imperial court politically, they increasingly succumbed to the elegant courtier style of life; and in Yoshimasa we find a scion of the great warrior house of Ashikaga who, though graced with the title of generalissimo, had scarcely any interest at all in military matters. In the 1460's, after more than twenty years as nominal head of the Shogunate, Yoshimasa sought to relinquish his official duties entirely in order to devote himself to what he regarded as the more pleasurable pursuits of life. Yet, far from slipping gracefully into retirement at this time, Yoshimasa helped precipitate a succession dispute between his brother and son that brought on a frightful holocaust of fighting known as the Ōnin War (1467–77).

Actually, the shogunal succession dispute was merely an excuse for two rival groups of daimyos to engage in a struggle for military supremacy, a struggle that the Shogunate, under the inept Yoshimasa, was powerless to check. Fought almost entirely in Kyoto and its environs, the Ōnin War dragged on for more than ten years, and after the last armies withdrew in 1477 the once lovely capital lay in ruins.

There was no clear-cut victor in the Ōnin War. The daimyos had simply fought themselves into exhaustion, and many returned home to find their domains in rebellion. Moreover, the Ashikaga Shogunate, although it continued in existence until 1573, was from this time on a government in name only. It was under such conditions that the country slipped into a century of conflict and disunion known as the "age of provincial wars."

Fig. 31　Despite the carnage of the Ōnin War and the widespread disorder that followed in its wake, the time of Yoshimasa was one of marvelous cultural achievement. Yoshimasa finally managed to transfer the office of shogun to his son in 1473—in the midst of the Ōnin War—and a few years after the end of hostilities, he began construction on a retreat, called the Silver Pavilion (in contrast to Yoshimitsu's Golden Pavilion), in the Higashiyama or Eastern Hills suburbs of Kyoto. Though a dismal failure as generalissimo, Yoshimasa was perhaps even more noteworthy as a patron of the arts than his grandfather, Yoshimitsu. In any case, his name is just as inseparably linked with the flourishing of culture in the Higashiyama epoch (usually taken to mean approximately the last half of the fifteenth century) as Yoshimitsu's is with that of Kitayama.

In certain cultural pursuits, most notably the nō theatre, the Higashiyama epoch added little to what had been accomplished earlier. Yoshimasa and his cronies loved the nō, and sometimes they arranged programs that lasted for several days. But the epoch produced no artists of the caliber of Kan'ami or Zeami, whose works proved to be so lofty that they tended to inhibit further development.

One art that was brought to its highest level of perfection in Higashiyama times was linked verse (*renga*). The idea of two or more people alternately (or consecutively) composing the 5-7-5 and 7-7 syllable links of a *tanka* and stringing them together one after another was not new. The Heian courtiers had occasionally engaged in sessions of linked verse composition for their own amusement, and the pastime became even more popular at court during the Kamakura period. But it was not until the fourteenth century that linked verse was given any serious consideration as an art. By this time, the creative potential of the traditional *tanka*, upon which countless generations of Japanese had lavished such unstinting love, was at length exhausted. The *tanka* cliques at court dictated such rigid rules of composition that they throttled the efforts of even the most imaginative poets. It was partly because linked verse offered freedom from such restrictions that poets and would-be poets turned increasingly to it in the Muromachi period.

Still another reason for the spread in popularity of linked verse from the fourteenth century on was that it stimulated social intercourse. The leisured Heian courtiers had, of course, been quite socially minded and indeed seem to have enjoyed a constant round of parties, including those that featured poetry recitations and competitions. But the other classes of premedieval times were, so far as we can discern, greatly restricted both in their opportunities to socialize and in the range of their social contacts. Peasants, warrior-peasants, townsmen, and others labored long hours, and apart from occasional shrine and harvest festivals probably had little time or inclination to engage in social relations of a purely convivial type with people outside their immediate families.

The medieval age brought a number of changes that greatly increased the socializing opportunities for people of all classes, especially the new ruling élite of samurai and the guilds of artisans and merchants that emerged in such urban centers as Kyoto, Nara, and the port city of Sakai on the Inland Sea. Records from the early fourteenth century reveal that among the pleasures these people enjoyed when they gathered together socially were *dengaku* and *sarugaku* (which we have already noted), communal bathing, the drinking of tea and sake, and the composition of linked verse.

It would be absurd to mistake a popular diversion for art, and we should not suppose that the extemporaneous *renga* poetizing by partygoing peasants, tradesmen, or common samurai produced very many immortal lines. Nevertheless, there are strong indications that the popularistic tastes of the lower classes did significantly influence the development of linked verse in the Muromachi period, just as they contributed (through *dengaku* and *sarugaku*) to the evolution of *nō*.

Linked verse was elevated to the status of a recognized art by the courtier Nijō Yoshimoto (1320–88), who in 1356 compiled the first imperially authorized *renga* anthology. But the greatest master of the linked verse form was Sōgi (1421–1502), a Zen priest of the Higashiyama epoch who rose from very humble origins and drew inspiration from his contacts not only with the courtier and samurai aristocrats of Kyoto but also with the myriad folk he encountered on his frequent travels into the provinces. In 1488, Sōgi and two other poets (Shōhaku and Sōchō) met at the shrine of Minase, a village south of Kyoto, where they engaged in what was probably the most famous session of linked verse composition in Japanese history. The opening lines of their hundred-verse poem, now known as "The Three Poets of Minase," go like this:

Sōgi: Snow yet remaining
The mountain slopes are misty—
An evening in spring.

Shōhaku: Far away the water flows
Past the plum-scented village.

Sōchō: In the river breeze
The willow trees are clustered.
Spring is appearing.

Sōgi: The sound of a boat being poled
Clear in the clear morning light.

Shōhaku: The moon! does it still
Over fog-enshrouded fields
Linger in the sky?

Sōchō: Meadows carpeted in frost—
Autumn has drawn to a close [30]

These poets have skillfully constructed their verses to provide flow and continuity from one link to another by the use of various associative devices: when Sōgi, for example, mentions spring, Shōhaku uses the vernal expression "plum-scented"; and when Shōhaku refers to the moon (which is always associated with the fall), Sōchō promptly shifts to the autumntime. Yet, however delightful such devices may be as employed by the Minase masters, their use was indicative of the fact that linked verse, like *tanka*, was becoming excessively restricted by conventions; and in time it too ceased to provide a means for truly creative expression.

Another cultural activity of the Higashiyama epoch that evolved even more obviously from both plebeian and aristocratic practices was the tea ceremony (*cha-no-yu*). Tea had been introduced to Japan as early as the Nara period, and the priest Saichō, patriarch of the Tendai Sect of Buddhism, is reported to have brought back a quantity of it to the court from China in the early ninth century. But there is nothing to indicate that the Japanese took more than a passing interest in tea until about the beginning of the medieval age, when Eisai (1141–1215), the founder of the Rinzai or "sudden enlightenment" school of Zen, reintroduced the beverage to Japan and recommended its use for medicinal purposes (and, incidentally, to help Zen acolytes remain awake during their long hours of meditative training).

By the early fourteenth century, tea drinking seems to have spread to people everywhere in Japan, most of whom presumably enjoyed it less for its purported medicinal value than for its satisfying taste. The Japanese of the fourteenth century not only came to enjoy tea but also to discriminate among the different types or brands. Imported tea from China was still very much prized among those who could afford it, but increasingly the products of Japan came into favor with even the most discerning people. For example, the tea grown at Uji (the site of the Byōdōin Temple) was personally praised by Yoshimitsu and even today is regarded as the finest in Japan.

The tea parties of this century were generally held as competitions in which contestants sought to identify various types of tea and to judge both their quality and the quality of the water in which they were brewed. Such competitions, which indeed became something of a craze in early Muromachi times, were often accompanied by linked verse sessions and, afterward, by sake, communal bathing, and gambling.[31] In all, the competitions and their sequels must have been very gay, frequently bawdy, occasions. A certain parvenu daimyo named Sasaki Dōyo became especially notorious about mid-fourteenth century for the gala tea parties he threw, in the course of which he ostentatiously displayed his collection of Chinese *objets d'art*, including ceramicware and other articles used in the preparation and drinking of tea, samples of calligraphy, and painted screens and hanging scrolls.

Dōyo's flaunting of his "foreign pieces" was symptomatic of the general passion for all things Chinese among the newly affluent samurai leaders of the fourteenth century. Envoys who went to China on behalf of these leaders eagerly purchased all the works of art they could find, particularly paintings attributed to Sung and Yüan masters. In the process, they exercised very little critical judgment, accepting many pictures simply on verbal guarantees of their authenticity or on the basis of seals that could easily have been forged. As a consequence, many of the most dearly cherished items in the Chinese art collections of men like Sasaki Dōyo were quite likely of dubious value.

Not until the Higashiyama epoch did the Japanese begin to take careful stock of the numerous artworks and antiques they had so randomly imported from China for several centuries. Yoshimasa assigned members of a group called the "companions" (*dōbōshū*) to survey and catalog the shogunal collection, by this time the largest single accumulation of Chinese treasures in Japan. The companions were artistically talented and discriminating men who were on very intimate terms with the shogun and who were entrusted with the general conduct of his cultural affairs. They included the "three ami" [32] (Nōami, 1397–1471; his son Geiami, 1431–85; and the latter's son Sōami, d. 1525); and in tasks such as the cataloging of the shogunal art collection, which was done chiefly by Nōami and Geiami, these men set the standards for subsequent art connoisseurship in Japan.

Nōami also played an important role in the development of the tea ceremony during the Higashiyama epoch. Until his time, tea had been prepared in one room and brought to the guests in another. Nōami combined the procedures of preparing and serving tea in the same room. Moreover, he formalized each act—from the handling of utensils to the manner of walking while in the presence of guests (slowly, like *nō* actors, with the feet nearly brushing the floor)—and thus helped transform the offering of tea from a party function to a true ceremony.

An even more important molder of the tea ceremony was Shukō (d. 1502), a man of modest background from Nara who was an earnest student of Zen Buddhism. Nōami's style of tea ceremony had been aristocratic, inasmuch as he and other members of the shogun's coterie delighted in employing imported Chinese utensils and in making their gatherings as elegant as possible. Shukō, on the other hand, minimized the surface elegance of the tea ceremony and stressed such simple qualities as *sabi* (agedness) and *wabi* (poverty).

So many trite and gushing things have been written about the Japanese tea ceremony, especially the style of "poverty tea" that has come down to us from Shukō's time, that it is difficult to comment objectively on the subject. The fact remains that the Japanese have expended an extraordinary amount of time and affection on its cultivation and indeed have come to regard participation in it as a profound spiritual experience.

The classical tea ceremony is held in a small room, usually about 9 feet square, which is decorated in a severely simple, even stark, manner. The guests enter it by a doorway so low they are obliged to crawl on their hands and knees, an act taken to symbolize their humility and their acceptance of at least temporary social equality. The mood sought in the ceremony is one of utter tranquility and detachment from worldly concerns. It is expected that the guests will savor in silence the slow and deliberate movements of the host as he prepares and serves the tea. Only after the ceremony has been completed is there likely to be any conversation, and then probably only the exchange of a few comments on the beauty of the utensils used.

Evolution of the tea ceremony was accompanied by the development of new styles in interior design and decoration. The rooms of the earlier *shinden* mansions of the Heian courtiers had been little more than spaces enclosed by sliding doors or other removable partitions. Their floors were bare, and most had no built-in fixtures. During the medieval age, rush matting (*tatami*) was increasingly employed to cover floors, and walls were interspersed with sliding doors to form the sidings of rooms. The sliding doors of this age were of two basic types: the traditional *fusuma*, used in homes (and decorated with Yamato pictures) from at least the Heian period; and the newer and lighter *shōji*, which consisted of lattice-like wooden frameworks with translucent rice paper pasted on one side.

The kind of room created for the tea ceremony was known as the *shoin* or den. Derived from the study chambers built for priests in medieval Zen temples, the *shoin* became the prototype for the main living room of the modern Japanese house. Its chief features, apart from wall-to-wall *tatami*, were a floor-level writing desk built into one wall, overhanging shelves (often of the asymmetrical *chigaidana* type), and an alcove or *tokonoma*.

Fig. 32

The *tokonoma* was the most distinctive feature of the *shoin*, since it lent itself to the display of such things as paintings, flower arrangements, porcelain, and ceramicware. The shape of the average *tokonoma* was especially suitable for vertical hanging scrolls known as *kakemono*, decorated either with pictorial scenes or with samples of calligraphy. The arranging of cut flowers for exhibition in *tokonoma*, moreover, was developed during the medieval age into an art that came to take its place alongside the tea ceremony as one of the most basic of the polite accomplishments of the Japanese.

Another art that flourished in the Muromachi period was monochrome painting done in the manner evolved several centuries earlier by artists of the Sung dynasty in China. Like their Japanese counterparts of this later age, the Sung monochrome artists painted a variety of subjects, including Zen abbots, folk deities, and flowers and birds. But their primary interest lay in landscapes (known in Japanese as *sansui* or pictures of mountains and water). And indeed Sung monochrome landscapes are among the more striking works of Chinese art. They are, moreover, perhaps the most supremely moving tributes of any people to the grandeur and vastness of nature.

The Sung masters made no attempt to reproduce nature as it really was; rather, they employed bold and even daring brushwork to capture in stylized outline misty scenes of forests, jagged cliffs, waterfalls, and awesome mountains (the most distant of which often seem to be on the point of vanishing into remote space). Human figures sketched into these landscapes are usually antlike in size. We see them, insignificant figures engulfed by the cosmos, as lone travelers moving slowly along mountain trails or as recluses seated in pavilion-like huts nestled on the sides of towering peaks.

Sung brushwork owed much to the techniques of calligraphy, and it is in fact common to discuss such brushwork in terms of the three main styles of Chinese calligraphic writing, the "standing," "walking," and "running" styles. The first of these is distinguished by thick, angular strokes, the second by lines that are thinner and more cursive, and the third—the running style—by impressionistic flourishes and splashes of ink. Some artists preferred to paint chiefly in one style or another. But many used all three simultaneously, typically doing foregrounds in the standing style, middle distances in the walking, and backgrounds in the running.

A number of Japanese authorities have asserted that the monochrome landscapes of the Muromachi Japanese are the equal in excellence to the best of those by the Sung masters. Perhaps this is so, but much of the Japanese work in this genre may also be criticized as excessively imitative. After observing how Japanese artists had made the gradual transition in the Heian period from "Chinese pictures" to a native form of painting known as "Yamato pictures," it may be perplexing to find them once again copying an alien art with such seeming indiscrimination. Yet the enthusiasm for Sung-style monochrome painting was simply one example of the powerful effect on Japan of the renewal of cultural influence from China that began in late Heian times and continued almost unabated throughout the medieval age.

The two most distinguished monochrome painters of medieval Japan were Shūbun (d. 1450) and Sesshū (1420–1506), both Zen priests of the Shōkokuji, one of the Gozan or Five Zen Temples of Kyoto. Shūbun, with whom Sesshū later studied, is reputed to have painted many different subjects in a variety of mediums; but the only extant works attributed to him are monochrome landscapes, mostly on folding screens and sliding doors. *Fig. 33*

However great his artistic talents may have been, Shūbun epitomized the cultural Sinification of the age. His paintings were in essence "Chinese pictures"; and, although specialists may detect certain individualistic aspects of style in them, his landscapes represent more of a testament to the recurrent over-responsiveness of the Japanese to foreign cultural influences than to any indigenous creative genius. It was not until the advent of Sesshū that monochrome landscape painting in Japan was finally rendered to some extent native.

Although originally affiliated as a priest with the Shōkokuji, Sesshū left Kyoto shortly before the outbreak of the Ōnin War and journeyed to Yamaguchi in the western provinces of Honshu, where he came under the patronage of the daimyo family of Ōuchi. With Ōuchi backing, Sesshū went to Ming China in 1467 and remained there until 1469. During his two-year stay abroad, he traveled widely and did many sketches and paintings of the Chinese countryside. Curiously perhaps, Sesshū was little inspired by the work of contemporary Ming artists. He professed that his idols remained the venerable Sung monochrome masters and his own countryman, Shūbun.

By Sesshū's time, it had become standard practice for artists to sign or affix their personal seals to all of their works. Hence, there is little doubt about the authenticity of the many paintings of his that have been preserved. One of Sesshū's most famous pieces, still owned by the successor family to the Ōuchi in Yamaguchi, is a horizontal landscape scroll some 52 feet in length and 16 inches in height known as the "Long Landscape Scroll." It leads the viewer, as he runs his eyes from right to left, through an ever-shifting but perfectly integrated series of landscape settings and changing seasons. Sesshū's special love for the axlike, angular strokes of the standing style of brushwork is particularly evident in this painting. Also clearly observable is his inclination, similar to that of many Japanese artists from at least the time of the twelfth-century painters of the Genji Scrolls, to flatten surfaces and thus give a strongly decorative appearance to his work. *Fig. 34*

Another outstanding painting by Sesshū is the hanging scroll or

Fig. 35 *kakemono* that depicts Ama-no-Hashidate, a bay on the Japan Sea coast to the northeast of Kyoto. Sesshū's use of a soft style to reproduce this lovely setting of mountains, water, and an unusual pine-covered sandbar extending nearly across the mouth of the bay seems especially appropriate. More important from the standpoint of the development of Japanese monochrome painting is the fact that he has here drawn an actual site in Japan and not simply an idealized representation of some Chinese-looking scene.

It would be pleasurable to discuss other types of paintings done by Sesshū—including portraits and studies of flowers and birds—that have also contributed to his reputation among many critics as Japan's greatest artist. But space allows only a few comments on still another kind of monochrome landscape in which he excelled, the landscape executed entirely in the running or "splashed ink" style. The best *Fig. 36* known of these is a hanging scroll in the Tokyo National Museum that Sesshū painted in 1495. It is a highly abstract representation of trees on a small island or jut of land with great mountains just faintly visible in the background. Although at first glance this picture may appear to be something that Sesshū simply "dashed off," closer examination reveals how superb a creation it is. One detects, for example, such details as the rooftops of buildings near the water's edge and rowers in a boat just offshore. Indeed, it is in extremely abbreviated, impressionistic paintings of this sort that one perceives most directly the intense feeling for nature that motivated artists like Sesshū.

A major form of art that came to be strongly influenced by monochrome painting in the Muromachi period was landscape gardening. The chronicles indicate that Japanese aristocrats from at least the mid-eighth century on customarily had gardens near their homes; and during the Heian period, as we observed, a fairly standard type of garden evolved in conjunction with the rambling *shinden*-style of courtier mansion. Situated directly in front of the mansion, the garden was built around a stream-fed pond with a small, artificial island in its center. For the pleasure-loving Heian courtiers, such a garden was both a source of visual delight and an excellent setting for outdoor parties.

Later in the Heian period, with the growth in popularity of Pure Land Buddhism, both the *shinden* style of architecture and garden were adapted to the construction of temples that were conceived as representations on earth of Amida's paradise in the western realm of the universe. One of the earliest and finest examples of this kind of temple was, of course, the Byōdōin at Uji.

During the medieval age, the Japanese, while still retaining such features of their traditional garden as the pond, stream (often dammed at some point to create a small waterfall), and artificial island, began to experiment in new and abstract ways with the use of rocks. The pioneer in this kind of experimentation was the Zen priest Musō Soseki (1275–1351), designer of the famous moss garden at the Saihōji in Kyoto. Musō and his successors increasingly used rocks of varying shapes and textures to represent both natural formations and man-made structures, such as mountains, cliffs, waterfalls, and bridges. In addition, they employed sand and white pebbles as "water" and thus, in some of their works, eliminated the pond, which for so many centuries had been the central feature of the Japanese garden.

It was during and after the Higashiyama epoch that the finest of the medieval rock or "dry" gardens were built, many on the grounds   *Fig. 37* of Zen temples. These gardens were reproductions in miniature of great natural scenes; and the more formal of them—made up chiefly, if not exclusively, of rocks and white sand—were very much like three-dimensional monochrome paintings. Not surprisingly, some of the leading monochrome artists of the age, such as Sesshū and Sōami, were also noted designers of gardens.

Perhaps the most famous Japanese rock garden, whose builder and precise date of construction are unknown, is the garden at the Ryōanji   *Fig. 38* in Kyoto. Consisting of a flat, rectangular surface of raked white sand with fifteen rocks scattered about singly and in clusters, the Ryōanji Garden is ostensibly a representation of the ocean with islands protruding above its surface. But it is so extraordinarily severe and abstract in layout that we cannot be certain what its creator actually intended the garden to symbolize or "mean." Presumably it is this very uncertainty that makes the Ryōanji Garden so perennially fascinating to Japanese and foreign tourists alike.

Many of the major arts discussed in this chapter, including the tea ceremony, monochrome painting, and landscape gardening, have come to be regarded as constituents of a distinctive "Zen culture" of Muromachi Japan. There is no question that members of the Zen priesthood were among the leaders in the development of Japan's medieval culture. Moreover, nearly all of the arts of the middle and late medieval age were governed by aesthetic tastes—such as simplicity, restraint, and a liking for the weathered, imperfect, and austere (*sabi* and *wabi*)— which, although not exclusively Zen in origin, certainly came to be associated with the Zen attitude. The only serious objection to the term "Zen culture" is that it may be interpreted to mean a religious culture. Obviously one can argue that all true art must somehow be spiritually or religiously moving. Nevertheless, apart perhaps from certain paintings that portrayed Zen holy men or depicted scenes associated with the quest for *satori*, the Zen culture of Muromachi Japan was essentially a secular culture. This seems to be strong evidence, in fact, of the degree to which medieval Zen had become secularized: its view of nature was pantheistic and its concern with man was largely psychological.

6

The Country Unified

THE LAST CENTURY of the Muromachi period, following the devastating Ōnin War of 1467–77, has been fittingly labeled the age of provincial wars. Although its first few decades witnessed the blossoming of Higashiyama culture, the age was otherwise the darkest and most troubled in Japanese history. Fighting raged from one end of the country to the other. The Ashikaga shoguns became totally powerless, and the domains of many daimyos were torn asunder either by the internecine warfare of vassals or by great peasant uprisings.

Among those most directly and adversely affected by the Ōnin War were the Kyoto courtiers, so long the bearers of traditional culture in Japanese history. Many courtiers had already departed from the capital during the war for safety elsewhere, and others followed after the end of hostilities. A number of prominent courtiers with special artistic and scholarly abilities accepted invitations to visit the more stable and prosperous provincial daimyos, who wished to infuse some of the cultural brilliance of Kyoto into their domainial capitals.

The cultural interests of the courtiers of the late fifteenth century were overwhelmingly antiquarian. They produced very little literature or art of note but rather devoted themselves to exegetical studies of the glorious poetry and prose works of their Heian predecessors, works such as the *Kokinshū*, *The Tales of Ise*, and *The Tale of Genji*. Ever more covetous of their role as custodians of the past, they even established secret or arcane interpretations of these classics which, in their increasingly straitened financial circumstances, they eagerly sought to purvey for cash.

Like the courtier class in general, the imperial family also suffered grievously in the age of provincial wars. Emperors, although still theo-

95

retically sovereign over the land, had long been mere figures of ceremony at court. From about the time of the Ōnin War they gradually withdrew from participation in all but the most essential courtly functions, and often they found themselves embarrassingly unable even to defray the costs of the latter. The coronation of an emperor of the early sixteenth century, for example, was postponed for more than twenty years for lack of funds.

Still another group whose influence was greatly reduced by the Ōnin War was the Zen priesthood of the Gozan temples of Kyoto. Along with the courtiers, the Zen priests depended heavily on the patronage of the Ashikaga Shogunate, especially the opportunity this patronage gave them to accompany the cultural and trading missions to Ming China. With the collapse of the Shogunate as a central governing body in the Ōnin War, initiative in the Ming trade was more and more assumed by certain daimyo houses based in Kyushu and the region of the Inland Sea. We have observed that the Zen priest and artist Sesshū, although formally associated with the Shōkokuji Temple in Kyoto, left the capital during the Ōnin War to take up residence in the Ōuchi domain and subsequently journeyed to China under Ōuchi auspices. Sesshū was simply the most outstanding personality attracted by the Ōuchi during these years in their attempt to make Yamaguchi, their domainial capital, the "Kyoto of the west."

Although the age of provincial wars was a time of great upheaval and seemingly endless disorder, we can see in retrospect that important institutional processes were under way, especially in the evolution of rule at the regional level of Japanese society, that were to make possible a rapid reunification of the country at the end of the sixteenth century. Certain daimyos, such as the Ōuchi, had managed to weather the Ōnin War and its aftermath; but most of the other great daimyo houses of the early Muromachi period were destroyed in the final decades of the fifteenth century. Gradually, during the early sixteenth century, a new class of regional barons emerged as the masters of domains which, although generally smaller than the territorial possessions of the pre-Ōnin War daimyos, were more tightly organized as autonomous units capable of survival in a time of constant civil strife.

These new daimyos of the age of provincial wars were a sturdy and in many ways progressive breed of men, who devoted all their energies to strengthening and expanding their domainial rule. They gathered their vassals into more permanent fighting units, compiled legal codes to cover the altered conditions of the age, and adopted a variety of policies to encourage both agricultural and commercial development and even to exploit, through mining operations and the like, the non-agrarian natural resources of their domains.

By mid-sixteenth century, much of Japan had been brought under the control of this new class of daimyos, and the stage was set for a general competition among the more powerful of them to undertake the task of restoring order to the entire country. Unification and the establishment of a lasting military hegemony was ultimately carried out by three great chieftains—Oda Nobunaga (1534-82), Toyotomi Hideyoshi (1536-98), and Tokugawa Ieyasu (1542-1616)—all of whom came from the region of modern Nagoya, midway between the central provinces and the Kantō.

Nobunaga took the first important step toward unification when he led his armies into Kyoto in 1568. Five years later he deposed the puppet Ashikaga shogun and thus officially dissolved the long-moribund Muromachi Shogunate. Nobunaga then set about expanding his power outward from Kyoto, dealing in turn with various enemies that included other daimyos, the members of Buddhist sects, and militant peasant bands. A hard and ruthless campaigner, Nobunaga often inflicted savage punishment on those who opposed him. Perhaps the most conspicuous example of this was his attack in 1571 on the Enryakuji Temple of Mount Hiei, whose monks had refused either to join him or to remain neutral in the struggle for control of the central provinces. Circling Mount Hiei, Nobunaga's forces marched up its sides, not only destroying the thousands of buildings that comprised the temple complex but also killing everyone they found from monks to the many folk who had been drawn from nearby villages for sanctuary on the mountain. Thus, in an orgy of slaughter, Nobunaga virtually obliterated the greatest scholarly and religious center of ancient Japan.

In 1582, while he was in the process of directing his armies against the western provinces, Nobunaga was assassinated at the age of forty-nine by one of his generals. His death was speedily avenged by another general, Hideyoshi, who thereupon assumed the mantle of unifier and, within eight years, brought the remainder of Japan under his control. Hideyoshi, probably the greatest military commander in Japanese history, rose by sheer ability and drive from the ranks of the peasantry to become national overlord, a career record that was exceptional even in this dynamic age.

Although invincible in his march to power in Japan, Hideyoshi ignominiously failed in two attempts to invade Korea in 1592 and 1597. He was apparently motivated to undertake these foreign adventures both from the desire for new lands to conquer and the wish to open by force new avenues of trade with the continent. The first invasion attempt was repulsed by Chinese armies that poured down from the north across the Yalu River, and the second was terminated upon Hideyoshi's death in 1598.

When Hideyoshi died he left an infant son to succeed him, and before long a struggle for power ensued in which two great leagues of daimyos came to confront each other. The head of one of these leagues was Tokugawa Ieyasu, a daimyo now based at Edo (modern Tokyo) in the Kantō, who had faithfully served Nobunaga and had later reluctantly submitted to Hideyoshi. The victory of Ieyasu's league over its coalition of opponents in a decisive clash of arms at Sekigahara in 1600 enabled the Tokugawa chieftain to impose a new hegemony over Japan and to establish a military government, known as the Tokugawa Shogunate, that was to endure until the beginning of modern times in the late nineteenth century.

The age of unification under Nobunaga, Hideyoshi, and Ieyasu was a particularly lively and exciting one in premodern Japanese history, not only because of the spectacular military exploits of these three great unifiers but also because of the arrival of Europeans in Japan. It was the Portuguese who led the European maritime explorations of the fifteenth century down the coast of Africa and into Asian waters. They rounded the Cape of Good Hope and touched India in 1498; and within another fifteen years or so they reached China, where they established a permanent trading station at Macao in 1559. Portuguese traders first set foot on Japanese soil about 1543, landing in a Chinese junk on the small island of Tanegashima off the coast of Kyushu.

Christian missionaries followed shortly in the wake of Portuguese traders to Japan. Europe was at the time aflame with the fervor of the Counter Reformation, and the king of Portugal had undertaken sponsorship of the recently formed and militantly aggressive Society of Jesus. It was, in fact, one of the leaders of the Jesuits, St. Francis Xavier (1506–52), who inaugurated Christian missionary activity in Japan. During his stay there from 1549 until 1551, Xavier developed a strong liking for the Japanese people as well as high optimism for the prospects of conversion among them. No doubt one reason why he and other European visitors of this age to the Far East felt a certain preference for the Japanese over other Asiatics they encountered was that the warring, feudal conditions of sixteenth-century Japan reminded them so much of home. The Jesuits in particular, with their special liking for martial order and discipline, could readily appreciate the rigorous life style of Japan's ruling samurai class.

Most of the missionary work of the Jesuits in the first decade or so after their arrival in Japan was restricted to those daimyo domains in Kyushu where the Portuguese trading ships made their calls. Not until the rise of Nobunaga were conditions sufficiently settled to allow them to extend their proselytizing activities to other parts of the country, especially to the central provinces. Nobunaga showed himself to be quite well disposed toward the Christian fathers, and on several occasions granted them personal interviews. One apparent reason for his cordiality was his hope that the Jesuits might be useful in combating, at least doctrinally, those Buddhist sects of the capital region that opposed his advance to national power.

Hideyoshi was also friendly toward the Jesuits in his early years as military hegemon. He was keenly interested in foreign trade and, through courtesies extended to the missionaries, sought to lure an ever greater number of Portuguese ships to Japan. Hideyoshi also sent forth his own trading vessels (known as vermilion seal ships from the documents of authorization they carried bearing such seals) and Japanese traders were seen during these years in ports of countries as distant as the Philippines, Cambodia, and Siam.

Portuguese ships had in the beginning dropped anchor in various harbors on the northern and western coasts of Kyushu. More often than not, they selected their ports of call on the basis of whether or not the local daimyos were tolerant of or welcomed Christianity. Undoubtedly the conversion of a number of Kyushu daimyos to Christianity about this time was motivated partly, if not entirely, by their desire to attract Portuguese trade. One of the most prominent of the Christian daimyos was Ōmura Sumitada, who in 1570 opened the harbor of Nagasaki in his domain to Portuguese commerce and ten years later ceded it as a territorial possession to be administered by the Jesuits.

By the late 1580's, when Hideyoshi carried his campaign of unification to Kyushu, Nagasaki had been transformed from a small coastal village into a flourishing port city with a high percentage of Christian converts among its population. The future prospects of both Portuguese traders and Jesuit missionaries in Japan were bright indeed. Then, in 1587, without warning or intimation, Hideyoshi declared the "nationalization" of Nagasaki and ordered the Jesuit missionaries to leave the country within twenty days. Hideyoshi never fully implemented his decree against the missionaries, since he feared that it might drive away the Portuguese traders as well. Yet, the fact that he issued it at all suggests a growing anti-Christian feeling in Japan's ruling circles, a feeling that was to reach great intensity several decades later.

The Portuguese and other Europeans, including Spanish, Dutch, and English, who visited Japan in the late sixteenth and early seventeenth centuries were loosely labeled by the Japanese (in accordance with Chinese practice) as *namban* or "southern barbarians," since they came from the seas to the south. For practical purposes, however, the so-called *namban* culture of this age consisted of the forms of Western technology, culture, and general knowledge introduced to Japan by the Jesuits. By far the leading center of *namban* culture was Nagasaki, which remained strongly under Jesuit and Portuguese influence even after Hideyoshi's nationalization of it in 1587.

Among the very first things the Portuguese introduced to the Japanese were Western firearms, and before long these weapons were in great demand among the daimyos contending for national power. But supply fell far short of demand and only the more strategically located daimyos were able to acquire firearms (chiefly muskets) in numbers sufficient to be decisive in battle. In his drive toward Kyoto, for example, Nobunaga seized the two most important foundries for musket production in the central provinces—one in the port city of Sakai and the other in the province of Ōmi to the east of the capital—and thereby ensured his superiority in firepower over his most immediate enemies.

It is often assumed that the Portuguese also influenced the Japanese in the construction of castles in the late sixteenth and early seventeenth centuries. Certainly this was the great age of castle building in Japan, but there is little evidence that the Japanese received any direct Portuguese instruction or aid in the building of these fortresses. Rather, the castles of the era of unification appear to have evolved as a natural product of conditions of accelerated warfare and the formation of more firmly and rationally controlled daimyo domains.

Fig. 39

In the early centuries of the medieval age, the samurai had apparently felt very little need for strong defensive fortifications. Although occasionally a force of warriors would attempt to hold a position against great odds, medieval armies usually withdrew when the tide of battle turned against them in order to regroup and fight again another day. In the style of warfare that prevailed until at least the Ōnin War, even the occupation of key cities, such as Kyoto, was seldom regarded as absolutely crucial from the standpoint of overall strategy. Thus, during the war between the Northern and Southern Courts in the fourteenth century, the Ashikaga on several occasions temporarily relinquished possession of the capital to the forces of the Southern Court when it seemed impractical or excessively difficult to defend it. Fighting in those days was done almost entirely by the samurai, and few peasants or townsmen were impressed into military service. Since supplies were readily accessible in the countryside, moreover, cities were not essential over the short term even for economic reasons. Hence Kyoto, until the Ōnin War, seldom suffered great physical damage as a direct result of warfare. Armies came and went and the city continued to function more or less as usual.

The new breed of daimyos who emerged in the age of provincial wars expanded their domains by stages and at each stage developed new types of fortifications to meet their military, economic, and administrative needs. In the early sixteenth century the most common fortress or "castle" was a kind of wooden stockade built atop a hill, a site selected solely because of its defensibility. The master, his family, and personal retinue lived at the base of the hill and used the castle only when attacked.

As daimyos spread their hegemonies over larger territories, they began to move their castles to level land. Some picked locations with protective mountains or bodies of water to the rear; but others—particularly the more successful daimyos from about the time of Nobunaga's rise—placed their castles on open land or plains. Daimyos who constructed castles in settings of the latter type obviously felt sufficiently secure in their positions as baronial rulers to sacrifice the military advantages of less exposed terrain in order to make these strongholds the administrative and commercial centers of their domains.

Nobunaga built a great castle at Azuchi on the shore of Lake Biwa; and Hideyoshi constructed three: one in Kyoto, another at Momoyama immediately to the south of the capital, and a third (a particularly massive fortification) at Osaka. Unfortunately, none of these structures has survived. Indeed, there are few castles remaining in Japan today and all postdate the period of unification. Warfare and natural disasters, combined with the policy of the Tokugawa Shogunate to restrict the possession and repair of castles, have taken their toll over the centuries. In addition to those torn down or allowed to decay in Tokugawa times, a number of fortifications were reduced in the fighting that accompanied the Meiji Restoration of 1868; and an especially splendid castle at Nagoya was demolished during an air attack in World War II.

Although no longer in existence, Nobunaga's castle at Azuchi and Hideyoshi's at Momoyama have given their names to the cultural epoch of the age of unification. The designation of this epoch as Azuchi-Momoyama (or, for the sake of convenience, simply Momoyama) is quite appropriate in view of the significance of castles—as represented by these two historically famous structures—in the general progress, cultural and otherwise, of these exciting years. For castles served not only as fortifications but also as centers of urban growth in the form of castle towns and as the symbols of daimyo authority and material opulence.

Apart from moats and great protective walls of stone, the most conspicuous feature of the Japanese castle was the many-storied keep or donjon. The typical keep had white plastered walls and complexly arranged, hipped and gabled roofs of tile, designed so that each roof was smaller in size than the one directly below it. Although the keeps were relatively safe from attack by incendiary missiles, owing to the composition of their walls and their sloped roofs, they were highly vulnerable to cannon. But Western-style artillery was not introduced into warfare in Japan until the late 1580's, shortly before Hideyoshi completed unification. And, in any case, the keeps of these late-sixteenth-century Japanese castles were not primarily designed as last-ditch military strongholds. Rather, they were intended to symbolize the power and eminence of their masters. Their exteriors were imposing and their interiors were carefully arranged into private living quarters, decorated according to the prevailing tastes of the age. As we shall see, some of the finest artwork of the Momoyama epoch was done on screens and sliding doors for use and display in castles.

Before examining further the Momoyama epoch of domestic culture, however, let us return to the foreign and exotic *namban* culture of the Portuguese traders and Jesuit missionaries that also flourished briefly during these years.

One of the most noteworthy projects undertaken by Europeans of this age in Japan was the opening of a Jesuit Press. During the period from 1591 until 1610, the Jesuits, using chiefly movable type which they introduced to the Japanese, printed some fifty books in Latin, Portuguese, and Japanese (in both the Romanized and native orthographies). Most of the Jesuit publications were Christian religious tracts, but some dealt with language and literature. Among the few examples of literary works that have been preserved are a Japanese translation of *Aesop's Fables* and a rendering into *romaji* or Roman letters of the famous medieval war tale *The Tale of the Heike*. The *Heike* and other Japanese narratives, known from the records to have been done in *romaji* at this time, were primarily intended for the use of missionaries as aids in learning the native language.

Another cultural activity in which the Jesuits were prominent was the introduction of Western pictorial art to Japan in the form of oil painting and copper engraving. The Jesuits were especially anxious to provide votive pictures for newly established Christian churches and for individual converts to Christianity who wished to display them in their homes. So great was the demand for these pictures that it could not be met solely by the importation of works from Europe, and the Jesuits were obliged to instruct Japanese artists in Western-style painting. All indications are that the Japanese learned the foreign style quickly and soon produced the desired pictures in more than adequate quantity. Yet, regrettably, the great bulk of such pictures by Japanese artists, as well as those brought from Europe, was destroyed in the Christian persecutions of the seventeenth century, and we have only a relatively few works remaining from which to judge Japan's "Christian art" during and after the period of unification.

Although much of *namban* art was either iconographic or religious in nature, there are extant a number of paintings and engravings done in the Western manner of such secular subjects as European cities, landscapes, and non-clerical people. Some of the latter are shown in portrait-like poses, but others are depicted in genre scenes performing everyday activities of work and leisure. These foreign genre pictures are particularly interesting because, as we shall see, it was about this time that the Japanese evolved a new style of genre painting of their own, a style that led ultimately to the famous *ukiyo-e* or "floating world" pictures of the Tokugawa period.

One kind of Japanese genre painting that dates from the late sixteenth century is the so-called *namban* screen. Although designated as *namban* because they depict Europeans in Japan, these screens are actually the creations of Japanese artists working entirely within the native tradition of painting.

The *namban* screens commonly come in pairs and are often very similar in subject matter, one showing the departure of the Portuguese carrack (great ship) from Goa or Macao and the other its arrival at Nagasaki. In the latter, the passengers are usually shown proceeding from the shore toward town, where they mingle with people, both Japanese and Europeans, who have come to greet them. The Portuguese traders are drawn with exceedingly small heads, thin legs, and huge pantaloons, and the Jesuits are shown attired in flowing black clerical robes. In some of the *namban* screens, the Portuguese are accompanied by black servants (who greatly delighted the Japanese) and are leading such animals as Arabian horses, deer, peacocks, and elephants. Also frequently shown in these screens are Christian churches, constructed in the architectural style of Buddhist temple buildings.

Fig. 40

It is impossible to date these rather stereotyped *namban* screens precisely, although most of them were probably painted in the early or mid-1590's when the fad for Western things was at its height in Japan. Hideyoshi had established his military headquarters near Nagasaki for the invasion of Korea in 1592, and this proximity aroused a new curiosity about the foreigners and their ways among Japan's samurai leaders. The Jesuits sought to capitalize on such curiosity in the hope of gaining better understanding and offsetting Hideyoshi's anti-Christian acts of recent years. They were fortunate to have available an exceptional "public relations" group of four Japanese Christians from Kyushu who had gone as youths in 1582 on a mission to Europe where they had visited Pope Gregory XIII in Rome.

Returning in 1590, these young men possessed not only first-hand knowledge of Europe but also various mementos of their trip, such as artworks, mechanical devices, and maps.

Hideyoshi and his advisers, then planning their invasion of Korea, were much impressed by the foreign maps and techniques of cartography; and the making of maps, many of them painted in bright colors on folding screens and even fans, became as popular about this time as the production of the *namban* pictures showing the arrival of the Portuguese great ship. Most of these *namban* maps were depictions either of the world or of Japan alone, and, apart from a distorted rendering in the world maps of the Americas and the northern and northeastern regions of Asia, they appear to be respectably accurate. The world maps, moreover, make manifestly clear by the varying perspectives from which they were drawn that the earth is round (although the Jesuits in their preaching refused to endorse the still heretical Copernican theory of earthly rotation around the sun).

The most frivolous aspect of the craze for things Western in the 1590's was the aping by Japanese, including Hideyoshi himself, of the Portuguese style of dress and personal adornment. The degree to which these became fashionable can be seen in a letter written by a Jesuit father about this time:

> Quambacudono (i.e., the Kwambaku, Toyotomi Hideyoshi) has become so enamored of Portuguese dress and costume that he and his retainers frequently wear this apparel, as do all the other lords of Japan, even the gentiles, with rosaries of driftwood on the breast above all their clothing, and with a crucifix at their side, or hanging from the waist, and sometimes even with kerchiefs in their hands; some of them are so curious that they learn by rote the litanies of *Pater Noster* and *Ave Maria* and go along praying in the streets, not in mockery or scorn of the Christians, but simply for gallantry, or because they think it is a good thing and one which will help them to achieve prosperity in worldly things. In this way they order oval-shaped pendants to be made containing reliques of the images of Our Lord and Our Lady painted on glass at great cost.[33]

But none of the interests the Japanese displayed in *namban* culture and Portuguese styles was, as we shall see, able to stem the mounting tide of anti-Christian sentiment that led in the seventeenth century to severe persecutions and, finally, to the expulsion of foreigners and adoption of a national seclusion policy. Although the Dutch were allowed to trade at Nagasaki, Christianity and Western ways were in general so thoroughly rooted out that few traces of *namban* culture were to be found in Japan after about the mid-seventeenth century.

There remained some things, like firearms, tobacco, and eyeglasses, and a few Portuguese words, such as *pan* (bread), *karuta* (playing card), and *kappa* (a straw cape used as a raincoat), to attest to the fact that the Jesuits and their patrons had really been in Japan for nearly a hundred years. Otherwise, their presence and cultural influence was to a remarkable extent expunged from the memory of the Japanese until modern times.

Along with architecture, painting was the art that most fully captured the vigorous and expansive spirit of the Momoyama epoch of domestic culture during the age of unification. It was a time when many styles of painting and groups of painters flourished. Of the latter, by far the best known and most successful were the Kanō, a school that was maintained by lineal and adopted descendants from medieval until modern times.

The origins of the Kanō school can be traced from Masanobu (1434–1530), a member of a samurai house who purportedly studied under Shūbun. Masanobu accepted the post, first declined by Sesshū, of official artist to the Ashikaga Shogunate in the *kanga* or Chinese manner of Sung and Yüan monochrome painting. He thus established the Kanō as a line of professional painters who worked on commission to meet the demands of their warrior patrons.

Although Masanobu founded the Kanō school, it was his son and successor, Motonobu (1476–1559), who was most responsible for defining its character and course of development. Motonobu was by all accounts a true eclectic. He continued the Kanō tradition of *kanga* monochrome painting, which still dominated the attention of nearly all Japanese artists until well into the sixteenth century; but Motonobu also made free use of the colorful Yamato style of native art that had evolved during the Heian period and had reached its pinnacle in the great narrative picture scrolls of the twelfth and thirteenth centuries.

The Yamato style had declined in early Muromachi times with the renewal of trade with the continent and the growing (and finally consuming) interest of Japanese artists, especially members of the Zen priesthood, in Chinese monochrome work. A line of painters called the Tosa school, who were engaged as official artists by the imperial court just as the Kanō were employed by the Shogunate, formally sustained the Yamato tradition throughout the Muromachi period. But the Tosa artists produced little work of distinction, and it was not until Kanō Motonobu eclectically blended the Yamato and *kanga* styles that indigenous achievements in the development of painting were restored to the mainstream of artwork in Japan. As if formalistically to seal the merger of the native and foreign ways of painting, Motonobu married the daughter of Tosa Mitsunobu, probably the best of his school in the Muromachi period and the person most responsible for the modest revival of Tosa painting about Motonobu's time.

The greatest representative of the Kanō school in the Momoyama epoch was Kanō Eitoku (1543–90), who, after dissolution of the Ashikaga Shogunate in 1573, was successively employed by the new military hegemons, Nobunaga and Hideyoshi. It was a cardinal event in the history of Japanese art when Eitoku was invited by Nobunaga in 1576 to decorate the interior of his new castle at Azuchi. Although Azuchi Castle no longer stands, we know from the chronicles the great variety of paintings in both monochrome and color it contained, including pictures of flowers, trees, birds, rocks, dragons, phoenixes, Buddhist themes, and Chinese sages.

Probably no other people has sought more assiduously than the Japanese to adapt their art—most notably painting—to developments in domestic architecture. From at least the Heian period on, much of Japanese secular painting had been done on folding screens and sliding doors, the chief devices used for the partitioning of space in the mansions of the Heian aristocracy. Even with the transition from the *shinden* to the *shoin* style of architecture in the Muromachi period, painting was readily adjusted to meet the additional decorative needs of the *shoin* room through the production in greater numbers of vertical hanging scrolls (*kakemono*) for display in the new alcoves or *tokonoma*. But it was not until the Momoyama epoch that the claims of architecture most conspicuously influenced the course of painting in Japan. To decorate the larger wall spaces, sliding doors, and screens of the living quarters of the typical Momoyama castle, the Kanō and other contemporary painters were forced to create a new, monumental style of art.

The practice of painting on folding screens (which in Japan was also adapted to the *fusuma*-type sliding doors) was originally derived from China, and a great number of Chinese-style screen paintings have been preserved from the eighth century in the Shōsōin at Nara. But with the development of Zen-inspired monochrome painting in the Sung period, Chinese artists abandoned the folding screen as a medium for their work. These artists, who were chiefly members of the literati class, saw that the monochrome style of landscape painting could more effectively be rendered on smaller formats, such as hanging scrolls, and by and large they left the decorating of screens to house painters and other lower-class artisans. In medieval Japan, on the other hand, the folding screen remained an extremely popular format for art among both the courtier and warrior aristocracies, and even the most prominent landscape painters, including Shūbun, were obliged to do much of their work on the larger areas of screen panels. This presented considerable difficulty, since the typical subtlety and suggestiveness of landscapes in ink were apt to appear as signs of weakness or insipidity on, say, a six-panel screen that measured some 5 or more feet in height and perhaps 12 feet in width.

Sesshū partly solved the problem of painting monochrome landscapes on large surfaces by employing an exceptionally strong brush stroke, a technique that was also adopted by the artists of the Kanō school. In addition, the Kanō turned increasingly from the painting of landscapes to flowers and birds, which provided them greater opportunity for close-up detailing and the decorative placement of objects. Although Sesshū and other Muromachi artists had earlier done scenes of flowers and birds on screens, it was the Kanō and their fellow painters of the Momoyama epoch who most fully exploited this traditional subject category of Chinese art.

But what screen painting really called for was color, and it was this that the Kanō artists, drawing on the native Yamato tradition, added to their work with great gusto during the Momoyama epoch. The color that these artists particularly favored was gold, and compositions done in ink and rich pigments on gold-leaf backgrounds became the most characteristic works of Momoyama art. It has been hypothesized that this extremely free use of gold leaf, which had been known but seldom employed by artists of the Muromachi period, was partly dictated by the need for greater illumination in the dimly lit reception halls of Momoyama castles. In any case, there could hardly be a more striking contrast between the spirits of two ages than the one reflected in the transition from the subdued monochromatic art of Japan's medieval era to the blazing use of color by Momoyama artists, who stood on the threshold of early modern times. The Kanō and other Momoyama artists continued also to paint in black and white, but their greatest and most original contribution to Japanese art was their heroic work in color done on screens.

Many Momoyama screens are unsigned, and it is only from an analysis of their styles or from contemporary accounts that the artists who did them can with any certainty be identified. The most likely reason for this anonymity is that Momoyama screen painters often worked in teams, and no doubt it was regarded as inappropriate for a single individual to take credit for a picture done jointly by affixing his personal signature or seal to it. Tradition has it that when Kanō Eitoku did large projects, like the decoration of Nobunaga's castle at Azuchi, he simply sketched in the outlines of pictures—often using a brush that was like a large straw broom—and left the detailing to his assistants.

Momoyama screen painting developed into a fully decorative style of art in which overall design and the placement of objects were of paramount importance. The boldness with which the Momoyama masters executed their works is readily observable in Kanō Eitoku's composition of a twisting, gnarled cypress tree set against a background of rocks, azure water, and gold-leaf clouds. Later decorative artists of the seventeenth and early eighteenth centuries were to scale down Eitoku's handling of objects and to soften his use of color. But they lived in an age when peace and stability were taken for granted in Japan, whereas Eitoku and his contemporaries displayed in their art the tremendous, if often impetuous, energy of the epic Momoyama years of unification.

Another major artist of the Momoyama epoch was Hasegawa Tōhaku (1539–1610). Like all Momoyama painters, Tōhaku worked in a variety of styles, including the colorful decorative manner that was so closely associated with his rivals, Eitoku and the Kanō school. He had a special fondness, however, for the monochrome art of the Muromachi masters and in fact declared himself to be the true successor to the tradition of Sesshū. In several of his major works, including the picture of pine trees on a pair of six-panel screens, Tōhaku demonstrated how a new and imaginative approach to the use of monochrome on large areas could produce extremely satisfying results. His *Fig. 41*   clusters of pine trees, presented without supporting motifs in either the foreground or background, do not seem at all inadequate for the decoration of these multi-paneled screens. Rather, they strikingly enhance, in the best Zen-like tradition, the emptiness of the remainder of the screens' surface.

Apart from the decorative style, the most significant art form to evolve during the Momoyama epoch was genre painting. Genre scenes —that is, portrayals of people in their everyday activities—can be found in Yamato pictures from the Heian period on and are particularly common in the later horizontal scrolls of the medieval era. Yet, for the most part, the genre scenes in these scrolls have been placed within the context of running narratives and were not intended to stand alone as depictions of how people of the age characteristically behaved. A major exception is a scroll reputedly painted at the end of the Heian period (although only copies done many centuries later in the manner of the original survive today) entitled "Important Events of the Year" (*nenjū-gyōji*), which shows Heian aristocrats in the cycle of elegant activities that filled their social calendars. Because the "Important Events" Scroll deals only with courtiers, however, its value as social history is limited. True genre art, picturing all classes at work and play, did not appear in Japan until the sixteenth century.

The oldest extant genre painting of the sixteenth century is a work, dating from about 1525, called "Views Inside and Outside Kyoto" (*rakuchū-rakugai zu*). Done on a pair of six-panel screens, it provides a bird's-eye, panoramic scene of the capital and its environs. Temples, mansions of the élite, mountains, and other famous points of interest in and about the city are clearly distinguishable, and people can be seen everywhere, promenading on the streets, relaxing in courtyards, visiting temples, carrying goods for sale and delivery, and attending the innumerable shops and stalls that stretch in rows along the busy thoroughfares. Because of the picture's obvious stress on the bustling commercial life of the city, a number of scholars have speculated that it was either produced or commissioned by merchants anxious to commemorate the crucial role of trade in the rebuilding of the capital after the devastation of the Ōnin War.

Many other pictures on the theme of "Views Inside and Outside Kyoto," including a particularly detailed one by Kanō Eitoku, were produced during the following two centuries. In addition to their artistic merits, these pictures are invaluable records of the changing *Fig. 42* features of the ancient capital in an age (at least until 1600) when it was more than ever the vital administrative as well as cultural center of the country.

With the coming of the Momoyama epoch and the general re-establishment of tranquility in the land, genre artists turned increasingly to studies of people at leisure and in the pursuit of pleasure rather than engaged simply in daily chores or as members of a passing scene (as in the pictures of "Views Inside and Outside Kyoto"). Among the great variety of subjects shown in genre works of the Momoyama epoch are picnics, flower-viewing excursions, festivals, horse races, dancing, actors of the popular theatre (*kabuki*), and women of the pleasure quarters. Of these, the *kabuki* actors and courtesans came especially to attract the attention of artists of the seventeenth-century urban scene, a clear indication of the emergence among them of what may be called a spirit of bourgeois or popular humanism.

Changing techniques in the handling of subjects also indicated the growing humanistic concerns of genre artists of this age. From distant, elevated perspectives that encompassed wide vistas and often huge throngs of people, they gradually shifted to intimate portrayals of small groups of men and women—or even of single individuals—viewed directly from close range. Moreover, by eliminating settings entirely and using stark gold-leaf backgrounds, these late Momoyama and early Tokugawa period genre artists presented their subjects, most of whom were denizens of the demimonde, as directly and candidly as possible.

Fig. 43

Although it differs from many of the others, which are frankly erotic, one of the finest of these portrait-type genre works of the Momoyama epoch is the so-called Matsuura Screen. It depicts eighteen women engaged in various casual activities and pastimes, some of which reveal the special fashions and fads of the day. Two women, for example, are playing cards, a game introduced by the Portuguese; another accepts from a companion a long-stemmed pipe containing tobacco, which was also brought to Japan by Westerners in the sixteenth century; and still another woman plucks the *samisen*, a three-stringed, banjo-like musical instrument of the Ryukyus that first became popular in Japan around the 1590's. Apart from the activities in which its subjects are engaged, the Matsuura Screen is notable for at least two reasons: first, for the skillful manner in which the artist has arranged his women, so that they strike an exceptionally varied and rhythmically interlocking series of poses; and second, for the dazzlingly patterned kimonos the women are wearing. Some authorities have conjectured, on the basis of the studied placement of the figures and the particularly flat appearance of their attire, almost as though it consisted of pieces of material pasted onto the surface of the picture, that the Matsuura Screen was actually produced as an advertisement or a merchant's display poster. In any event, it reveals the great skill that artists of this age were capable of in handling the genre-type portraits that were to serve as forerunners of the famous "pictures of the floating world" (to be discussed in the next chapter).

One of the most prominent people of the Momoyama cultural scene was the noted tea master and arbiter of taste, Sen Rikyū (1521-91). Descended from a Sakai merchant house, Rikyū became a devoted practitioner of the classical tea ceremony of *wabicha*, based on standards of severe restraint, humility, and "poverty," that Shukō had originated a century earlier.

The rise of Rikyū was in one respect an indication of the expanded influence, in cultural as well as commercial matters, of the merchant class of the Momoyama epoch. Rikyū, who came to serve both Nobunaga and Hideyoshi, appears indeed as a herald of the coming age of bourgeois culture that flourished under the Tokugawa after 1600. Yet, despite his bourgeois background, Rikyū remained essentially a medieval man. He was not reluctant to take advantage of the new opportunities for social and political advancement that the times presented; but in the realm of culture, Rikyū proved to be a necessary restraining force against the excessive exuberance of the Momoyama spirit.

Momoyama screen art, although bold and showy, was saved from becoming vulgar by its firm grounding in the earlier, more traditional *kanga* and Yamato styles of painting. The tea ceremony, on the other hand, was greatly threatened by the urge to ostentation it aroused among the newly risen military leaders of the age of unification. In their desire to demonstrate their cultural as well as martial grandeur, these swashbuckling chieftains went to extravagant lengths to engage specialists in the "way of tea" and to collect rare and unusual tea utensils and accessories. They frequently purchased these at astronomical prices and greatly coveted them. One daimyo, Matsunaga Hisahide, is said on a certain occasion to have saved his life by presenting Nobunaga with a priceless tea caddy. Some years later, after Matsunaga had joined a plot against Nobunaga and was faced with imminent destruction, he purportedly smashed to bits another highly treasured piece, a kettle, to prevent its falling into his adversary's hands.

When Nobunaga in his march to power imposed his control over the city of Sakai, then the main port in the lucrative foreign trade with China, he acquired a number of valuable tea pieces from the collections of wealthy Sakai merchants and took into his service several of the better known tea masters of the city, including Sen Rikyū. In addition to having these masters design the tearoom for his castle at Azuchi, Nobunaga used them to preside over the frequent and elaborate tea parties he held. It became his custom, moreover, to bestow prized tea utensils on his lieutenants for meritorious service; and he even went so far as to make the right of these men to hold formal tea parties a distinction which he alone could bestow. It is recorded that Hideyoshi, when granted this honor in 1578 after an important military victory, was overcome with gratitude toward Nobunaga.

Upon his accession to national overlordship, Hideyoshi displayed an especially strong fondness for mammoth social affairs and is particularly remembered for the great tea party he held at the Kitano Shrine in Kyoto in 1587. The party was scheduled to last for ten days, weather permitting, and everyone, from courtiers and daimyos to townsmen and peasants and even foreigners, was invited. Guests were required only to bring a few utensils to serve themselves and mats to sit on. An outbreak of fighting in Kyushu brought cancellation of the party after only one day; yet it seems to have been thoroughly enjoyed by the great throng of people who attended. Hideyoshi put many of his most valued tea pieces on display and, along with Rikyū and two other tea masters from Sakai, personally served a large number of the assembled guests.

Although Rikyū was an active participant in the Kitano extravaganza, the experience was no doubt inherently painful to him. Intensely committed to *wabicha*, Rikyū is noted for having carried this style of tea ceremony to its farthest extreme. Shukō had suggested that the ceremony be held in a small room, preferably four and a half mats in size, and that it be conducted with a minimum of utensils and decorative accessories. Later *wabicha* masters went so far as to arrange their teahouses to appear like the huts of the most humble of farmers, building them with mud walls and unpainted wood, and eliminating all decoration save a single display of flowers or calligraphy in the *tokonoma*. Rikyū, however, achieved the ultimate in *wabicha* settings by adopting as his preferred teahouse a stark hut of only two mats in size, which could at most accommodate two or three people in one gathering.

Despite his penchant for the grandiose, Hideyoshi was also a fond admirer of *wabicha* and he and Rikyū became intimate companions. As a result, Rikyū was one of the most influential people in Japanese ruling circles during the late 1580's. Then, suddenly, disaster struck. In 1591, for reasons that remain to this day obscure, Hideyoshi ordered his distinguished tea master to commit suicide. Hideyoshi, who was noted for his impetuosity and who was fully capable of ghastly and capricious acts of tyranny, may have imposed this punishment for some personal slight or because he genuinely feared the power Rikyū had acquired. It is said that Hideyoshi later much lamented having caused the tea master's death. At any rate, the passing of Sen Rikyū removed from Japan's cultural scene the last great medieval figure and accelerated the advent of the already rapidly approaching early modern age.

7

The Flourishing of a Bourgeois Culture

THE GREAT PEACE of more than two and a half centuries that followed the founding of the Tokugawa Shogunate in 1600 was made possible largely by the policy of national seclusion which the Shogunate adopted during the late 1630's. To many historians this policy, carried out amid fearful persecutions of both native and foreign Christians, has appeared as an arbitrary and extraordinarily reactionary measure whereby the Tokugawa, in order to preserve their national hegemony, terminated a lively century of intercourse with the countries of Western Europe and reinstituted harsh and repressive feudal controls over Japan.

It has been held that the Japanese paid a tremendous price in progress by cutting themselves off from the West just as it was entering fully into its great age of technological and scientific advancements. No doubt this is in some measure true. Yet, we cannot simply assume that, in the absence of the Tokugawa seclusion policy, Japan would have moved steadily or smoothly into more intimate relations with the West. To the Westerners, Japan still lay at the farthest extremity of the known world; and quite possibly the Western trade of this age with Japan had already passed its zenith. Japan, moreover, was not alone in acting as it did, but was only one of several countries of the Far East—including China, Korea, and Vietnam—that effectively minimized or restricted trade and cultural ties with the West during the seventeenth century. In their first major encounter, the East as a whole thus managed to hold the West at arm's length. Two centuries later when the West, having undergone its industrial revolution, sought once more to intrude into the Far East, its impetus was such that it could not be stopped by unilateral seclusion or restriction policies.

The Tokugawa, of course, did not conceive of participating in a historical movement by which the East rejected the West. They pursued their seclusion policy for essentially two reasons: first, the fear, smoldering since Hideyoshi's day, that Christianity was by its nature antithetical to Japan's traditional social order and religious beliefs; and secondly, the apprehension that the daimyos of western Japan, who had been the leading opponents of the Tokugawa before the battle of Sekigahara, might ally themselves with the Europeans and attempt to overthrow the Edo regime. Although it is questionable how realistic the Tokugawa concern over Christianity was, there can be no doubt that the presence in Kyushu ports of Europeans capable of providing arms and other military supplies to the western daimyos was a very real threat to national peace. Short of seeking to assert more complete military overlordship of the country than had been achieved at Sekigahara, especially in the western provinces, the Tokugawa actually had no practical alternative other than to impose some sort of seclusion policy if they wished to ensure the security of their regime.

The Tokugawa held approximately one-quarter of the agricultural land of Japan. In addition, they directly administered a number of the major cities, including Kyoto, Osaka, and Nagasaki, as well as certain important mining sites. The remainder of the country was divided into the domains or *han* of the daimyos. During the Tokugawa period, there were two principal kinds of territorial lords: hereditary or vassal (*fudai*) daimyos, who had pledged personal loyalty to the Tokugawa before Sekigahara and were raised to daimyo status after this great victory; and "outside" (*tozama*) daimyos, who had been peers of the Tokugawa family head before 1600 and, whether friends or foes at Sekigahara, submitted to him only after he became national hegemon. Because of their long-standing allegiance to the Tokugawa, the *fudai* daimyos were allowed to serve in the shogunal government; the *tozama* daimyos, on the other hand, were barred from all participation in the ruling affairs of Edo.

In theory, the daimyos remained autonomous rulers of their *han*. In practice, the Shogunate came not only to dictate general rules of conduct for them but also to place severe restrictions on their personal freedom of action. Daimyos, for example, were not allowed to marry or to repair castles in their domains without shogunal permission. Moreover, especially during the first half-century or so of Tokugawa rule, the daimyos were frequently shifted from one domain to another or were deprived of their domains entirely for various acts proscribed by the Shogunate. But the most important measure by which the Tokugawa controlled the daimyos was the system of "alternate attendance" (*sankin kōtai*), which required that the daimyos spend approximately half their time in attendance at the shogunal court in Edo and leave their wives and children behind whenever they returned to their domains. In addition to discouraging any separatist or other seditious thoughts, the system of alternate attendance placed a heavy financial burden on the daimyos that further served to reduce the feasibility of their opposing the Shogunate.

Tokugawa society was officially divided into four classes: samurai, peasants, artisans, and merchants. The main social cleavage, however, was between the ruling samurai class—which from Hideyoshi's time on had been called upon to leave the countryside (if they had not already done so) and to take up residence in the castle towns and cities—and the commoners. The samurai received fixed annual stipends based on the rice harvest of their former fiefs, and enjoyed a variety of special privileges, including the exclusive right to wear swords and to cut down on the spot any commoners who offended them. Because they were the primary producers of food, the peasants were honored with second place in the official social ordering. But the life of the average peasant was one of much toil and little joy. It was, on the contrary, the socially despised artisans and merchants—known collectively as *chōnin* or townsmen—who, apart from the favored upper strata of samurai, enjoyed the greatest prosperity in Tokugawa times.

Although in the long run the seclusion policy undeniably limited the economic growth of Tokugawa Japan by its severe restrictions both on foreign trade and on the inflow of technology from overseas, it also ensured a lasting peace that made possible a great upsurge in the domestic economy, especially during the first century of Shogunate rule. Agricultural productivity, for example, was increased markedly in the seventeenth century; transportation and communication facilities were extensively improved; urban populations in the key trading and administrative centers of the country rose dramatically; and commerce, stimulated by a sharp expansion in the use of money, spread at a rate that would have been inconceivable a century earlier when it had been largely confined to the central provinces and the foreign entry ports of Kyushu.

It is ironic that the prosperity of the Tokugawa period most greatly benefited that class, the townsmen, which the authorities had emphatically relegated to the bottom of the social scale. Yet, this was inevitable. Both samurai and peasants were dependent almost solely on income from agriculture and constantly suffered declines in real income as the result of endemic inflation; only the townsmen, who as commercialists could adjust to price fluctuations, were in a position to profit significantly from the economic growth of the age.

We should not be surprised, therefore, to find this class giving rise to a lively and exuberant culture that reached its finest flowering in the Genroku epoch at the end of the seventeenth and the beginning of the eighteenth centuries. The mainstays of Genroku culture were the theatre, painting (chiefly in the form of the woodblock print), and prose fiction, all of which, while drawing heavily on Japan's aristocratic cultural tradition, evolved as distinctly popular, bourgeois forms of art.

Before turning to the *chōnin* arts, let us note first the principal cultural activities of the ruling samurai class during the early Tokugawa period. Although the samurai served as custodians of such venerable pursuits as the *nō* theatre, the tea ceremony, and flower arrangement, their most important cultural contribution was in the realm of Confucian philosophy. The Japanese had, of course, absorbed Confucian thinking from the earliest centuries of contact with China, but for more than a millennium Buddhism had drawn most of their intellectual attention. Not until the Tokugawa period did they come to study Confucianism with any great zeal.

One of the most conspicuous features of the transition from medieval to early modern (Tokugawa) times in Japan was the precipitous decline in vigor of Buddhism and the rise of a preponderately secular spirit. The military potential and much of the remaining landed wealth of the medieval Buddhist sects had been destroyed during the advance toward unification in the late sixteenth century. And although Buddhism remained very much a part of the daily lives of the people, it not only ceased to hold any appeal for Japanese intellectuals but indeed even drew their outright scorn and enmity.

The vigorous and colorful outburst of artistic creativity in the Momoyama epoch was the first major reaction to the gloom of medievalism. With the advent of the Tokugawa period, this reaction spread to the intellectual field and stimulated a great Confucian revival. Interestingly, as we observed in an earlier chapter, it was the Buddhist church—and especially the Zen sect—that paved the way for the upsurge in Confucian studies during Tokugawa times. Japanese Zen priests had from at least the thirteenth century on assiduously investigated the tenets of Sung Neo-Confucianism, and in ensuing centuries had produced a corpus of research upon which the Neo-Confucian scholarship of the Tokugawa period was ultimately built.

Neo-Confucianism had evolved during the Sung period in China partly as a reaction against Buddhism, which from mid-T'ang times had increasingly come to be criticized as an alien and harmful creed, and partly as an attempt to revitalize native Confucian values and institutions. In the process of its formulation, however, Neo-Confucianism absorbed much that was fundamentally Buddhist, including an elaborate cosmology and metaphysical structure. Of the various schools

Fig. 29 Golden Pavilion (*photograph by Joseph Shulman*)

Fig. 30 Scene from a *nō* play (*Japan National Tourist Organization*)

Fig. 31 Silver Pavilion (*photograph by Joseph Shulman*)

Fig. 32 *Shoin*-style of interior architecture: at the right end of the far wall is the alcove (*tokonoma*); to the left of it is the "desk" with overhanging shelves; the floor is covered with *tatami* matting, and *fusuma* and *shōji* sliding doors can be seen in the left and right walls (*drawing by Arthur Fleisher*)

Fig 33 Landscape attributed to Shūbun (*Seattle Art Museum*)

Fig. 34 Winter landscape by Sesshū (*Tokyo National Museum*)

Fig. 35 Ama-no-Hashidate by Sesshū (*Consulate General of Japan, New York*)

Fig. 36 "Splashed ink" scroll of Sesshū (*Tokyo National Museum*)

Fig. 37 Garden at the Daisenin of the Daitokuji Temple (*photograph by Joseph Shulman*)

Fig. 38 Garden at the Ryōanji Temple (*photograph by Joseph Shulman*)

Fig. 39 Himeji Castle (*Consulate General of Japan, New York*)

Fig. 40 *Namban* ("southern barbarian") screen showing the arrival of the Portuguese great ship at Nagasaki (*Cleveland Museum of Art*)

Fig. 41 Pine Trees Screen by Hasegawa Tōhaku (*Tokyo National Museum*)

Fig. 42 Screen of "Views Inside and Outside Kyoto" (courtesy of the Brooklyn Museum, gift of W. W. Hoffman)

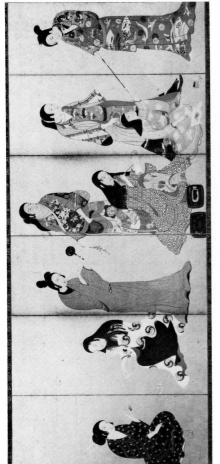

Fig. 43 Matsuura Screen
(*Museum Yamato Bunkakan*)

Fig. 45 Tōshōgū Shrine at Nikkō (*Japan National Tourist Organization*)

Fig. 44 Poem scroll by Sōtatsu and Kōetsu (*Seattle Art Museum*)

Fig. 46 Katsura Detached Palace (*photograph by Joseph Shulman*)

Fig. 47 Scene from a *kabuki* play (*Consulate General of Japan, New York*)

Fig. 48a,b Scenes from the puppet theatre (*Consulate General of*

Japan, New York)

Fig. 49 "Street Scene in the Yoshiwara" by Moronobu (*Metropolitan Museum of Art, Harris Brisbane Dick Fund, 1949*)

Fig. 50 "Waterfall" by Harunobu (*courtesy of the Brooklyn Museum, gift of Louis V. Ledoux*)

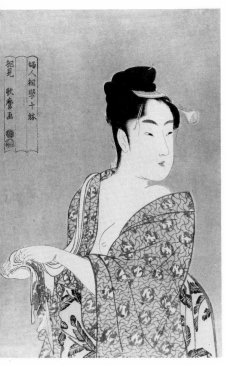 

Fig. 51 Half-length portrait from the "Studies in Physiognomy: Ten Kinds of Women" by Utamaro (*Cleveland Museum of Art, bequest of Edward Loder Whittemore*)

Fig. 52 Otani Oniji III as Edohei by Sharaku (*Art Institute of Chicago*)

Fig. 53 "The Great Wave at Kanagawa" by Hokusai (*Metropolitan Museum of Art, Howard Mansfield Collection, Rogers Fund, 1936*)

Fig. 54 "Cutting a Log" from "The 100 Poems Explained by the Nurse" by Hokusai (*courtesy of the Brooklyn Museum*)

Fig. 55 "Evening Rain at Azuma no Mori" by Hiroshige (*courtesy of the Brooklyn Museum*)

of Neo-Confucianism that emerged in China, it was the teachings of the great twelfth-century philosopher Chu Hsi (1130–1200) that eventually were accepted as the orthodox doctrine of Confucian learning. From the early fourteenth century until the abolishment of the examination system in 1905, Chu Hsi's brand of Neo-Confucianism was painstakingly studied and rehashed by countless generations of candidates for the degrees of official preferment and entry into the ministerial class that were traditionally bestowed by the Chinese court.

In Japan, too, it was Chu Hsi's Neo-Confucianism that came to be accepted as doctrinally orthodox by the Tokugawa Shogunate. Although Shogunate authorities and Tokugawa period intellectuals in general had relatively little interest in the purely metaphysical side of Chu Hsi's teachings, they found his philosophy to be enormously useful in justifying or ideologically legitimizing the feudal structure of state and society that had emerged in Japan in the seventeenth century.

Orthodox Neo-Confucian philosophy has been aptly and succinctly described as a doctrine of reason or principle (in Japanese, *ri*; in Chinese, *li*). Chu Hsi asserted that all things were governed by their underlying principles, and that, if men wished to determine what these principles were, it was incumbent upon them to pursue with diligence the "investigation of things." In contrast to Buddhism, which urged individuals to renounce this world of suffering and perpetual flux and to seek entry to a transcendent realm of pure bliss and tranquility, Neo-Confucianism held that the physical world was based on an inherently perfect (and, therefore, moral) order. It was only when men lost sight of or failed to comprehend the *ri* of things that social disorder occurred. Rulers and their ministers were in particular charged with the responsibility of investigating the lessons of history in order to chart a proper course of governance. Quite apart from any practical guidance to good rulership it may have provided, this Neo-Confucian stress on historical research proved to be a tremendous spur to scholarship and learning in general during the Tokugawa period,[34] and thus, as we shall see in the next chapter, it also facilitated the development of other, heterodox fields of intellectual inquiry.

A second major feature of Neo-Confucianism, which harked back to the most fundamental teaching of Confucius himself, was its humanism. Again, in contrast to the otherworldliness of much medieval Buddhism, Neo-Confucianism was primarily concerned with the conduct and affairs of men in the here and now. Social order demanded a strict hierarchical structuring of the classes and conformance by all people with the obligations imposed by the five primary human relationships: that is, the relationships between father and son, ruler and subject, husband and wife, older and younger brother, and two friends. It can readily be imagined how appealing the feudal rulers of Tokugawa Japan found these highly conservative social strictures that called upon people everywhere to accept without question their lots in life and to place highest value in the performance of such duties as filial piety to their parents and loyalty to their overlords.

The most important Neo-Confucianist of the early Tokugawa period was Hayashi Razan (1583–1657), a man of great and diverse scholarly accomplishments who served four shoguns over a period of more than fifty years. Noted as a Confucian theorist, historian, and specialist in legal precedence, Razan did more than anyone else to gain acceptance of the Chu Hsi school of Neo-Confucianism as the orthodox creed of the Tokugawa state; and by the end of the seventeenth century, the Hayashi family itself had become securely fixed as the official Confucian advisers to the Shogunate and the hereditary heads of a Confucian academy in Edo.

Although Neo-Confucianism was unquestionably a valuable ideological tool for the Shogunate and a powerful stimulus to learning in the Tokugawa period, it also exerted a certain stultifying influence on literature and the arts in general. Confucianists have always been absorbed first and foremost with morality, and their liking for didactic literature has often led to very dull writing. But perhaps the most telling example of how the Confucian sense of propriety and reserve stifled artistic creativity in the Tokugawa period can be observed in the history of the distinguished Kanō school of painters.

From the time of Masanobu in the late fifteenth century, the Kanō artists had served the successive military rulers of Japan—the Ashikaga, Nobunaga, and Hideyoshi—and shortly after the founding of the Tokugawa Shogunate they entered into the employ of the country's new warrior chieftains in Edo. Kanō Eitoku's son, Mitsunobu (1565–1608), who had assisted his father in the decoration of Nobunaga's castle at Azuchi and later did much work for Hideyoshi, was in his later years summoned by Ieyasu to decorate the Tokugawa castle in Edo. But the true founder or "restorer" of the Kanō as the official school of shogunal painters in the Tokugawa era was Eitoku's grandson, Tan'yū (1602–74), who moved permanently to Edo in 1614. In time, there came to be four major and twelve minor branches of the Kanō engaged on a stipendiary basis by the Shogunate. Moreover, many other bearers of the Kanō name were employed by daimyos as their official *han* artists. The various Kanō schoolmen thus secured a virtual monopoly of the appointments open to painters among the new Tokugawa military élite. Anxious to please their masters—who were strongly imbued with Confucian moralism—and reluctant to innovate, the Kanō artists after Tan'yū produced little work of real distinction. On the contrary, the best painting of the Tokugawa period was done by others.

The outstanding artist of the early seventeenth century and one of the finest painters in all of Japanese history was Tawaraya Sōtatsu (d. 1643), a man of merchant stock who drew his inspiration from the ancient cultural tradition of the imperial court. Although we know almost nothing about Sōtatsu's personal life, we can deduce some of the influences that worked upon him from his close association with another distinguished craftsman and artist of the age, Hon'-ami Kōetsu (1558–1637).

Kōetsu, the son of a Kyoto merchant family that dealt in fine swords, was a person of many skills, including the tea ceremony, the making and adornment of pottery and lacquerware, painting, and—perhaps most notable of all—calligraphy. Indeed, some of the most treasured works of art to come down from this period are "poem scrolls" done jointly by Kōetsu and Sōtatsu, scrolls in which Kōetsu inscribed *tanka* (often taken from such admired anthologies of the ancient period as the tenth-century *Kokinshū* and the early thirteenth century *Shinkokinshū*) over the painting of flowers, grass, and animals by Sōtatsu.

Fig. 44

Both Kōetsu and Sōtatsu were representatives of the upper merchant class of those cities—especially Kyoto, Nara, and Sakai in the central provinces—that had flourished commercially during the late medieval and Momoyama periods. A number of noted artists and men of culture, from the Higashiyama tea master Shukō to Sen Rikyū of Hideyoshi's day, emerged from the successful merchant houses of these cities to gain acceptance in the highest social circles of Japan's courtier and warrior élites. The Tokugawa period, of course, witnessed a continuation and expansion of commerce (at least domestically) and the rise of new and even greater urban centers at Osaka and Edo, cities which in the seventeenth century produced a bourgeois culture that catered especially to the great bulk of their middle- and lower-class townsmen. Hence, the art of Kōetsu and Sōtatsu was part of the "higher" or more traditional line of cultural development from pre-Tokugawa times, and the men themselves were members of a former class of privileged merchants whose influence and status were entering into decline.

Although Sōtatsu employed various styles on many different formats, including horizontal scrolls and folding fans (his family were apparently fan makers), he is noted chiefly for his work in the monumental decorative tradition of Kanō Eitoku and his contemporaries of the Momoyama epoch. Sōtatsu, however, was far more of a "Yamato artist" than his Momoyama predecessors, insofar as he selected the themes for many of his greatest paintings from the Japanese, rather than directly from the Chinese, cultural past. Two of his best-known works are screen paintings based on *The Tale of Genji* and on the *bugaku* form of dance that was popular during the Nara period.

Sōtatsu was a superb master of his craft, not only in his use of a strong and sure brush line and in the matching of colors (including the characteristic gold-leaf backgrounds of the mature decorative style), but also in his sense of design and capacity to exploit to a greater degree than any who came before him the geometrics of screen painting. Such works as the Genji Screen are particularly striking to the modern viewer as studies in form and the placement of objects that seem extraordinarily similar in approach, if not subject matter, to those of Western artists from at least the time of Cézanne and the Post-Impressionists.

Sōtatsu's immediate followers were mere imitators, but the decorative school produced one more great master at the end of the seventeenth century in Ogata Kōrin (1658–1716).[35] Like Sōtatsu and Kōetsu (to whom he was distantly related), Kōrin was the scion of a merchant family that had prospered in Kyoto since the Momoyama epoch and had even had personal and business ties with Hideyoshi and, later, the Tokugawa and imperial families. The Ogata were dealers in textiles, many richly decorated in styles that became popular for clothing during the late sixteenth and seventeenth centuries: no doubt Kōrin's exceptionally powerful sense of design came in part from familiarity with the family wares. In fact, Kōrin himself later became one of the most widely imitated designers of the *kosode* (small sleeve) type of kimono that was a main item of clothing in the Tokugawa period.

Kōrin's great grandfather had married Kōetsu's sister, and his grandfather had participated in the activities of an artists' colony that Kōetsu founded at Takagamine in the outskirts of Kyoto. His father, Ogata Sōken, had also maintained the family interest in the Kōetsu-Sōtatsu school of art. But unfortunately, Sōken was less able than his predecessors to afford the leisure from business that the pursuit of art required, and it was during his time that the Ogata family fortunes declined. Nevertheless, Kōrin was amply provided for during his youth and, by all accounts, became a true Genroku profligate, frequenting the pleasure quarters and pursuing a life of idleness and debauchery.

Not until he ran out of funds sometime about 1693 and was forced to secure a loan from his younger brother Kenzan (1663–1743), who became a distinguished potter and painter in his own right, did Kōrin think seriously about the need to find permanent employment. He began by teaming up with Kenzan—in much the same way that Sōtatsu had teamed with Kōetsu—and decorating a number of the fine ceramic pieces his brother produced. But although he did this and many other varied kinds of artwork, Kōrin, like Sōtatsu, achieved his greatest fame as a painter of folding screens.

Kōrin was the last of the great decorative artists of early modern Japan and might be said to have brought the decorative style to its highest level of perfection. He much admired the painting of Sōtatsu and even copied a number of the earlier master's works. But, whereas Sōtatsu had based works such as the Genji Screen on familiar and easily recognizable themes, Kōrin's best-known paintings are in a purely design-like and decorative manner. This is clearly observable in his Iris Screen, one of the most famous of all Japanese paintings. The screen was actually inspired by an episode from *The Tales of Ise* of the tenth century in which Narihira, who is having a wayside lunch near where some irises are growing, is challenged by a companion to compose a *tanka* poem on "A Traveler's Sentiments" and to use the syllables in the word "iris" (*kakitsubata*) to begin each of its five lines. Kōrin made no attempt to reproduce the narrative itself, but simply placed irises in "disembodied" fashion against a stark gold-leaf background. With their blue blossoms and green leaves providing a striking contrast to the dominant golden coloring of the screen, the flowers seem almost to dance before the viewer's eyes.

Architecturally, the Tokugawa period was not a time of great vigor or activity. Nevertheless, two of the most famous, and possibly most dissimilar, sets of buildings—the Tōshōgū Shrine and mausoleum of Tokugawa Ieyasu at Nikkō and the Katsura Detached Palace in Kyoto—were constructed during the first century of this age. The present-day visitor to Japan who takes the excursion of several hours by train from Tokyo to Nikkō will be enchanted by its beautiful mountain and forest setting. At the same time, he is apt to be puzzled and perhaps repelled by the elaborately embellished and garish buildings of the Tōshōgū Shrine. There can be no question that these *Fig. 45* brilliantly colored buildings, almost completely encased in a profusion of carvings and other ornamentation, are marvels of craftsmanship; but they also represent the antithesis of the aesthetic qualities that have inspired the finest works of Japanese art and architecture.

The Katsura Detached Palace, on the other hand, is the most *Fig. 46* splendid remaining example of traditional domestic architecture in Japan. Constructed as a villa by a prince of the imperial family, it has had a profound influence in recent years on both Japanese and foreign architects, for here in the structures at Katsura are combined those elements of Japanese architecture, including cleanness of line, simplicity of adornment, harmony of buildings to surrounding gardens and ponds, and the flow of space through rooms with readily removable partitions, that will forever be a source of aesthetic wonder and delight.

The calendrical era of Genroku lasted from 1688 until 1703, but the Genroku cultural epoch is usually taken to mean the span of approximately a half-century from, say, 1675 until 1725. Setting the stage for this rise of a townsman-oriented culture was nearly a century of peace and steady commercial growth. Such growth was, of course, almost entirely domestic and, owing in large part to the strict limitations on foreign trade imposed by the seclusion policy, it had begun to taper off markedly even during the Genroku epoch. Nevertheless, the commercial advances of the first century of Tokugawa rule were sufficient to bring to the fore for the first time in Japanese history a numerically significant and prosperous class of merchants who, although still regarded as inferior by their samurai masters, came increasingly to assert their social and cultural independence.

Other factors that contributed to the flourishing of Genroku culture were the rapid spread of learning and literacy among all classes in the seventeenth century and the transformation of warfare from a practical reality, which it had been throughout the medieval age, to little more than a distant memory. The samurai still sported their swords and flaunted their martial ways, but they were generally resigned to the fact that their proper, and apparently permanent, function was to practice the arts of peace rather than those of war.

The spawning grounds of townsman culture were the pleasure and entertainment quarters that formed, almost like extra-territorial enclaves, within the great cities: the Yoshiwara of Edo, the Shinmachi of Osaka, and the Shimabara of Kyoto. Abounding in brothels, theatres, teahouses, public baths, and sundry other places of diversion and assignation, these quarters were the famous "floating worlds" (*ukiyo*) of Tokugawa fact and legend. *Ukiyo*, although used specifically from about this time to designate such demimondes, meant in the broadest sense the insubstantial and ever-changing existence in which man is enmeshed. To medieval Buddhists, this had been a wretched and sorrowful existence, and *ukiyo* [36] always carried the connotation that life is fundamentally sad; but, in Genroku times, the term was more commonly taken to mean a world that was pleasurable precisely because it was constantly changing, exciting, and up-to-date.

In view of the tremendous pressure that Tokugawa society placed on the individual to conform to the rigid rules of Confucian behavior, sections like the pleasure quarters, offering escape from the heavy responsibilities of family and occupation, were almost essential safety valves against overt social unrest. Although the Shogunate always maintained careful surveillance over them, the quarters were to a great extent self-governing. Social distinctions based on birth or status meant little within their precincts: indeed, it was money, not pedigree, that usually carried the day in the floating world.

One of the first and greatest chroniclers of townsman life was the poet and author of prose fiction, Ihara Saikaku (1642–93). Born into a merchant family of Osaka, Saikaku did not begin to write the fiction that brought him his most lasting fame until he was past forty. His main literary interest during his earlier years was devoted, rather, to the composition of *haikai*, a form of poetry derived from the linked verse of medieval times. As a result of the efforts of various innovating schools (to be discussed later), *haikai* had been freed from the stylistic and topical restraints that had rendered linked verse, like the classical *tanka* before it, virtually devoid of the potentiality for original expression. And, in the hands of a facile manipulator of words like Saikaku, it served as an effective device for lively and witty poetizing. Saikaku the poet, however, seems to have been more interested in quantity than quality. Engaging in one-man poetry marathons, he came to compose the staggering total of 23,500 *haikai* in a single twenty-four-hour period, and thus established a presumably unbeatable, if not necessarily enviable, record for concentrated poetic output.

Frivolous as they appear, the poetry marathons may still be interpreted as an effort by the exuberant and energetic Saikaku to overcome the limitations of even the liberated *haikai* form of poetry, and thus to have been a kind of prelude to the prose writing that took up the last decade or so of his life. Saikaku's firm background in *haikai* is evident in his prose works, which are replete with poetic passages of alternating five- and seven-syllable lines.

Saikaku created a new genre of prose literature called *ukiyo-zōshi* or "books of the floating world," derived from writings known as *"kana* books" (*kana-zōshi*) that had evolved from the late medieval age. As their name implies, these latter writings were done largely in the *kana* syllabary in order to appeal to as wide a reading audience as possible. Advances in printing during the early Tokugawa period also helped increase the circulation of *kana* books, which included purely didactic pieces, adaptations of classics, travel accounts, and supernatural tales, as well as pleasure books on subjects such as loose women and the escapades of lecherous priests and samurai. Yet, by and large, the *kana* books retained a strongly medieval character, either in actual content and style or in the use of outmoded literary devices for presenting moralistic instruction. Saikaku's books of the floating world, by contrast, are realistic and up-to-date and are written in a style that, although occasionally didactic, is essentially detached and analytical.

Most of Saikaku's prose fiction falls into three major categories, the so-called erotic (*kōshoku*), townsman, and samurai books. Since Saikaku was never entirely at home when writing about the samurai class, he did his best work within the erotic and townsman categories. His first book, published in 1682, was entitled *The Life of a Man Who Lived for Love* (*Kōshoku Ichidai Otoko*) [37] and was an "erotic" work, although the term *"kōshoku"* in its title might more accurately be taken to mean rakish rather than simply erotic. Indeed, as variously used by Saikaku, *kōshoku* came to have a wide range of meanings, from rakish or romantic on the one hand to lecherous or perverted on the other.

The Life of a Man Who Lived for Love is the story of Yonosuke, a townsman who commences a long life of sexual adventures by making advances to a maid at the age of eight; at sixty-one, after having enjoyed all the delights that Japanese women can provide him, he sets forth by boat to find an island inhabited only by females. Divided into fifty-four chapters, each of which deals with a year in Yonosuke's life, *The Life of a Man Who Lived for Love* is little more than a collection of spicy episodes brought together as the doings of an indefatigable rake.

In 1686, Saikaku wrote another erotic work entitled *Five Women Who Chose Love* (*Kōshoku Gonin Onna*), which contains five fairly lengthy and well-structured tales that may properly be called novelettes. Whereas *The Life of a Man Who Lived for Love* deals mostly with life in the pleasure quarters, *Five Women Who Chose Love* concerns women of respectable townsman and peasant origins who, because of their excessively passionate natures, become involved in affairs that lead in all cases but one to dishonor and death. In this work, then, Saikaku shifted from accounts of the artificial world of the pleasure quarters to stories, based on real events, of people in everyday life. He also treated one of the most important social themes in all of Tokugawa literature, the conflict between human feelings (*ninjō*) and the heavy sense of duty (*giri*) imposed on the individual by the feudal laws and mores of the age.

In the same year that he wrote *Five Women Who Chose Love*, Saikaku produced still another major erotic work entitled *The Life of an Amorous Woman* (*Kōshoku Ichidai Onna*). This is a tale of the darker side of love, told in the first person, of uncontrolled lust and depravity. The heroine is, in fact, a nymphomaniac (descended on her father's side from the courtier class of Kyoto), who makes her way through life largely on her own ingenuity and resourcefulness, engaging in a variety of occupations, including those of dancer, parlormaid, seamstress, and calligraphy teacher, as well as courtesan and, finally, common streetwalker. After noting that as a girl she had become intoxicated with love (of the sort she observed being practiced at court) and had come to regard it as the most important thing in life, she recounts her first affair at the tender age of twelve:

There is naught in this world so strange as love. The several men who had set their affections on me were both fashionable and handsome; yet none of them aroused any tender feelings in me. Now, there was a humble warrior in the service of a certain courtier. The fellow was low in rank and of a type that most women would regard askance. Yet from the first letter that he wrote me his sentences were charged with a passion powerful enough to slay one. In note after note he set forth his ardent feelings, until, without realizing it, I myself began to be troubled in my heart. It was hard for us to meet, but with some cunning I managed to arrange a tryst and thus it was that I gave my body to him.

Our amour was bound to become the gossip of the court and one dawn it "emerged into the light." In punishment I was banished to the neighborhood of Uji Bridge. My lover, most grievous to relate, was put to death. For some days thereafter, as I lay tossing on my bed, half asleep, half awake, his silent form would appear terrifyingly before me. In my agony I thought that I must needs take my own life; yet, after some days had passed, I completely forgot about him. From this one may truly judge that nothing in this world is as base and fickle as a woman's heart.[38]

The years take their toll, and in the end the "Amorous Woman," old and destitute, ventures forth yet again in the dark of night with the forlorn hope of attracting unwary customers:

In these days people have become so canny that, though it be only a matter of ten coppers, they exercise more care in their choice of a harlot from the streets than does a rich man in selecting a high-class courtesan. Sometimes they will wait until a passer-by appears with a torch, sometimes they will conduct the woman to the lantern of a guard box—in either case they scrutinize her closely, and nowadays, even when it is only a matter of hasty diversion, a woman who is old or ugly is promptly turned down. "For a thousand men who see, there are a thousand blind." So the saying goes; but on that night, alas, I did not meet a single one who was blind!

Finally dawn began to appear: first the eight bells rang out, then seven. Aroused by their sound, the pack-horse drivers set forth with a clatter in the early-morning light. Yet I persisted in walking the streets, until the hour when the blacksmith and the bean-curd dealer opened their shutters. But no doubt my appearance and demeanour were not suited to this calling, for during the entire time not a single man solicited my favours. I resolved, then, that this would be my last effort in the Floating World at plying the lustful trade, and I gave it up for once and all.[39]

Saikaku's two great themes were love and money, and in his townsman books, written mostly after his erotic studies, he examined the *chōnin* ethic of working hard, being clever, and becoming a financial success. *The Eternal Storehouse of Japan* (*Nihon Eitaigura*), a collection of stories on the making and losing of fortunes, is perhaps his most celebrated work in this category. Yet, in the same way that he shifted in his erotic works from the romanticization of love to a Defoe-like recounting of the corrupting effect of sexual passion in *The Life of an Amorous Woman*, Saikaku turned his attention in his later townsman writings to the life of the middle- and lower-class merchant, which was generally one of unceasing drudgery and the struggle to keep one step ahead of the bill collector.

While Saikaku was perfecting a new kind of prose fiction, two forms of popular drama that had been evolving from at least the early seventeenth century—the *kabuki* and the puppet theatre—also blossomed into maturity.

Kabuki owed much to both *nō* and *kyōgen*, the main theatrical forms of the medieval age. This is obvious not only in the kinds of plays, acting techniques, and musical and narrative accompaniments used in early *kabuki*, but also in the physical staging of these productions. Even more immediate influences, however, can be traced that help explain how *kabuki* became the vigorous and popular type of entertainment it was during its first great flourishing in Genroku times.

The acknowledged "originator" of *kabuki* was a woman named Okuni, whose background is obscure but who was quite likely a former attendant at the great Shinto shrine at Izumo. Sometime in the late 1590's or the early years of the seventeenth century, Okuni led a troupe of female dancers in Kyoto in a kind of outdoor musical entertainment that was labeled (by others) "*kabuki* dancing" and, as a result of its commercial success, soon gave rise to competing troupes. The term *kabuki* was derived from *katamuki*—"slanted" or "strongly inclined"—and was used in this age to describe novel or eccentric behavior. Its application to the dancing of Okuni and her girls is a clear indication that the first *kabuki* company was regarded as a daring and not very proper undertaking.

One thing the Okuni troupe performed was "*nembutsu* dancing" (*nembutsu odori*), a type of religious ecstaticism (in which people danced around and chanted their praise to Amida buddha) that dated back to the tenth-century evangelist of Pure Land Buddhism, Kūya, but was especially popularized among people everywhere by Ippen during the Kamakura period. By the late medieval age, *nembutsu odori* had become a form of folk dance that was performed more for entertainment than for religious purposes, and it survives in Japan today in the dancing done annually in the midsummer *bon* festival for the dead.

In addition to dances of this sort, the Okuni troupe also performed farcical skits in which they portrayed encounters between men and prostitutes or re-enacted assignation scenes in teahouses and bathhouses. (No doubt the girls did these skits very professionally, since they were all apparently practicing harlots on the side.) Shogunate officials sternly disapproved of both the onstage and offstage behavior of female performers such as these, and in 1629, after a period of indecision, they banned their participation in *kabuki* altogether. This had the immediate effect of giving impetus to the rise of another form of entertainment known as "young men's *kabuki*" that had gradually been developing in the shadow of "women's *kabuki*." The performances of these attractive young men included certain kinds of acrobatics and flashing swordplay that were eventually to be incorporated into the mainstream of *kabuki* acting; but, to the dismay of the authorities, the youths were as much of a social nuisance as the female *kabuki* performers since they aroused the homosexual passions that had been widespread in Japan (particularly among samurai and Buddhist priests) from the medieval age on. Finally, in 1652, after a number of unseemly incidents including public brawls in the midst of performances over the affections of the actors on stage, the Shogunate also banned young men's *kabuki*. Henceforth, only adult males (or youths who had shaved their forelocks to give the appearance that they were adults) were allowed to perform on the *kabuki* stage.

Throughout the Tokugawa period, *kabuki* was subjected to a greater or lesser degree of official suppression, and this suppression had an extremely important influence on the way in which it developed. Shogunate officials hesitated to ban *kabuki* entirely for at least two reasons. First, they regarded *kabuki*, like the floating world of which it became an integral part, as a necessary outlet for the more elemental drives of the masses, even though these grossly offended their Confucian sensibilities. And second, they no doubt realized that like prostitution itself (both male and female), it could never be completely eradicated and might just as well be held to some kind of formal account.

The banning of women from *kabuki* gave rise to the unique personage of the *onnagata*, or male performer of female roles. So special are the acting qualities cultivated over the centuries by the *onnagata* that, even if women were permitted to perform in *kabuki* today, they would have little or no advantage over men in learning the *onnagata* art.

One of the reasons why young men's *kabuki* was not prohibited until as late as 1652 was that the third Tokugawa shogun, Iemitsu (1604–51), had a great fondness for the youthful actors. In finally taking the step after his death, Shogunate authorities made clear that, although they could hardly hope to convert the *kabuki* actors and their patrons into puritans, they intended to restrict the extreme promiscuity that had been so blatantly apparent on the *kabuki* stage. At the same time that they banished young men from the stage, the authorities also called upon the people in *kabuki* to devote their attention to becoming real actors instead of just vaudeville-like performers whose main business was illicit sex.

The injunction apparently had some effect, for *kabuki* thereafter was gradually transformed into a truly dramatic art. Actors came to assume specialized roles (such as those of *onnagata*), draw curtains were introduced and plays divided into acts, more scenery and stage props were used, and the physical theatre was altered and adapted to the special needs of *kabuki*. Yet, although the particular prohibitions imposed by the Shogunate may have helped it to become a more legitimate form of theatre, official treatment of *kabuki* throughout the Tokugawa period as a kind of necessary evil probably also prevented it from rising to a higher level of refinement. *Kabuki* has been and remains a conspicuously plebeian theatre.

Fig. 47   In *kabuki*, as it developed from the late seventeenth century, the actor is supreme. The texts of the plays are hardly more than scenarios or guides for the actor, who is expected to embellish or alter them as he sees fit. The typical *kabuki* play consists of a series of dramatic high points or tableaux that are made exciting by the broad gesturing, posturing, and declamations of the actors.

Although *kabuki* prospered in both the Edo and Osaka-Kyoto regions, it was particularly among the citizens of Edo, whose number included a far greater percentage of samurai and whose tastes tended to be more robust and unrestrained, that it enjoyed its greatest patronage. In the early and mid-seventeenth century, *kabuki* had competed for popularity in Edo with the puppet theatre (*bunraku*), but after a great fire in 1657 had destroyed much of the city and brought about the reconstruction of the Yoshiwara pleasure quarters in the present-day Asakusa section of Tokyo, most of the puppet chanters (who were the principal functionaries in *bunraku*) moved to the Kansai (Kyoto-Osaka region) and left *kabuki* unchallenged in the theatre world of Edo.

The two most famous names in *kabuki* during the Genroku epoch were Ichikawa Danjūrō (1660–1704) of Edo and Sakata Tōjūrō (1647–1709) of the Kansai. Ichikawa, who was influenced by an early form of puppet theatre that dealt with the martial exploits of a semi-legendary hero named Kimpira, developed a style of acting called "rough business" (*aragoto*). So great was Ichikawa's success and fame that this rough business was widely imitated among Edo performers and became probably the most characteristic feature of that city's brand of *kabuki*. Sakata Tōjūrō, on the other hand, practiced "soft business" (*wagoto*) in his acting and thus demonstrated the Kansai preference for the more intimate and feminine (rather than heroic and masculine, as in Edo), a preference that can be seen even more obviously in the Kansai approach to *bunraku*.[40]

The earliest recorded practitioners of puppetry in Japanese history were groups of people in the late Heian period known as *kugutsu*, who moved about from place to place in gypsy-like fashion and staged entertainments in which the men manipulated wooden marionettes and performed feats of magic and the women sang. In addition, the women apparently also liberally purveyed their physical charms, further proof that from early times prostitution and the theatre (to use the term loosely) were closely linked in Japan. Little is known about puppetry during the next few centuries, although there appears to have been a revival of interest in it during the fourteenth century as a result of the importation of string-operated puppets from China.

The mature art of *bunraku*, as it was developed in the late sixteenth and seventeenth centuries, has been defined by Donald Keene as "a form of storytelling, recited to a musical accompaniment and embodied by puppets on a stage."[41] Of the three main elements of *bunraku*—storytelling, musical accompaniment, and the use of puppets —it is the storytelling (and, to a lesser extent, its musical accompaniment) that is of greatest importance in the history of Japanese culture. Puppetry was a minor theatrical form that was used to supplement the traditionally derived art of the *bunraku* chanters.

Storytelling as performed by itinerant chanters, who were often Buddhist priests, had been popular throughout the medieval age. Among the most important literary sources from which the chanters drew their material were the great war chronicles, including *The Tale of the Heike* and *Taiheiki*. For accompaniment, the chanters generally used a mandolin-like four-stringed instrument called the *biwa*. But by the late sixteenth century, another instrument, the three-stringed *samisen*, which had its origins in China and was introduced to Japan via the Ryukyu Islands, was coming into vogue among chanters. Roughly akin to the banjo, the *samisen* gives off a rather brittle, twanging sound (in contrast to the languid tone of the *biwa*) and is particularly well suited for the accompaniment of the vocal techniques of chanters. During the Tokugawa period, the *samisen* became the principal musical instrument in both the *kabuki* and *bunraku* theatres.

It was thus the adaptation of the *samisen* to the ancient art of chanting and the employment of puppets to depict the narrative action declaimed by chanters that gave rise to *bunraku*. The two men most responsible for effecting the final evolution of *bunraku* to a serious dramatic form in Genroku times were the chanter Takemoto Gidayū

(1651–1714) and the playwright Chikamatsu Monzaemon (1653–1724). In 1684, Gidayū, whose distinctive chanting style became the most widely admired of its day, opened a puppet theatre called the Takemoto-za in Osaka and engaged the services of Chikamatsu, a writer of samurai origins from Kyoto who had already achieved some note as the author of plays for the renowned *kabuki* actor Sakata Tōjūrō.

Although Chikamatsu wrote for both the *kabuki* and *bunraku* theatres, his work for the latter won for him the great stature he enjoys in the history of Japanese literature. His *bunraku* plays are of two general types, historical plays (*jidaimono*) and domestic or contemporary plays (*sewamono*). The historical plays are derived from the same kinds of narrative materials that Japanese chanters had used for centuries and are by their very nature rousing tales of derring-do and romantic love. To increase further the excitement of their presentation on stage, Chikamatsu and other *bunraku* playwrights also provided in their scripts for the performance of fabulous tumbling acts and supernatural feats, which their audiences loved and which the puppets, unlike the live actors of *kabuki*, could convincingly do. Chikamatsu's best-known historical play is *The Battles of Coxinga* (*Kokusenya Kassen*), based on the story of a Chinese loyalist who held out against the Manchus after they invaded China and overthrew the Ming dynasty in 1644.

Chikamatsu did not write his first domestic play, *The Love Suicides at Sonezaki* (*Sonezaki Shinjū*), until 1703. With this work, derived from actual events that had recently occurred in Osaka, Chikamatsu not only created a new category of puppet plays but also found the precise medium in which he was to do his finest writing. *The Love Suicides at Sonezaki*, which was enormously popular with Genroku audiences, is constructed around a simple plot that Chikamatsu used, with variations and embellishments, as the basis for a number of his subsequent domestic plays. It tells the story of a soy sauce salesman named Tokubei who is in love with Ohatsu, a courtesan of the Osaka pleasure quarters. As the play opens, we learn that Tokubei has quarreled with his employer and must return a sum of money that the employer (actually Tobukei's uncle) had advanced as a dowry for his daughter, whom Tokubei now refuses to marry. The kindhearted although dull-witted Tokubei has temporarily loaned the money to a friend, and, when he seeks to reclaim it, the erstwhile friend not only denies that he ever received any money but even charges that Tokubei has forged his seal. In the ensuing argument, Tokubei is soundly thrashed. Distraught and utterly at a loss what to do, he proceeds to Ohatsu's place where the two lovers, without even considering an alternative course of action, decide to commit double suicide. That night they set forth on a *michiyuki* or "lovers' journey" to their deaths at Sonezaki Shrine.

As a writer of domestic plays for the puppet theatre, Chikamatsu was, like Saikaku, a major chronicler of townsman life during the Genroku epoch. Unlike Saikaku, who in his townsman works examined virtually all aspects of the behavioral patterns and standards of value of the emergent bourgeoisie of Tokugawa Japan, Chikamatsu concerned himself chiefly with the lives of lower-class townsmen and specifically with the conflict between duty or obligation (*giri*) and the dictates of human feelings (*ninjō*) to which the members of all classes were subject in this feudal age.

Even though Chikamatsu is famous for his treatment of this *giri-ninjō* conflict, it is not in fact so strongly presented in his plays as it is in other literary works of the Tokugawa period, such as vendetta stories in which samurai unhesitatingly forsake their own personal interests and even sacrifice their lives to meet the exacting demands of their warrior's code of honor. Tokubei and Ohatsu of *The Love Suicides at Sonezaki*, although in difficult straits, do not seem to be under any unique or overwhelming pressure to act as they do. Rather, they appear to be neurotically obsessed with the "purity" of their love for each other and with the religious urge to perpetuate it through death for Buddhist eternities to come. In later "love suicide" plays, Chikamatsu made the pressures of *giri* more explicit; even so, his favorite theme might better be described as one of "all for love" rather than of fundamental conflict between duty and human feelings.

The literary high point of the love suicide play is the *michiyuki*, the journey of the lovers to their predetermined fate. Chikamatsu's *michiyuki* passages are composed in richly textured and often hauntingly beautiful poetry. Perhaps the most memorable is the one from *The Love Suicides at Sonezaki*, which begins:

Narrator: Farewell to this world, and to the night farewell.
We who walk the road to death, to what should we be
likened?
To the frost by the road that leads to the graveyard,
Vanishing with each step we take ahead:
How sad is this dream of a dream!

Tokubei: Ah, did you count the bell? Of the seven strokes
That mark the dawn, six have sounded.
The remaining one will be the last echo
We shall hear in this life.

Ohatsu: It will echo the bliss of nirvana.

Narrator: Farewell, and not to the bell alone—
They look a last time on the grass, the trees, the sky.
The clouds, the river go by unmindful of them;
The Dipper's bright reflection shines in the water.

Tokubei: Let's pretend that Umeda Bridge
Is the bridge the magpies built
Across the Milky Way, and make a vow
To be husband and wife stars for eternity.

Ohatsu: I promise. I'll be your wife forever.

Narrator: They cling together—the river waters
Will surely swell with the tears they shed.
Across the river, in a teahouse upstairs,
Some revelers, still not gone to bed,
Are loudly talking under blazing lamps—
No doubt gossiping about the good or bad
Of this year's crop of lovers' suicides;
Their hearts sink to hear these voices.

Tokubei: How strange! but yesterday, even today,
We spoke as if such things did not concern us.
Tomorrow we shall figure in their gossip.
If the world will sing about us, let it sing.[42]

Fig. 48   *Bunraku* enjoyed its greatest prosperity in the half-century after Chikamatsu's death, from about 1725 until the 1780's. An important technical innovation during this period was the introduction in 1734 of the puppet manipulated by three men, one responsible for the back, right hand, head, and eyebrows; another for the left hand; and a third for the feet. So vigorous was the puppet theatre that its influence was strongly felt even in *kabuki* circles, where actors imitated the stiff body movements of the puppets and producers adopted *bunraku* methods of staging and presentation. One sad development, however, was the decline in popularity of Chikamatsu's plays, regarded as too wordy and slow-moving for the new, more lively puppets.

If Saikaku was a realist and Chikamatsu a romantic, the third great literary figure of the Genroku epoch, the poet Matsuo Bashō (1644–94), was something of a mystic. Born into a low-ranking samurai family, Bashō became a *rōnin* or "masterless samurai" at the age of twenty-two upon the death of his lord. Rather than seek similar employment elsewhere, the young Bashō, who had long been interested in poetry, abandoned his samurai status and, after studying for a while in Kyoto, moved to the military capital of Edo. Edo remained his nominal home for the rest of his life, although Bashō, like several famous poets of the past (including Sōgi of the Higashiyama epoch), sought inspiration for his verses in frequent travels into the provinces. He died of illness in Osaka at the age of fifty while on a final journey whose ultimate destination was Nagasaki.

Linked verse, the major form of poetry in the late medieval age, had, as we have seen, suffered the same fate as the classic *tanka* from which it was derived by becoming oppressively burdened with rigid stylistic and topical conventions. In the late sixteenth and seventeenth centuries, efforts, motivated by the rise of a townsman culture, were made to liberate linked verse from the shackles of the past. One of the most important figures in this movement was Matsunaga Teitoku (1571–1653), whose Teimon school of poets asserted their right to go beyond the restricted vocabulary of the traditional linked verse and to use more prosaic and even vulgar language in versification. Yet, even though the members of the Teimon school were significant innovators in the language of their poetry (commonly called by this time *haikai* or "light verse"), they remained staunch traditionalists in their fidelity to the topical dictates of earlier poets and to what they regarded as the inviolable spirit of the aristocratic linked verse of medieval times. Not until the meteoric rise in the late 1670's and early 1680's of another group of poets called the Danrin school was *haikai* finally freed, in terms of both language and subject matter, from the heavy hand of the linked verse masters of the past. It was as a member of the Danrin school that Saikaku poured forth his great and indeed overflowing stream of *haikai* verse.

But the newly risen Danrin movement, despite its importance in making possible the subsequent flowering of *haiku*, was itself seriously restricted by the fact that its followers concentrated mainly on clever word-plays, allusions, and references to current fads and fashions. The Danrin poets soon exhausted the possibilities of such an ephemeral approach to poetry and found themselves left with a corpus of verse that held little prospect of appealing to posterity.

It was Bashō who led Japanese poetry out of the Danrin impasse. Although he never fully abandoned the writing of *haikai*, Bashō adopted as his principal medium of expression the seventeen-syllable *haiku*. Certainly one of the world's briefest verse forms, *haiku* derives from the first phrase or link of the classic *tanka* and consists of three lines of five, seven, and five syllables. Since the rules are simple, almost anyone can compose these seventeen-syllable poems, and indeed Japanese of all classes have written *haiku* through the centuries from Bashō's time. But the *haiku* is something like the ultimate in deceptive simplicity, and out of a vast number of "acceptable" ones only a fraction are apt to be truly fine. Bashō's output of *haiku* was not numerically great (perhaps a thousand or so have come down to us), but it is of such an extraordinary quality as to make him without question one of the greatest of Japanese poets.

With little more than a handful of syllables at his disposal, the writer of *haiku* obviously cannot hope to enter into extended poetic dialogue. He must seek to create an effect, to capture a mood, or to bring about a sudden and sharp insight into the truth of human existence. Bashō found much of his inspiration in Zen Buddhism, and many of his best *haiku* are the product of his intuitive and profoundly mystical response to life and nature. Bashō's insights are not explicitly presented. His best-known *haiku*, for example, is

> An ancient pond
> A frog jumps in
> The sound of water.

Bashō has not said how wondrous it is to observe the meeting of that which is eternal, as embodied in the ancient pond, and that which is fleeting, as represented by the frog's jump. In the best Zen and *haiku* spirit, he has simply juxtaposed the two images without subjective comment and has left it to the reader to draw whatever meaning or meanings he can from the poem.

Of all Bashō's many journeys, the most famous was one he took with a companion into the remote northern provinces in 1689 and later immortalized in the travel account, *The Narrow Road of Oku* (*Oku no Hosomichi*). Bashō's travel accounts, of which this is by far the finest example, were not intended to be accurate, diary-like records of his journeys. They are highly poetic evocations of his feelings and sentiments as he visited places famous for their natural beauty, for their association with former poet-travelers, or for their roles in the great events of Japanese history. As Bashō journeyed through the provinces, his fame preceded him and he was often met by people who asked him to write *haiku* or to join them in a round of linked-verse composition. But Bashō did not need others to inspire him, and the most beautiful passages in *The Narrow Road of Oku* are those in which he was moved to compose *haiku* upon encountering some memorable scene or viewing a surpassingly lovely setting:

We first climbed up to Castle-on-the-Heights, from where we could see the Kitagami, a large river that flows down from the north. Here Yoshitsune once fortified himself with some picked retainers, but his great glory turned in a moment into this wilderness of grass. "Countries may fall, but their rivers and mountains remain. When spring comes to the ruined castle, the grass is green again." These lines went through my head as I sat on the ground, my bamboo hat spread under me. There I sat weeping, unaware of the passage of time.

Natsugusa ya	The summer grasses—
Tsuwamono domo ga	Of brave soldiers' dreams
Yume no ato	The aftermath.

In the domain of Yamagata is a mountain temple called the Ryūshaku, a place noted for its tranquility. People had urged us "just to take a look," and we had turned back at Obanasawa to make the journey, a distance of about fifteen miles. It was still daylight when we arrived. After asking a priest at the foot of the mountain for permission to spend the night, we climbed to the temple at the summit. Boulders piled on rocks had made this mountain, and old pines and cedars grew on its slopes. The earth and stones were worn and slippery with moss. At the summit the doors of the hall were all shut, and not a sound could be heard. Circling around the cliffs and crawling among the rocks we reached the main temple. In the splendor of the scene and the silence I felt a wonderful peace penetrate my heart.

Shizukasa ya	Such stillness—
Iwa ni shimiiru	The cries of the cicadas
Semi no koe	Sink into the rocks.[43]

Perhaps Bashō's true greatness lay in the fact that, at a time when other Japanese poets (i.e., of the Danrin school) were recklessly rejecting the poetic traditions of the past in the pursuit of artistic freedom and modernity, he sought to bring together the old and the new. His inquiry into Zen brought him into communion with the very essence of the aesthetic spirit of medieval culture. At the same time, as a former member of the Danrin movement, he was fully liberated from the restraining conventions of medieval poetry and was very much a part of the great *haikai-haiku* movement of the seventeenth century, which accompanied and was made possible by the economic and cultural, if not political, burgeoning of the townsman class. He was thus as much a Genroku man as either Saikaku or Chikamatsu. But to a far greater degree than either of his distinguished contemporaries, Bashō dealt with the eternal verities and spoke to all people of all ages.

Still another major art to emerge from the Genroku epoch—and indeed the form of Japanese art probably best known in the West—was the woodblock print, used to depict *ukiyo-e* or "pictures of the floating world." Any attempt to trace the precise origins of the *ukiyo-e* would necessitate a detailed investigation of the many streams of development in painting in Japan from at least the late medieval era on, and so complex are these streams that the task could probably not be definitively done. But the immediate precursor of the *ukiyo-e* was clearly the genre painting, discussed in the last chapter, that flourished in the late sixteenth and early seventeenth centuries. In fact, it is debatable what criteria should be used to distinguish the earlier genre works from the *ukiyo-e*, although one crucial distinction is certainly the fact that the former were painted (so far as we know) by members of the "aristocratic" schools such as the Kanō whereas the *ukiyo-e* were done by townsman artists.

The establishment of *ukiyo-e* as an independent art form was, to an exceptional degree, the work of one man, Hishikawa Moronobu (1618–94). Little is known of Moronobu's background, although he may have been the son of a Kyoto embroiderer. It is certain, in any case, that he grew up in the region of the ancient imperial capital, where he studied the various schools of art still flourishing there. Moronobu probably moved to Edo in the 1660's, at a time when the city was being extensively rebuilt after the great fire of 1657. This was a critical period in the history of Edo, for in the rebuilding of it much of the influence of the older, more traditional Kansai culture was cast off and the city was allowed to assume an appearance and style uniquely its own. It was from about this time, for example, that *kabuki* became the theatre par excellence of Edo; and in Moronobu the newly reconstructed city found an artist who perfectly captured in visual form its vital and engaging spirit. Throughout the Tokugawa period, the art of *ukiyo-e* remained, first and foremost, the art of Edo.

Moronobu possessed two qualities which, apart from his natural artistic ability, made him a successful pioneer in *ukiyo-e*. He had an intimate and personal interest in townsman life, unlike the detached curiosity of most earlier genre painters; and he was sufficiently self-confident and assertive to demand recognition as an independent artist. Much genre painting had been done by unknown people, and in Moronobu's younger years about the only opportunity for aspiring painters, unless they were members of the officially patronized schools like the Kanō and Tosa, was the relatively humble chore of drawing anonymous illustrations for popular books. Moronobu not only insisted upon signing his paintings, he emphatically identified himself on them with such signatures as "The Yamato artist Hishikawa Moronobu." Moreover, he was the first artist of his kind to go beyond the secondary function of illustrating books and to produce both picture albums and "single-sheet" artworks.

But Moronobu's greatest innovation was to make the shift from painting to woodblock printing. Although he and other *ukiyo-e* artists continued to do some of their work in paint, it was their use of the woodblock print that gave the *ukiyo-e* its special character. Not only did woodblock printing make possible the production of pictures in numbers sufficient to meet the great demand for this plebeian art form; it also provided a medium—that is, pictures printed in ink by means of carved woodblocks—that made *ukiyo-e* unique and instantly distinguishable from all other kinds of Japanese art.

The earliest *ukiyo-e*, done by Moronobu and others, were simply black and white prints known as "primitives." Gradually, however, artists began to have colors (usually red or reddish brown and green) painted in by hand on their prints, although these early efforts at the use of color generally added very little to the artistic merit of the *ukiyo-e*. Nevertheless, the urge to employ color persisted, and shortly after the mid-eighteenth century the technique of printing in multi-colors and even half tones was perfected. The multi-colored print, known as *nishiki-e* or "brocade picture," necessitated close cooperation among three people, the artist, the woodblock carver, and the printer, and thus became in a very real sense a joint artistic endeavor. *Fig. 49*

From the beginning, *ukiyo-e* artists were primarily interested in two subjects—women of the pleasure quarters and *kabuki* actors—and throughout the Tokugawa period the overwhelming majority of prints they produced were of these two representative types of Edo nightlife, sometimes done with detailed backgrounds but more commonly with few if any background elements. Not surprisingly, the *ukiyo-e* representations of pleasure women and actors usually stress the sensual and erotic, in contrast to the earlier genre paintings in which people were for the most part portrayed objectively and with little infusion of emotion on the part of the artist.

To some lovers of *ukiyo-e*, the early primitive works in plain black and white or black and white with slight coloring are the most vigorous and exciting of all Japanese woodblock prints. But the greatest names in *ukiyo-e* are of artists who flourished after development of the multi-colored "brocade" print, first used in 1765 by Suzuki Harunobu (1725–70). Harunobu achieved widespread popularity not only for his superb use of color but also for his portrayals of beautiful young women in dreamlike settings. Harunobu's women, unlike those of other *ukiyo-e* artists, are more charming than erotic in appearance. In addition, their faces and expressions are almost all identical. Most *ukiyo-e* masters, in fact, drew stereotyped faces; but in the prints of Harunobu, where it is often impossible even to distinguish between young boys and girls, this convention may appear, as it does to me, as an artistic failing. *Fig. 50*

Although a number of artists of the *ukiyo-e* school are noted for their depiction of feminine beauty, the most celebrated is Kitagawa Utamaro (1753–1806). Utamaro's typical beauties are long and willowy and have about them a languid and sensual air. Often they are portrayed in great intimacy, with one or both breasts bare and with hair and *Fig. 51* clothing in casual disarray. To many later—and often unabashedly puritanical—critics Utamaro has epitomized the decadence into which they believe *ukiyo-e* sank at the end of the eighteenth century. It is true that Utamaro lapsed into a kind of mannerism in his final years and that, with the exception of the work of two early nineteenth-century artists—Hokusai and Hiroshige, who were in any case unusual in that they specialized chiefly in landscapes—the traditional *ukiyo-e* did in fact lose most of its vitality about this time. Nevertheless, Utamaro's art, as observable in his better prints, is clearly of superior quality. In sureness of line, overall composition, and delicacy of handling subject matter, he ranks with the best of the *ukiyo-e* masters.

One of Utamaro's contemporaries was a mysterious genius named Tōshūsai Sharaku (no dates). Almost nothing is known with certainty about Sharaku's identity or activities apart from the astonishing fact that he did his entire corpus of surviving work—some 145 prints, *Fig. 52* mostly of *kabuki* actors—during a concentrated period of less than ten months in 1794. Whereas Utamaro specialized in pictures of the courtesan, Sharaku was the master chronicler of the actor. Both artists had a penchant for doing close-up, bustlike portraits of their subjects, and both frequently left the backgrounds of their prints blank; otherwise, they had virtually nothing in common. Utamaro's prints are sophisticated and restrained, with composition and coloring precise. Sharaku's, by comparison, are stylistically crude. His colors sometimes clash and he seems to lack the sureness of placement of his subject matter that is so characteristic of Japanese artists. But these ostensible failings seem only to enhance Sharaku's forte: the bursting, elemental energy he has infused into his actors, whose faces and bodies are contorted with dramatic emotion. Unlike most *ukiyo-e* artists, Sharaku sought to portray real people, not simply stereotypes. It has even been speculated that he stopped producing prints so abruptly because actors were outraged at being so unflatteringly drawn. This seems absurd, since no other artist has ever captured the spirit of *kabuki* as Sharaku did, and it seems much more likely that the actors he drew fully appreciated having their dramatic skills depicted in such a vivid, exciting manner.

8

Heterodox Trends

THE TOKUGAWA SHOGUNATE was a thoroughly conservative regime. Once having established itself in power in the early seventeenth century, it made every effort to prevent any change in its system of rule or in the structure of society upon which it rested. The very concept of change was anathema to the rulers of Tokugawa Japan. Nevertheless, despite the Shogunate's official attitude, much change did occur in Japan, even during the strong early years of Tokugawa rule. The flourishing of a bourgeois culture, for example, brought the modification or alteration of many of the traditional canons of taste in Japanese literature, theatre, and the visual arts. In philosophy, too, scholars expressed much diversity or heterodoxy of opinion in opposition to the supposedly orthodox body of Neo-Confucian thought that was officially championed by the Hayashi family of advisers to the Shogunate.

Most of the early heterodox thinkers, if they may be so loosely designated, did not deliberately set out to refute the Neo-Confucian orthodoxy in the same way that Tokugawa period intellectuals in general vociferously denounced medieval Buddhism. Rather, they gradually came to oppose the orthodoxy on at least two major grounds: first, that it was excessively academic and not readily applicable to the everyday, practical problems of man and society; and secondly, that as a foreign creed it did not account for the peculiar social conditions of Tokugawa Japan (for example, the existence of a hereditarily entrenched governing class of samurai warriors).

The first important scholar to challenge the Neo-Confucian orthodoxy was Nakae Tōju (1608–48). After serving in his youth as a samurai retainer, Nakae denounced the rigidities of such service and retired at the early age of twenty-six to a life of study and contemplation at his birthplace on Lake Biwa in Ōmi Province. As a scholar, Nakae had at first been a keen student of Chu Hsi Neo-Confucianism, but from his observations of people of all classes in Japan he came to question whether certain of its basic tenets were truly meaningful when applied to them. Neo-Confucianism, for one thing, endorsed a hierarchical structuring of society in which all people were expected to accept without question the obligations attendant upon predominantly inferior-superior relations among men. But was it proper for the ruling class of Tokugawa Japan to enjoy its privileges solely on the basis of birth rather than, as in China, on intellectual or scholarly merit?

At an even more fundamental level, Nakae questioned the orthodox view of the moral perfectibility of man. According to this view, man's nature is basically good and is governed by *ri* or reason. Although there is the danger that he may be led astray by certain inner cravings and outside forces, if his basic nature is properly cultivated through moral training, man will automatically act in a good and upright fashion. Nakae Tōju observed that, despite their claim that man should be allowed to act with complete freedom once his inherently moral nature has been cultivated, the orthodox Neo-Confucianists in fact made sure that he acted rightly by dictating to him elaborate rules of social conduct.

Nakae asserted that the most important consideration was man's mind or will to action (*shin*). In other words, whereas the orthodox Neo-Confucianists talked about the *ri*-nature and prescribed how man should behave to prove that he had it, Nakae said that man should act according to the dictates of his mind or "intuition," and should not be fettered by the need to conform to arbitrary norms of social behavior. The creed he thus came to espouse was formally based on the writings of the Ming dynasty philosopher, Wang Yang-ming (1472–1529). The Neo-Confucianism of Wang Yang-ming, which stressed that man had the inherent or intuitive capacity to act morally, held a powerful attraction for many Japanese of the Tokugawa period, especially samurai whose class background and outlook made them logically receptive to a doctrine of personal independence and direct action. Yet, the Wang Yang-ming emphasis on intuition was also close to the spirit of Zen Buddhism and, toward the end of his life, Nakae Tōju became less concerned with social action than with the cultivation of a Zen-like inner tranquility. It remained for others, particularly in the tumultuous final years of the Tokugawa period, to employ Wang Yang-ming Neo-Confucianism as a rationale for political activism.

Another group of scholars who came to attack the Neo-Confucian orthodoxy was the so-called School of Ancient Studies (*kogaku-ha*). The leading members of the *kogaku-ha* had such diverse personalities and viewpoints that it may at first seem inappropriate to group them together as a school. Nevertheless, they were similar at least insofar as each sought to go back beyond Neo-Confucianism—and indeed beyond all the major accretions to Confucianism of the preceding two millennia—to rediscover the original teachings of the Confucian tradition. Of course, the Neo-Confucianists in China had started out to do the very same thing and had ended in producing intellectual syntheses that were far removed from the down-to-earth humanism of Confucianism and the sages of early China. The Ancient Studies scholars of Tokugawa Japan also differed widely in their interpretations of what constituted the original teachings of Confucianism and how they should be applied to the conditions of their own country and age.

The first major figure of the Ancient Studies School was Yamaga Sokō (1622–85). Of samurai origin, Yamaga earned a reputation as a brilliant scholar, delving into such varied subjects as Shinto, Buddhism, and Japanese poetry, as well as Confucianism, which he studied in Edo under Hayashi Razan. Yamaga was also greatly interested in military science, and it was probably this interest as much as anything that eventually led him to attack the Neo-Confucian orthodoxy as irrelevant to Japan in the seventeenth century. He observed that Confucius had lived during an age when conditions in China were far closer to the feudal system of Tokugawa Japan than to the centralized bureaucratic state for which the Neo-Confucianists of the Sung dynasty had shaped their doctrines. Yamaga accordingly believed that, rather than the metaphysically based and overly idealistic tenets of orthodox Neo-Confucianism, the practical ethics for everyday living that Confucius had preached should be used for the moral training of the Japanese of his time.

Yamaga was also one of the first thinkers of the Tokugawa period to address himself to the problem of justifying the existence of the samurai as a largely idle, stipendiary class. After the founding of the Tokugawa Shogunate in 1600, there had been little opportunity for the samurai to pursue their principal calling, and it became a historical anomaly that a class of fighting men should come to preside over Japan during its longest age of peace. Some samurai became bureaucratic administrators of the Shogunate and *han* governments, but others had very little in the way of formal assignments or responsibilities to occupy their time. In the first provisions of its "Laws for the Military Houses," issued in 1615, the Shogunate had enjoined the samurai to pursue with singleminded devotion the arts of "peace and war"; and it was in line with this injunction that Yamaga formulated his code for samurai conduct. The samurai, he asserted, must not only cultivate his physical skills as a warrior, but also his mind and character. In particular, he must serve as the exemplar of high moral purpose for Japanese of all classes. Central to such moral purpose was the samurai's sense of duty or obligation—that is, *giri*. This was the same *giri* that we observed affecting the behavior of townsman characters in the domestic plays of Chikamatsu. When set forth by Yamaga as a moral imperative for the samurai, however, it implied an absolute loyalty to one's overlord and devotion to duty that far transcended what could realistically be expected of the members of the other classes of Tokugawa society.

On the basis of views such as these, Yamaga Sokō, who at one time had had as a student the leader of the famed Forty-seven Rōnin,[44] is generally credited as the formulator of the code of *bushidō*, or the "way of the warrior." Certainly he was a pioneer in analyzing the role of the samurai as a member of a true ruling élite and not simply as a rough, and frequently illiterate, participant in the endless civil struggles of the medieval age. In his later years, Yamaga also turned more and more to another theme—the greatness of Japan—that was to endear him to the followers of *bushidō* as well as the nationalists of modern Japan.

The study of Confucianism naturally imbued Japanese scholars with a greater or lesser degree of enthusiasm for the civilization of China: some became outright Sinophiles, and although other Confucian scholars of the early Tokugawa period, including Hayashi Razan, had gone beyond their study of Chinese philosophy to investigate Shinto and the Japanese tradition, Yamaga Sokō was the first thinker of stature to claim the superiority of Japanese culture and ethical values over those of China. By exalting the sacred origins of Japan and by claiming that Japan, rather than China, should be regarded as the Middle Kingdom of the world, Yamaga gave early voice to an attitude that was to gain wide acceptance after the rise to prominence in the eighteenth century of the Neo-Shintoist School of National Learning (*kokugaku-ha*).

Another outstanding scholar of the Ancient Studies School was Ogyū Sorai (1666–1728), who went even farther back into Chinese history than Yamaga to find the "true" Confucian way in the age of ancient sages who lived before Confucius. Yamaga Sokō had criticized the abstract Neo-Confucian stress on cultivating man's inherently moral nature and had urged the inculcation of more practical, "fundamental" ethics as a means for maintaining social order in Tokugawa Japan. But both Yamaga and the Neo-Confucianists were, in the best Confucian tradition, interested chiefly in the subject of morality. Ogyū Sorai, on the other hand, paid less attention to morality than to the legal and institutional controls necessary for governing society.

Although there were antecedents for it in Confucianism, Ogyū's greater emphasis on controlling men than on trying to elevate them to the utopian state where they would be sufficiently moral to exist without external controls is generally associated with schools of thought in China other than the Confucian. That Ogyū Sorai should take such a position was in part a response to new social and political problems that came to beset Tokugawa society about the time of the Genroku epoch and in part simply a reflection of the strongly practical, pragmatic approach of many heterodox thinkers of this age.

Many of the problems that the Tokugawa Shogunate encountered as it approached its second century were the result of what today we would call progress. The Shogunate, for one thing, was increasingly perplexed about how to deal with the great flourishing of commerce which peace and tranquility brought. While the townsmen enjoyed to the fullest their Genroku prosperity, the Shogunate and the samurai class in general, still overwhelmingly dependent on agriculture for income, found themselves more and more financially hard-pressed as the result of market fluctuations and the inflationary drift of the times. In 1695, the Shogunate even resorted to the desperate expediency of currency debasement in an attempt to solve its financial difficulties.

Another problem that troubled the Shogunate was bureaucratization. The Tokugawa Shogunate had been founded on the basis of direct military controls to govern a country that in 1600 had known only warfare for generations. The original structure of the Shogunate, although it proved to be remarkably durable, was inevitably altered and expanded with the passage of time to meet changing conditions. One of the most important changes was in the office of shogun. The three great founding shoguns, who ruled until 1651, had been personally dominant figures. But with the growth in complexity of Shogunate affairs and the appearance of weak men in the hereditary line of its headship, the shogun's powers came to be exercised by others, and open struggles over these powers among men and groups within the Shogunate became increasingly frequent. Although a particularly strong-willed shogun could still exert his personal influence, the tendency toward a diffusion of power (apparently characteristic of all bureaucracies) can be observed in the history of the Tokugawa Shogunate from the late seventeenth century on.

It was precisely to the question of strengthening the Shogunate institutionally in order to meet the new demands of the eighteenth century that the Ancient Studies scholar Ogyū Sorai turned his attention. And it is interesting to note that Shogunate authorities were not so enamored of the orthodox Neo-Confucianist view of the Tokugawa government as a purely moral agent that they did not lend an attentive ear to the heterodox, legalistic views of Ogyū.

Although I have stressed that one of the features common to many heterodox thinkers of the Tokugawa period was their desire to approach things in a more direct and rational fashion, it should be noted that certain scholars who remained within the Neo-Confucian orthodoxy exhibited a similar bent. The best example is Arai Hakuseki (1657–1725), a *rōnin* who served as the personal adviser to two shoguns from 1709 until 1715. Arai was noted for certain bold and forceful policies he initiated, including his efforts to restore the value of the coinage after the currency debasement of 1695, to revise the Shogunate's "Laws for the Military Houses," and to restrict the outflow of gold and silver bullion from Japan through the foreign trade with the Dutch and Chinese at Nagasaki. But, from the standpoint of cultural history, Arai's rationalism is best observed in the field of pure scholarship, where he wrote books on such wide-ranging subjects as archeology, sociology, philology, history, and even conditions in the West.

In all of his scholarly work, Arai exhibited a degree of rationality and a quest for empirical evidence that make his writings valuable secondary reference sources even today. When dealing with Japan's prehistory, for example, he urged the investigation of Chinese and Korean accounts of early Japan and not simply acceptance of the mythical versions of the country's origins as recorded in the *Kojiki* and *Nihon Shoki* of the eighth century. In perhaps his best-known work, *Observations on History* (*Dokushi Yoron*), Arai presented a careful analysis in terms of cause and effect of Japanese history from the time of the establishment of the Fujiwara regency in the Heian period until Hideyoshi's unification of the country in the late sixteenth century (with particular emphasis on the rise of the military class to pre-eminence).

Whereas Arai Hakuseki employed techniques of historical methodology that we would consider quite modern, other scholars of the early and mid-Tokugawa period undertook histories of Japan of a more traditional kind, written in Chinese and based on classical Chinese models of textual organization. One of these was *The Comprehensive Mirror of Our Country* (*Honchō Tsugan*)[45] of the Hayashi family; another was *The History of Great Japan* (*Dai Nihon Shi*), compiled by a school for historical studies established in the Mito *han*. The Mito work, which was not actually completed until 1906, is a chronicle of Japan's imperial line from the time of the mythical founding of the state by the first emperor in 660 B.C. until unification of the Northern and Southern Courts in 1392. Strongly moralistic in tone, it was greatly admired by loyalists of the late Tokugawa period, who attacked the Shogunate and urged a restoration of the emperor to power. In fact, the early Mito scholars, whose daimyo was related to the Tokugawa family, had by no means intended their history to be subversive of the Shogunate. Nevertheless, *The History of Great Japan,* which stresses the continuity and sanctity of the imperial institution in Japanese history, greatly aroused the nationalistic sentiments of those who finally carried out the Meiji Restoration of 1868.

Another source of inspiration for the loyalists of the Meiji Restoration was the collected writings of the School of National Learning (*kokugaku-ha*). This school arose in the eighteenth century as an antiquarian literary movement whose members investigated such ancient masterpieces as the *Man'yōshū* and *The Tale of Genji* in the search for a true and original Japanese spirit untainted by those alien systems of thought and behavior, including Buddhism and Confucianism, that had been introduced to Japan from China during the previous thousand years.

Despite its inflammatory appeal to later imperial loyalists, the National Learning movement in its origins was not a radical or aberrant phenomenon at all but a logical development in Japanese intellectual history that owed much to the various schools of Tokugawa Confucianism. The forerunners of the movement, participating in the general upsurge in scholarship stimulated by Confucianism in the seventeenth century, undertook philological studies into the origins of the Japanese language that paved the way for the subsequent work of the two leading National Learning scholars of the eighteenth century, Kamo Mabuchi (1697–1769) and Motoori Norinaga (1730–1801).

Kamo Mabuchi, the son of a functionary at a Shinto shrine who rose to become lecturer to the head of a branch family of the Tokugawa, was much taken with the *Man'yōshū,* and asserted that the poems of this eighth-century anthology were imbued with the true spirit of the Japanese. He identified this spirit as one of pure naturalness, spontaneity, and manly vigor, and charged that the influx of Chinese culture into Japan had perverted it to a way of life, exemplified by the courtiers of the Heian period, that was both artificial and effeminate. Kamo urged people to compose poems in the manner of the *Man'yōshū* and thereby seek to recapture or "restore" the native temper of ancient times. As we have seen, restorationism—that is, the desire to return to an earlier, golden age in history—was also a strong sentiment among scholars of the Ancient Studies School, although some Sinophiles among them, like Ogyū Sorai, may have wished to revive only the conditions of ancient China. Kamo Mabuchi, on the other hand, insisted unequivocally that the golden age to be sought in the past was a Japanese age.

Although he only met Kamo Mabuchi once, Motoori Norinaga

claimed to be his true disciple and never directly challenged Kamo's glorification of the *Man'yōshū* as the repository of the original Japanese spirit. But Motoori's own investigation into courtier literature, especially *The Tale of Genji* and the *Shinkokinshū*, led him to adopt a quite different view of that spirit. Motoori believed that the most important quality native to the Japanese was their sensitivity, as embodied in the aesthetic term *mono no aware*. He attacked what he regarded as the excessive rationalism of the Confucianists and claimed that the Japanese were fundamentally an emotional people. To his mind, *The Tale of Genji* was a classical delineation of this emotionalism as it revealed itself in the courtier society of the Heian period. In contrast to Kamo Mabuchi, Motoori thus extolled the highly refined, indeed effeminate, aestheticism that characterized the behavior of individuals in *The Tale of Genji* and the poems of the thirteenth-century *Shinkokinshū* and proclaimed it to be the finest product of Japanese civilization.

In an effort to get to the origins of the Japanese tradition, Motoori also went back beyond Kamo's much-esteemed *Man'yōshū* to undertake research on the oldest extant Japanese book, the *Kojiki*. Whereas the *Nihon Shoki* was composed in Chinese and had been studied by courtier scholars through the centuries, the *Kojiki* was so complexly written by means of Chinese characters to reproduce Japanese sounds that it had long been regarded as almost indecipherable. In what was one of the greatest achievements of scholarship in Japanese history, Motoori devoted nearly thirty-five years to an analysis and annotated translation of the *Kojiki*. The end result is a testament to the exceptionally high standards of scholarly work that had been cultivated in Japan by the eighteenth century.

Although Motoori approached his translation of the *Kojiki* with an attitude of strict scholarly neutrality, his personal interest in the work went beyond the cultural to the religious. He sought, in fact, to establish the *Kojiki* as a basic scripture of Shinto. Motoori's own theology was founded on absolute faith in the native *kami* of Japan. Rejecting the various Shinto schools that had emerged in the medieval age and had absorbed varying amounts of Buddhism, Confucianism, and sundry Chinese lore, Motoori insisted that the ways of the *kami* were inscrutable and that the accounts of them in such writings as the *Kojiki* and *Nihon Shoki* must be accepted as gospel.

Enriched by the great contribution of Motoori, the National Learning movement evolved in several directions during the late Tokugawa period. Some scholars continued to devote themselves to Japanese literature and history; others gave their attention chiefly to the Shintoist elements in National Learning; and still others moved into the field of political activism and became advocates of imperial restoration.

By far the most influential member of the National Learning (or Neo-Shintoist) movement of the early nineteenth century was Hirata Atsutane (1776–1843). Hirata never had the opportunity to meet Motoori Norinaga, but he deeply venerated the work of the older master and always claimed that he was Motoori's true successor. Nevertheless, Hirata was of a very different temperament and outlook from Motoori. He was, for one thing, a fiery Shintoist and Japanophile, who reviled alien teachings and foreign countries in order to glorify the superiority of Japan and its native learning. Motoori had combined impeccable scholarship with an abiding religious faith (even though we may regard as excessively naïve his acceptance of the mythical accounts of the age of the gods as literally true); Hirata, on the other hand, seems never to have hesitated to interpret and even to distort things to suit his purposes.

Two examples may be given to illustrate Hirata's penchant for specious argument. First, he asserted that the reason why the ancient Japanese had not articulated a Way of virtuous behavior (that is, a Way like Confucianism), as the early Chinese had, was because they had been inherently virtuous and had felt no need consciously to identify and preach virtue. Second, Hirata contended that the Japanese failure to develop the art of medicine independently stemmed from the fact that, unlike China and the Western countries, Japan had originally been pure and without disease and hence did not need medicines. Only after contact with the outside world were the Japanese also afflicted with diseases and obliged to seek remedies for them.

Hirata possessed a wide knowledge of many subjects, including the Western learning of the scholars of Dutch Studies (*rangaku*); in fact, his remarks about medicine were made in spite of (or because of?) a considerable familiarity with Western advances in the field of medicine. Hirata's religious views may also have been influenced by Christianity, even though that foreign creed had been rigorously proscribed throughout the Tokugawa period. With the rise of Dutch Studies in the eighteenth century, some knowledge of Christianity inevitably filtered once again into Japan despite efforts of the authorities to prevent it. Hirata's stress on the central importance of a Shinto god of creativity and his belief in a rather pleasant sounding, if vaguely defined, Shinto afterworld may both have been partly or wholly derived from Christianity. His positing of an afterworld was in particular an innovation for Shinto, which has always been notably deficient in eschatological speculation.

It is difficult to make a general assessment of Hirata Atsutane. Much of his thought is, at least to the outsider of another age, both highly irrational and repellent. Still, he was able to attract a wide following and his teachings were fervently propagated by disciples. This is undoubtedly attributable in part to the fact that his crudely expressed xenophobia, his pathetically Japan-centered myopia, and his indiscriminate eclecticism are tendencies observable in many Japanese of recent times.

The last major movement of heterodox learning in the Tokugawa period was the school of Dutch Studies. We have seen that, although the Japanese had engaged in a century of intercourse with Europeans, particularly the Portuguese, from the 1540's until the late 1630's, much of the Western knowledge they acquired in that period was lost during the anti-Christian persecutions that accompanied implementation of the national seclusion policy. From 1641 on, only the Dutch among Europeans were permitted to trade with Japan; and the Dutch, who shared the limited Japanese foreign trade with the Chinese, were virtually quarantined from all but a few officials and interpreters who dealt with them at their compound on the small island of Deshima in Nagasaki Harbor.

There was little opportunity under the seclusion policy, therefore, for the Japanese to gain access to Western knowledge. Most of the Dutch at Nagasaki were dour tradesmen who were concerned only with making a profit, and the linguistic talents of the Nagasaki interpreters (both in Portuguese, which remained the lingua franca of communication with the foreigners until the end of the seventeenth century, and in Dutch) were so limited as to make serious exchange with the Hollanders almost impossible. Even so, sufficient information about Dutch superiority in scientific, and especially medical, knowledge did seep out of Nagasaki to stimulate the imaginations of some Japanese scholars. One reason why Western medicine became the object of particular interest among the Japanese was that the doctors regularly assigned to the Dutch contingent at Nagasaki were, unlike the Dutch traders, often men of broad intellectual background and curiosity. One was the German physician Englebert Kaempfer (1651–1716), who was at Deshima in the early 1690's and twice traveled to Edo with the Dutch party that visited the shogun's court there annually. Kaempfer was a keen student of all aspects of Japan and Japanese life (as he could observe them), and he later published in Europe his *History of Japan*, a book that captured the minds of Europeans just then awakening to an interest in the Far East. It was used by Montesquieu and others in their writings as a primary source for observations on Japan.

By the early eighteenth century, the desire to learn about the West had become increasingly widespread among Japanese scholars and even government officials. The great Confucian rationalist and Shogunate adviser Arai Hakuseki, for example, produced a book about conditions in the West based on interviews with an Italian missionary named Sidotti who, after studying Japanese in Manila, had made his way alone to Japan in 1708. One reason for this renewal of interest in the West was the diversity in intellectual inquiry encouraged by the other heterodox schools of scholarship; another was the strong leaning on the part of Tokugawa intellectuals as a whole toward the kind of practical study that Western learning offered.

The actual start of the Dutch Studies movement was made possible by the eighth Tokugawa shogun, Yoshimune (1684–1751), who in 1720 was persuaded by his advisers to lift all restrictions on the importation of foreign books (i.e., Chinese and Dutch books) so long as they did not deal with the still forbidden subject of Christianity. Yoshimune is noted for his efforts to reform the Shogunate, including the rather futile policy of reviving the martial spirit of the samurai class. He was also a man who greatly admired learning and was willing to patronize scholars of all schools if he thought their ideas might be useful. He listened, for example, to the views of Ogyū Sorai, even though these were quite at variance with the orthodox Neo-Confucian attitude toward the state; and he agreed to allow the pursuit of Western learning and even sponsored the study of the Dutch language because he hoped they might be of practical value to the Shogunate.

Some information about Western science could be garnered through translations of Western books into Chinese by Jesuit scholars of the seventeenth and eighteenth centuries in China; but a working knowledge of Dutch was obviously essential to the new students of Western learning if they wished to go deeply into their studies. It is a tribute to the great zeal of the early pioneers of Dutch Studies that they persisted in the painfully tedious tasks of compiling Dutch-Japanese dictionaries and translating technical books, at first only a few lines at a time, with only the limited help they could obtain from the Dutch and their interpreters at Nagasaki. Nevertheless, by the late eighteenth century, the scholars of Dutch Studies had produced a respectable body of work, including dictionaries, translations, and treatises on Western subjects. And, in 1811, the Shogunate gave further impetus to their movement by opening an office for the translation of foreign books in Edo.

The overwhelming interest of the early scholars of Dutch Studies in medical and other scientific matters is attributable not only to the fact that these subjects were practical and safe (that is, unlikely to be connected directly with Christianity), but also, it appears, to the general temperament of the men drawn to study them. The *rangaku* scholars were of a type who had an insatiable curiosity about all manner of things, who loved to experiment simply for the sake of experimenting and, because of their instinctively pragmatic approach to life, were not especially attracted to questions of social or political ideology. Most of the early *rangaku* scholars dabbled in many fields, including medicine, botany, astronomy, and geography. As we shall see, they also practiced painting in the Western style by employing the techniques of realistic perspective and chiaroscuro; but their interest in Western ideas and philosophy was conspicuously slight, even allowing for their wish to avoid the topic of Christianity.

Toward the end of the eighteenth century and the beginning of the nineteenth, however, there appeared a number of scholars of Western learning who came to devote their attention increasingly to questions of military preparedness, economics, and foreign affairs, and who also advocated programs of action. Among the reasons for this were the perennial, although ever more pressing, problems of the Tokugawa period: the disequilibrium caused by the growth of commercial markets and a complex monetary system in a state still theoretically based on a natural economy; the inability, because of the seclusion policy, to alleviate domestic economic difficulties by increasing foreign trade; and continuance of the samurai as a largely idle class separated from their main source of income, the soil.

The Shogunate attempted to deal with these and other problems by undertaking a series of great reforms, the first of which was conducted by the shogun Yoshimune in the second quarter of the eighteenth century. But apart from some worthwhile programs, such as the encouragement of land reclamation, diversification of crops, and the adoption of more equitable and humane penal laws, these reforms were hopelessly traditionalistic and ill-suited to solving difficulties created chiefly by an expanding, dynamic economy. Shogunate reformers, for example, invariably sought to resolve the economic suffering in certain sectors of society by calling upon people everywhere to be more frugal; but, with very few exceptions, they did not consider the possibility of expanding the national wealth through an increase in foreign trade.

The apprehensions of Dutch Studies scholars of the late Tokugawa period were further intensified by the mounting incursion of foreigners, especially Russians, into the regions surrounding Japan. By the end of the eighteenth century, Russian explorers and traders had pushed eastward across the northern reaches of the world and, in addition to establishing colonies in places such as Kamchatka and the Aleutians, were making periodic probes into islands closer to Japan, including Hokkaido (until this time in Japanese history inhabited almost exclusively by the Ainu) and the Kurils. It is little wonder, therefore, that the Dutch Studies scholars should turn their eyes northward in assessing the challenges and opportunities presented by the outside world.

Among the most astute and imaginative of these later scholars of Dutch Studies was Honda Toshiaki (1744–1821).[46] Raised in one of the northern domains of Japan, Honda devoted his life to the study of a wide range of Western subjects from mathematics and astronomy to military science, geography, and navigation. He also traveled widely throughout Japan, observing the social and economic conditions of different regions, and even went by ship into the northern seas, perhaps as far as Kamchatka. Honda believed that Japan not only should seek to increase its foreign trade but also should expand territorially overseas. It was imperative first that Hokkaido, Sakhalin, and the Kurils be colonized to prevent them from falling into the hands of the Russians; then other islands and territories in Asia and North America could be absorbed to form a great Japanese empire whose capital, Honda felt, should be situated in Kamchatka. Honda was particularly fond of likening Japan to England, the island country of the West that had also founded a far-flung empire.

Honda was perhaps more blatantly imperialistic in his views than most, but he was certainly not alone among scholars of his age in advocating alteration of the seclusion policy to permit expansion of Japanese interests abroad. Yet, except for a brief period in the late eighteenth century, the opinions of Honda and like-minded men were not especially appreciated by the Shogunate. This was partly because of a clamping down on heterodox studies undertaken in 1790 by issuance of an edict calling upon the Confucian schools conducted by the Hayashi family to teach only the tenets of the orthodox creed of Neo-Confucianism. This edict was conceived by Shogunate officials who sincerely believed that the diversity of thinking in the country was having adverse effects upon society and who hoped to strengthen the moral fiber of the Japanese people by insisting upon propagation once again of an orthodox philosophical line in officially sponsored schools.

In addition to the various heterodox trends we have been examining in intellectual circles, the middle and late Tokugawa period also witnessed what may be called heterodox developments in painting, at least insofar as the main schools flourishing during this time were influenced to a greater or lesser degree by Western "scientific" techniques of realistic detailing, shading, and perspective. When one considers that, by the early Meiji period (say, the 1870's), the Japanese had become so enamored of Western-style painting that they were prepared almost totally to ignore their own rich artistic heritage, this turning to Western techniques from about the early eighteenth century on constituted a radical heterodoxy indeed.

One of the main schools of painting that arose in the eighteenth century, although under some Western influence, was in fact inspired by the so-called literati artists (*bunjin*) of China. From about the late Han period on, there had developed in China a distinction between professional artists on the one hand and, on the other, amateur artists who were also members of the ruling literati class and regarded painting as a natural and proper function of the cultivated man. In its origins, then, the *bunjin* distinction was a social one; but, from the fourteenth century on, a definite *bunjin* style emerged, distinguished chiefly by the use of soft colors and a thin and delicate brush stroke, and it was this style that was finally introduced to Japan in the eighteenth century. Interestingly, this was the first major school of Chinese painting to be emulated by the Japanese since painters of the early Muromachi period, some four centuries earlier, had succumbed to the beauty of Sung monochrome landscapes.

Unlike their Chinese counterparts, most of the leading Japanese *bunjin* artists painted to earn a living. They seem originally to have been inspired to adopt this particular style because of the influence of Chinese *bunjin* artists who came to Nagasaki in the seventeenth century. The fact that the fashion for *bunjin* art thus emerged from Nagasaki, which had been the center of Portuguese *namban* culture and in Tokugawa times included Dutch as well as Chinese in its foreign community, no doubt helps explain the Western influences that can be seen in much *bunjin* work.

The leading Japanese *bunjin* artists of the eighteenth century were Ike no Taiga (1723–76) and Yosa Buson (1716–83). Taiga, who was born into a peasant family in the outskirts of Kyoto, was an extremely precocious child and, at the age of fourteen, began painting fans in order to support his widowed mother. Although he subsequently became known as the founder of the *bunjin* school in Japan, Taiga's mature painting style is actually quite eclectic and reveals the influences not only of the Muromachi monochrome masters and the Sōtatsu-Kōrin (Rimpa) school but also of Western art (especially in the techniques of perspective and depth perception). Like all *bunjin* artists, Taiga did most of his paintings of Chinese-style landscapes and people. His pictures also often have a delightfully eccentric and witty quality that suggests they were done by one of the more joyous and refreshing personalities of the age.

Taiga's friend, Buson, was both a noted painter and a master of *haiku*. Like Taiga, he traveled frequently about the country and added much that was Japanese to his essentially "Chinese" landscapes. Also like Taiga, Buson did thoroughly charming caricature work that was undoubtedly influenced by the indigenous Japanese tradition of caricature, since Buson is known to have studied the great twelfth-century Animal Scrolls of the priest Toba. In the series of drawings he did to illustrate Bashō's *The Narrow Road of Oku*, Buson, as a writer of *haiku* who also traveled into the northern provinces, has captured the spirit of this great travel account so perfectly that, once having seen his illustrations of it, we have difficulty imagining how they could possibly have been done in any other way. Indeed, Buson's art might well be called the art of *haiku*, and some of his most appealing works are known as "*haiku* pictures" (*haiga*)—that is, pictures used to illustrate *haiku*, the texts of which are usually painted in calligraphic brush style in the upper right-hand corners.

Some comment on Buson as a poet may help to enhance appreciation of Buson the artist. In comparing Buson to Bashō, a Western critic has said, "Bashō was gentle, wise, loving, and mystic; Buson was brilliant and many-sided, not mystic in the least, but intensely clever and alive to impressions of the world around him. A foreign simile would be to liken Bashō to a pearl, and Buson to a diamond." [47] Two poems will illustrate both Buson's cleverness and his sensitivity to impressions of the world around him:

> Spring rain: and as yet
> the little froglets' bellies
> haven't got wet.

> Departing spring:
> with belated cherry blossoms
> shilly-shallying.[48]

Although Taiga and Buson had qualities that were unique and great, many other *bunjin* artists were mere Sinophiles, who turned to this style of painting as part of a greater craving for things Chinese. It is interesting to note that, even at a time when some Japanese were inaugurating a movement of National Learning with strongly xenophobic and nationalistic overtones, others—scholars as well as painters—were giving all their love to China. This is a paradox characteristic of the ambivalence with which the sensitive and highly adaptable Japanese have often confronted the dominant outside world, represented by China in premodern times and the West in the modern era.

A second new school of painting to evolve in the eighteenth century was the realistic or naturalistic school, whose most outstanding practitioner was Maruyama Ōkyo (1733–95). In this school, the influence of Western art was very strong, and in fact the followers of

Ōkyo were the forerunners of one of the mainstreams of painting in modern Japan. Ōkyo did many sketches and drawings from nature that are extremely detailed and realistic, but his most interesting works are his larger paintings in which he sought to blend traditional Far Eastern and Western artistic styles.

In contrast to the synthesizing efforts of Ōkyo and others of the naturalistic school, the Dutch Studies painters openly attempted to imitate Western models. The best-known, although perhaps also the most extreme, representative of these painters was Shiba Kōkan (1738–1818). Shiba did not actually study the Dutch language; but, in his diversity of interests and his love of Western scientific and utilitarian methods, he was very much the *rangaku* man. The paintings of Shiba, who was the first Japanese to produce a copper engraving, are technically excellent and are definitive proof that long before the Meiji Restoration the Japanese had become thoroughly familiar with the mechanics of Western art. Shiba's work is apt to impress one more for its technique than its inspiration, but there is no denying the great contribution he made to this area of Western learning.

The influence of Western techniques of painting was also felt by the later *ukiyo-e* school of artists. Certain devices, such as realistic perspective, had been employed on occasion by *ukiyo-e* artists from about the early 1700's, but it was not until the great nineteenth-century painters, Katsushika Hokusai (1760–1849) and Andō Hiroshige (1797–1858), that the Western influence became pronounced.

Hokusai was a phenomenon even in the prolific world of Tokugawa *ukiyo-e* art. Virtually unknown until he was about forty, Hokusai (who later styled himself the "old man mad with painting") absorbed the main features of all the major art styles, native and foreign, then known in Japan and produced literally tens of thousands of drawings and paintings of a great variety of subjects over an incredibly active career that continued until his death in 1849 at the age of eighty-nine. Hokusai is best remembered for his landscape prints, especially his "Thirty-six Views of Mount Fuji." Curiously, Fuji, Japan's greatest natural treasure and the object of countless lyrical flights by Japanese poets, had until this time received very little attention from Japanese painters. No doubt the chief reason for this was that Fuji's wonderful symmetry simply was not in keeping with the generally angular, jagged conception of mountains and rock formations in the highly influential Chinese tradition of monochrome landscape work. Significantly, the Western-oriented Shiba Kōkan was also attracted to Fuji and sought to apply scientific techniques to produce a truly realistic painting of the mountain. Hokusai's views of Fuji, on the other hand, are often startlingly conceived, as for example the world-famous glimpse of its snow-capped cone through a huge, curling wave. *Fig. 53*

Whereas Maruyama Ōkyo self-consciously tried to merge Far Eastern and Western art and Shiba Kōkan imitated Western painting outright, Hokusai, with his boundless energy and enthusiasm, simply absorbed the techniques of Western as well as other art styles and used them to shape his own unique style. Hokusai's better landscapes display a superb sense of design and proportion and a compassionately human concern for the figures, often from the lower classes, who inhabit them. Hokusai has enjoyed great favor in the West, and some of his prints, along with those of Hiroshige, have become as well known to Western art lovers as the more famous masterpieces of their own tradition. The case of Hokusai is an excellent illustration of cross-cultural exchange, for here was a Japanese artist who borrowed from the West and at the same time contributed, along with the *ukiyo-e* school in general, a new and exotic inspiration to the French Impressionists and other Western artists of the late nineteenth century.

Hiroshige, although he painted other subjects, was much more of a specialist in landscapes than the extraordinarily dynamic and versatile Hokusai. In a Hokusai landscape, attention is often divided between *Fig. 54* the setting and the people in it; but in Hiroshige's work, everything is *Fig. 55* subordinated to the setting and especially to the mood established by season, weather, time of day, and angle of view. Moreover, while Hokusai's figures, as they go about their business, frequently provide an element of genre interest to his landscapes, Hiroshige's are usually mere reminders of the insignificance of man against the vastness of nature. In this, Hiroshige would appear to be an inheritor of the spirit of the Chinese and Japanese masters of monochrome landscapes; and even though Hiroshige depicts far more dramatic seasonal and weather changes in his prints, there is an underlying tranquility to them that is also very reminiscent of the earlier monochrome work.

Hiroshige achieved his greatest fame in a series of prints entitled "The Fifty-three Stations of the Tōkaidō," depicting scenes along the great highway connecting Kyoto and Edo. By far the most important thoroughfare in Japanese history, the Tōkaidō during Tokugawa times was the scene not only of many great daimyo processions to and from the military capital but also of the coming and going of an unending stream of other people, including merchants, itinerant priests, pilgrims, entertainers, adventurers, and even the Dutch on their annual journey to the shogun's court. In response to this bustling traffic, the stations of the Tōkaidō flourished and each came to accumulate stories and legends about the famous people who had visited its inns, restaurants, brothels, and bathhouses, and about the unusual events it had witnessed. Hence, the Tōkaidō became a fertile source for both writers and artists. Hokusai, among the artists, tried his hand at a series of prints of the Tōkaidō stations, but no painter succeeded in immortalizing the highway and its famous stopping-off places like Hiroshige. To many people around the world who have seen copies of them, these Tōkaidō prints by Hiroshige constitute their most vivid impressions of Japan. And, in truth, they remain even to those long familiar with the country a constant source of delight as extraordinarily effective representations in art of the peculiar qualities of Japan's natural beauties and seasonal moods.

A significant development of the late Tokugawa period was the decisive shift in the center of cultural activity from the Osaka-Kyoto region to Edo. In the seventeenth and early eighteenth centuries, the Kansai had produced such leading figures of the world of art as Sōtatsu, Kōrin, Saikaku, and Chikamatsu. With the exception of Bashō, who moved to Edo, and the painters of the early *ukiyo-e* school, the most outstanding creative artists up through the Genroku epoch were the products of Japan's ancient center of cultural life. But by the Bunka-Bunsei epoch (the end of the eighteenth century and the first quarter or so of the nineteenth), Edo had taken over this central role in culture. It had become the principal home for writers, artists, and intellectuals, as well as the mecca for publishing and scholarship. The cultural primacy of Edo established at this time proved lasting, and indeed has been even more completely asserted in the modern era.

The Bunka-Bunsei epoch was a relatively placid time preceding the final, crisis decades of the Tokugawa period, when the Western powers exerted increasing pressure upon and finally succeeded in forcing Japan to open its doors and enter the modern world. In painting, the epoch was of course distinguished by men such as Shiba Kōkan, Sharaku, Utamaro, Hokusai, and Hiroshige. But in literature there was no such comparable brilliance. The efforts of late Tokugawa authors were, in fact, polarized rather sharply into the writing either of "witty" and "amorous" books (*kokkeibon* and *sharebon*) or of historical novels (*yomihon*). The distinction between the two categories was essentially one of the overly frothy versus the overly serious, of the pornographic versus the didactic.

Literature dealing with the floating world of the Tokugawa pleasure quarters had reached an early level of excellence in the writing of Saikaku. But the subject matter was too narrow in range to be a continuing source for true artistic inspiration and, with few exceptions, the successors to Saikaku produced distinctly inferior work. The examples of this sort of work in the Bunka-Bunsei epoch are interesting as social commentaries on contemporary styles and tastes, and particularly on the meaning of two much-admired qualities of people of fashion in Edo, *sui* and *tsū*, which Sansom has aptly rendered as *chic* and *savoir faire*. Otherwise, the literature of the floating world as observed in its later variants, including the witty. and amorous books, was merely a cheap, salacious type of writing that catered to low and vulgar tastes.

The most commercially successful author of this lighter type of literature in the early nineteenth century was Jippensha Ikku (1765–1831), who began his career as the writer of puppet plays in Osaka before he moved to Edo and turned his attention to prose literature. Ikku's most popular work, the picaresque *Hizakurige* (A *Journey by Foot*), recounts the adventures of two ribald and devil-may-care rogues as they make their way down the Tōkaidō from Edo. In contrast to the sophisticated inquiries of Saikaku's writings, *Hizakurige*, with its slapstick and its bawdy humor, portrays the world of lusty adventure and the irresistible pleasures of the flesh.

The second major category of literature in the Bunka-Bunsei epoch was the historical novel, whose most noted author was Takizawa Bakin (1767–1848). Like Ikku, but unlike many writers of the epoch, Bakin was able to earn his living solely by his literary efforts. His magnum opus, written over a period of some twenty-eight years and intended to be the longest novel in either Chinese or Japanese, was entitled *Satomi and the Eight Dogs* (*Nansō Satomi Hakkenden*). It is the tale of eight men who vow to restore the fortunes of the warrior family of Satomi in the fifteenth century. Against this heroic, medieval background, Bakin set about demonstrating how such ethical values as filial piety, loyalty, chastity, and selflessness actually function in the lives of men. Bakin's didacticism is all-encompassing, and each episode in *Satomi and the Eight Dogs* is designed to show how, inevitably, "virtue is rewarded and vice is punished." Compared to the literature of the floating world that was predominant through much of the Tokugawa period, this was indeed sober writing. But Bakin's great popular reception suggests that the temper of the times was turning more serious, at least in some circles; and many people were prepared and perhaps even anxious to rekindle Confucian traditions and some of the spirit of the more admirable behavior of the samurai.

From its beginning, the Tokugawa regime had attempted to impose an orthodoxy of attitude, not only socio-politically but also in the realm of art, as for example in its encouragement of moralistic, didactic literature and its patronage of the conservative Kanō school of painters. It was able to exert a particularly powerful check on foreign heterodoxies, like Christianity, through implementation of a national seclusion policy, which sealed Japan off more completely from foreign contacts than any other major civilization during the crucial centuries when the West was fashioning the modern world. Yet, despite official opposition or disapproval, Tokugawa artists, writers, and thinkers struck out in many unexpected directions. The achievement of the Dutch Studies scholars was particularly impressive because it exemplified the extraordinary inquisitiveness of the Japanese about foreign cultures and their capacity to adapt, a capacity that has been the most consistent feature of their conduct in modern times.

The failure of the anti-heterodox edicts of the 1790's was ample proof that the old orthodoxy was utterly inapplicable to a society grown as complex as Japan's in the late eighteenth century. Not only did the edicts fail; the orthodoxy itself faded soon thereafter from sight. Thus, as Japan was exposed to increasingly greater contact with the West in the first half of the nineteenth century, the response of Japanese officials and intellectuals was by no means uniform or orthodox. Even so, there were certain new beliefs that came to be widely shared. These beliefs were based on the conception of Japan as a mixed, Confucian-Shinto state. Like other Far Eastern peoples, the Japanese saw themselves as governed by the fundamental Confucian verities of ethical behavior; at the same time, they were superior to all people in the world because they were descended from the gods and had been ruled by an unbroken line of sovereigns from the founding of their country until the present. But the truly dynamic element in the Japanese world view in the early nineteenth century was that, to an infinitely greater degree than other non-Western people, they were both impressed and alarmed by the material superiority of the West. Certain scholars in the last years of the Tokugawa period proclaimed the need for a combination of "Eastern morals and Western technology," and thereby aphoristically suggested the central problem that was later to confront a modernizing Japan: how to retain the socially binding ethics of traditional behavior while at the same time resolutely acquiring the material benefits of the Western scientific and industrial revolutions.

9

Encounter with the West

IN 1844, KING WILLIAM II of Holland dispatched a letter to the shogun of Japan warning him that the quickening pace of world events made continuance of the Japanese policy of national seclusion both unwise and untenable. The development of steam navigation, for one thing, now enabled the ships of Western countries readily to penetrate the most distant waters of the world. China had already suffered military defeat at the hands of the British in the Opium War of 1839–42, and Japan could not expect to remain aloof from world affairs much longer.

Although they debated it among themselves, Tokugawa officials did nothing concrete in response to the letter of the Dutch king. The Shogunate was at the time engrossed in the last of its great traditionalistic reforms, and the failure of this reform, combined with vacillation in the face of a growing need to reconsider the seclusion policy, portended trouble for the Shogunate. The Edo regime was certainly under no immediate threat in the 1840's of being overthrown, but opinion was developing in the country that was eventually to be turned against it in the fervid movement for imperial restoration at the end of the Tokugawa period.

Interestingly, the seeds that gave growth to this opinion were first sown by scholars of the Mito school, whose daimyo was related to the Tokugawa family. For it is the Mito scholars who are usually credited with coining the slogan: "Revere the Emperor! Oust the Barbarians!" (sonnō-jōi) that was to become the rallying cry of loyalists in the Meiji Restoration. As originally used by the Mito scholars, this slogan was not intended to be either an attack on the Shogunate or a call for imperial restoration. "Revere the Emperor!" was a Confucian–

Shinto-inspired reminder of the ethical obligations within Japan's hierarchically ordered society: by revering the emperor, subjects would automatically be loyal to the shogun (to whom the emperor had delegated governing powers) and, at a lower level, would be obedient to their immediate superiors. "Oust the Barbarians!", on the other hand, was an injunction to the Shogunate to strengthen defenses against the threat of foreign aggression.

The debate over foreign defense and the seclusion policy became a national one with the arrival in Edo Bay in the summer of 1853 of Commodore Matthew Perry of the United States and his squadron of "black ships." Perry had been dispatched by President Millard Fillmore to inquire into the possibility of opening diplomatic and commercial relations with Japan, and in 1854 he achieved the first objective through the signing of a Treaty of Friendship that provided for an exchange of consular officials between Japan and the United States.

The first American consul, Townsend Harris, arrived in Japan in 1856, and it was he who finally secured a commercial pact. This pact, in addition to providing for the opening of certain Japanese ports to trade, contained a set of stipulations, previously worked out by the Western powers in their dealings with China, that came to be known as "the unequal treaty provisions." These included the principle of extra-territoriality, or the right of the Western signatory to try its nationals by its own laws for offenses committed on Japanese soil; the most-favored-nation clause, which provided that any additional treaty benefit acquired by one Western nation would automatically accrue to all other nations holding similar treaties; and the setting of a fixed customs levy of approximately 5 per cent on all goods imported to Japan, a levy that could be altered only with the consent of both parties to a treaty. It was on the basis of the Harris agreement, and especially its most-favored-nation clause, that the principal European powers also acquired commercial treaties with Japan during the next few months.

The coming of Perry and Harris brought to an end Japan's seclusion policy of more than 200 years, but it did not resolve differences of opinion about the policy. There was the question, for example, of the extent to which Japan should be opened. The Harris treaty specified only that a few ports be made available to foreign trade over a period of years. Should the rest of Japan, even the interior, also be opened to foreign merchants, missionaries, and residents, and if so over what span of time? Some diehards continued to insist that the treaties with the Western "barbarians" be regarded simply as tactical measures valid only until Japan could strengthen itself sufficiently to drive the foreigners once again from the divine land; but other Japanese began to consider more soberly the sweeping and long-term implications of their new relations with the West.

The final, chaotic years of the Tokugawa period are fascinating for the momentous political events that led to the overthrow of the Shogunate, but they are not especially important to Japanese cultural history and hence may be briefly summarized here. The first wave of opposition to the Shogunate's handling of foreign affairs came primarily from certain of the larger *tozama* or outside *han* of western Japan, especially Satsuma and Chōshū. These great domains regarded as anachronistic the Tokugawa governing system whereby they were theoretically excluded from all participation in the conduct of national affairs at Edo. In the early 1860's, the Shogunate sought a reconciliation by bringing some of the more important outside daimyos into its deliberative councils. At the same time, it attempted to strengthen relations with Kyoto by arranging a marriage between the shogun and an imperial princess.

With these developments, the initiative in opposition to the Shogunate's policies was assumed by younger, activist samurai from Satsuma, Chōshū, and other domains, many of whom renounced their feudal ties to become *rōnin* and thus free to pursue their own political convictions. These samurai, also known as *shishi* or "men of high purpose," formed the nucleus of the loyalist movement that grew in intensity during the next few years. By the middle of the decade, the loyalists were openly calling for the overthrow of the Shogunate on the grounds that, not only had it usurped the rightful ruling powers of the emperor, it had failed militarily to protect Japan against the intrusion of the Western barbarians. For them, "Revere the Emperor!" became a call for imperial restoration and "Expel the Barbarians!" a demand that the Shogunate do what in fact was no longer possible: drive the foreigners from Japanese soil.

The climax to the confrontation between the Shogunate and the loyalists, more and more of whom were congregating in Kyoto where they aligned themselves with anti-Tokugawa ministers at the imperial court, came in 1866 when the Shogunate attempted for the second time in two years to put down the loyalist faction in the most unruly of the domains, Chōshū. At this critical point, Satsuma, whose loyalists had already formed a secret alliance with Chōshū, refused to join the Shogunate's expedition, and in the ensuing conflict the Shogunate forces were defeated. Encouraged by this demonstration of military weakness on the part of the Shogunate, Satsuma and Chōshū loyalists, joined by men from other domains, carried out a coup in Kyoto at the end of the year and proclaimed an imperial restoration. The shogun, realizing the futility of further resistance, capitulated; and, although there was some scattered fighting by stubborn supporters of the Shogunate, the restoration was completed by early 1867 with very little loss of blood.

The Meiji Restoration, named after the Emperor Meiji (1852–1912) who ascended the throne in 1867 at the age of fifteen, was a political revolution from above carried out by younger, enlightened members of Japan's ruling samurai class.[49] These men and their supporters had called for a "return to antiquity" (*fukko*), and, in the early days following the Restoration, there was a certain heady excitement about recapturing the spirit and ways of the past, especially through temporary reinstatement of the ancient institutions of imperial government as originally set forth in the eighth-century Taihō Code. But the new Meiji leaders, who included some Kyoto courtiers along with samurai, were men of the future, not the past. They made this clear from the very outset of the Meiji period by quietly dropping the cry of "Expel the Barbarians!" which they had so recently used to embarrass the Tokugawa Shogunate. They may have continued to harbor personal animosities toward the West, particularly for forcing Japan to accede to the unequal treaties; but the Meiji leaders were by and large pragmatic men who respected the material superiority of the West and wished to emulate it by undertaking modernization. Sharing an overriding concern for Japanese territorial independence, they believed that, quite apart from the obvious benefits and enjoyments it would bring, modernization was essential if Japan was to be protected against possible future threats from the outside. Accordingly, they adopted as a general statement of their policy the slogan, taken from Chinese legalist thought, of "Enrich the country and strengthen its arms" (*fukoku-kyōhei*). Japan was to be enriched through modernization for the primary purpose of strengthening it militarily.

The devotion of the Meiji leaders to modernization can also be seen in the brief, five-article Charter Oath they issued in 1868 in the emperor's name. This may be regarded as a very broad statement of purpose by the new regime, and it is significant that at least two of its articles seem to be explicit commitments to modernization:

> Article 4. Evil customs of the past shall be broken off and everything based upon the just laws of Nature.
> Article 5. Knowledge shall be sought throughout the world so as to strengthen the foundations of imperial rule.[50]

In line with their determination to make Japan a modern state, the Meiji leaders took a series of steps during their first decade in power that together constituted a radical and sweeping reform of Japanese society. These included abolition of the feudal *han* and the institution of a centrally controlled system of prefectural government; and dissolution of the samurai class and the establishment of basic legal equalities for all people. One of the most severe blows to the old, rigid class system and particularly to the inflated samurai sense of superiority was the adoption in 1873 of universal military conscription.

Despite the inevitable stresses caused by social change and the specific grievances of many samurai as they were dispossessed of their traditional privileges, the Japanese by the early 1870's had in general abandoned their dreams of restoring the past and were caught up in an overwhelming urge to join the march of Western progress. This was the beginning of a period of nearly two decades during which the Japanese unabashedly pursued the fruits of Western "civilization and enlightenment" (*bummei-kaika*). That the government intended to take the lead in this quest for the holy grail of foreign culture can be seen in the dispatch in 1871 of a mission to visit the United States and Europe headed by a distinguished court noble, Iwakura Tomomi (1825–83), and including a number of other leaders of the new Meiji regime. So cherished was the opportunity to journey to the West at this time that one young boy who accompanied the Iwakura Mission in order to study in the United States wrote (years later) that he and his fellow students all fervently believed that one could not become a real human being without going abroad.

Although it may be debatable whether exposure to the West was a necessary qualification for full status in the human race, there is no question that it became the surest means for advancement among Japanese in the early Meiji period. Of the many youths who went to study in Europe and the United States, the great majority were sponsored by the government as part of its civilization and enlightenment policy. Upon returning home, these youths had virtually unlimited career opportunities. Meanwhile, for those who could not make the trip abroad, the government and other institutions invited a number of foreigners to Japan as teachers and technical advisers. Offering high wages, they were able to attract generally excellent people, who provided knowledge and expertise crucial to the modernization process.

Outward signs of modernity began to appear throughout the country, but particularly in the metropolitan centers like Tokyo and Yokohama: steamships, railroads, telegraph lines, a national postal service, industrial factories, and, especially exciting to the Japanese, gas-burning streetlamps that "made the night as bright as the day." Most of these innovations were, of course, indispensable to modernization; but many others were just marginally important or were even ludicrous fads reflecting the craze among some people to "become Western."

Western-style uniforms were first adopted by the Japanese military before the Restoration and were made standard for policemen, train conductors, and other civil functionaries within a few years after the beginning of the modern era. During the 1870's, Western clothes, deemed more practical and up-to-date, were increasingly worn by men in the cities, often combined amusingly with items of the native costume. Thus, it was not unusual to see men sporting kimonos over long pants or suit jackets and *hakama* skirts. Women and people in the rural areas, on the other hand, were much slower in adopting the sartorial ways of the West. Western shoes, moreover, presented a special problem, for the Japanese foot, splayed from the traditional wearing of sandals, frequently could not be fitted into footgear imported from abroad.

But whereas the shift to Western wearing attire was made erratically, and never completely, the transition to the Western custom of cropped hair for men became something of a national issue. The Japanese are by nature extraordinarily sensitive to ridicule by others. No doubt this sensitivity has been heightened by the minimal contact they have had with foreigners through much of their history. In the early Meiji period, as they sought to "catch up with the West," they also faced the practical problem that, so long as the Western nations regarded their ways as barbaric, it would be that much more difficult to secure revision of the unequal treaties and achieve complete independence. Hence, the Japanese Government either banned or tried to restrict practices, such as public bathing, tattooing, and the sale of pornography, that they thought the foreigners found offensive. And the wearing of the topknot, which had been the practice of Japanese men for centuries, also came to be looked upon as primitive and unbecoming to the citizens of a modern Japan.

Again, it was the Japanese military who first cut their topknots in order to wear the hats of their Western-style uniforms. By the early Meiji period, all prominent Japanese men, including the emperor, wore their hair cropped (and often grew fine beards and mustaches, like their Western counterparts): indeed, it was very much the sign of the progressive man to wear his hair this way, and a popular jingle claimed: "If you tap a cropped head, it will play the tune of civilization and enlightenment." But the fashion was not immediately accepted by the lower classes, and the Japanese Government felt constrained to issue occasional directives urging its adoption. Some headmen in rural villages are said to have walked around reading the directives while still sporting their own topknots; others cut the topknots but let their "hair of regret" hang down their backs. Not until about 1890 did the wearing of cropped hair by men become universal in Japan.

Among the many Western fads, none was more conspicuous or symbolic of the humorous side of foreign borrowing than the eating of beef. Owing to Buddhist taboos and a scarcity of game animals, the Japanese had traditionally abstained from eating red meat. With the coming of foreigners, however, restaurants specializing in beef dishes, especially *gyūnabe* or beef stew, began to crop up in the cities. A contemporary author of "witty books," Kanagaki Robun (1829–94), even wrote a collection of satirical sketches entitled *Aguranabe* (*Eating Stew Cross-Legged*) about the conversations of customers in a beefhouse who concluded that a man could not be regarded as civilized unless he ate beef. Kanagaki's description of one customer includes the observation that

> . . . he uses that scent called Eau de Cologne to give sheen to his hair. He wears a padded silken kimono beneath which a calico undergarment is visible. By his side is his Western-style umbrella, covered in gingham. From time to time he removes from his sleeve with a painfully contrived gesture a cheap watch, and consults the time.[51]

Meanwhile, this newly enlightened man commented to his neighbor that "We really should be grateful that even people like ourselves can now eat beef, thanks to the fact that Japan is steadily becoming a truly civilized country." Perhaps it was in celebration of the glory of beef that about this time some students invented sukiyaki, now the hallmark of Japanese cuisine to most foreigners.

Some of the more fervent advocates of *bummei-kaika* at the height of the Western fever in early Meiji times even went so far as to suggest that Japan should adopt English as its national language. But the most extreme suggestion was that, since Caucasians were observably superior to the people of all other races, the Japanese should intermarry with them as quickly as possible in order to acquire their higher ethnic qualities.

One of the most ultimately profound physical changes wrought by modernization in Japan was the gradual adoption of Western building materials and architectural styles. Throughout their history, the Japanese had constructed their dwellings and other buildings almost entirely out of wood. With the growth in recent centuries of great urban centers like Edo and Osaka, this gave rise to the constant danger—and all too frequent occurrence—of fires that consumed large portions of cities. For example, a devastating fire in 1657 made necessary the extensive rebuilding of Edo. In 1874, after a fire that gutted the Ginza area of central Tokyo, the government took the opportunity to order the construction of a row of some 300 two-story brick buildings for the use of merchants on this bustling thoroughfare. Contemporary woodblock prints show how grand and exotic these buildings appeared to the Japanese of that day. The government hoped that the Ginza would serve as a model to encourage others to build these new fireproofed buildings; and the newspapers declared that people who walked down the Ginza could enjoy the enchanted feeling of being in a foreign country.

Although more and more public and commercial buildings on Western lines were built in the cities, the construction of Western private homes was undertaken much more slowly. The higher cost of such homes was one reason; but another was the continuing, overwhelming preference of the Japanese for their traditional, native-style homes. This was one area in which Westernization made little headway in Japan, and even today the Japanese continue to live as they have for centuries in houses consisting chiefly of sparsely furnished rooms with matted floors upon which to sit and sleep.

In intellectual circles, the great national quest for civilization and enlightenment in early Meiji gave rise to a number of study and discussion groups devoted to the question of transforming Japan into a modern state. Of these, the most influential was the Meirokusha or "Meiji Six Society," founded in the sixth year of Meiji, 1873, by some ten of the more prominent Westernizers of the day. The members of the Meirokusha met twice a month to discuss such subjects as politics, the economy, education, religion, the Japanese language, and women's rights. In 1874, they began publication of the *Meiji Six Magazine* for the purpose of publishing articles on their views. A large percentage of the Meirokusha membership was comprised of men who had engaged in Western learning before the Restoration and had been employed as translators and teachers by the Tokugawa Shogunate in its Office for Barbarian Studies, established in 1855 after the arrival of Perry. Hence, the Meirokusha had as its legacy the venerable tradition of Dutch Studies begun nearly a century and a half earlier in Japan.

The leading figure in the Meirokusha, and indeed the most popular and widely read intellectual of the Meiji period, was Fukuzawa Yukichi (1835–1901). Fukuzawa was a low-ranking, but personally ambitious and opportunistic, samurai who began the study of Western gunnery and the Dutch language as a youth under the patronage of his feudal domain. Later, when Fukuzawa visited Yokohama shortly after the signing of the Harris treaty in 1858 and observed the newly arrived foreigners at first hand, he learned a sad fact that was to cause anguish for all students of Dutch Studies: Dutch was practically useless as a medium for dealing with most Westerners. Fukuzawa, we are told, switched the very next day to the study of English; and, two years later, in 1860, he was selected to accompany a Shogunate mission to the United States in what was the first transoceanic voyage of a Japanese-manned ship.

Fukuzawa made two other trips abroad, in 1861 and 1867. In between he published *Conditions in the Western World* (*Seiyō Jijō*), a book that established him as one of the foremost interpreters of the West. Fukuzawa was more of a popularizer than a pure intellectual, and as such he made a far greater impact on the people of his time. It is no exaggeration to say that he, more than any other single individual, influenced the minds of a generation of Japanese in the early, formative years of the modern era. His most successful book, *An Encouragement of Learning* (*Gakumon no Susume*), written between 1872 and 1876, eventually sold nearly 3.5 million copies. The opening paragraph set the tone for Fukuzawa's argument:

It is said that heaven does not create one man above or below another man. This means that when men are born from heaven they all are equal. There is no innate distinction between high and low. It means that men can freely and independently use the myriad things of the world to satisfy their daily needs through the labors of their own bodies and minds, and that, as long as they do not infringe upon the rights of others, may pass their days in happiness. Nevertheless, as we broadly survey the human scene, there are the wise and the stupid, the rich and poor, the noble and lowly, whose conditions seem to differ as greatly as the clouds and the mud. The reason for this is clear. In the *Jitsugokyō* we read that if a man does not learn he will be ignorant, and that a man who is ignorant is stupid. Therefore the distinction between wise and stupid comes down to a matter of education.[52]

Strongly influenced by British utilitarianism and by the then current Western idea of the perfectibility of man through education, Fukuzawa became a staunch advocate of modern education, with the emphasis particularly on practical subjects. He vigorously denounced the social inequities and indignities of Tokugawa feudalism and declared that all men should be free and all countries independent on the basis of "natural reason." The democratic idealism that Fukuzawa thus espoused was concurrently reflected in the new Meiji Government's attitude toward education. Dedicating itself to the goal of universal primary education on the American model, the government's 1872 ordinance founding a new public school system contained the vow that "in no village will there be a family without learning and in no household will there be an uneducated person."

Unlike most of the other members of the Meirokusha, Fukuzawa steadfastly refused to enter the service of the Meiji Government and insisted upon the importance of maintaining his independence as a social critic. The sensitivity of the Meiji Six enlighteners in general to changes in government attitude, however, was revealed in 1875 when, as the result of issuance by the government of a restrictive press law, they ceased publication of the *Meiji Six Magazine* and soon terminated the activities of its parent society. Amidst the continuing enthusiasm for civilization and enlightenment, the government had found itself faced in the mid-1870's with a newly organized political opposition; and the predominantly government-oriented membership of the Meirokusha deemed it prudent to dissolve an organization that might be viewed as sympathetic to that opposition.

The Meiji Restoration had been carried out under the euphoric slogan of a "return to antiquity"; in fact, the restorationists do not appear to have had any concrete political plan other than to wrest power from the tottering Shogunate. As leaders of the new Meiji Government, they launched the country on the road to civilization and enlightenment and encouraged aspirations among the Japanese people for "independence," "freedom," and "individual rights," concepts taken from British liberal democracy, which absorbed the thinking of Japanese officials and intellectuals during the first decade or so of the Meiji period. But, although a few extreme Westernizing enthusiasts suggested that Japan establish a republic, no one of importance went so far as to advocate that a "free" people should also have the right to select their own government. The new political and intellectual leadership of Meiji Japan came almost entirely from the samurai class; and, while vociferously attacking the evils of Tokugawa feudalism, they retained the feudalistic attitude that the masses were by nature inert and stupid. It was their purpose to enlighten the people, not to make them politically active but to "enrich the country" and thereby strengthen it *vis-à-vis* the nations of the West. Even the iconoclastic and utilitarian-minded Fukuzawa was not prepared to encourage a critical attitude on the part of the people toward the government. When political opposition did arise in the 1870's, it was not the result of a movement from without but of a factional dispute within the government itself.

The leaders of the Meiji Restoration were primarily samurai from the domains of Satsuma, Chōshū, Tosa, and Hizen. From the outset, however, the Satsuma-Chōshū men formed a separate clique, based on the pact between their two domains that had been so important in the overthrow of the Tokugawa Shogunate, and increasingly they came to monopolize real power in the new government. The dissatisfaction that this created among the samurai of Tosa and Hizen was transformed into a national issue in the so-called Korean invasion crisis of 1873. The ostensible issue in the 1873 crisis was how to deal with a rebuff by Korea to Japanese overtures to open diplomatic and commercial relations. Most of the Tosa and Hizen leaders in the government urged a hard line, including the possibility of invading Korea; but the Satsuma-Chōshū clique, with the notable exception of Saigō Takamori (1827–77) of Satsuma, counseled restraint on the grounds that Japan was still too weak to risk any foreign involvement. When the views of the "peace" party prevailed, Saigō and other members of the "war" party left the government.

Although the Satsuma-Chōshū clique had won a major victory and had further strengthened its hold on the government, it now had powerful enemies on the outside. Some of these enemies turned to open rebellion, leading armies composed of samurai who were discontented with the progressive policies of the Meiji Government. The most serious of these uprisings was the Satsuma Rebellion of 1877–78, led by Saigō Takamori. More than any other Restoration leader, Saigō felt a continuing attachment to the ideals of the samurai class. His bellicose attitude at the time of the 1873 crisis was based largely on his belief that the samurai of Japan could and should deal with a foreign insult by taking direct military action. In assuming leadership of the Satsuma Rebellion in 1877, Saigō made a last gallant gesture for feudal privilege and became the great romantic hero of modern Japan. At the same time, the failure of the Satsuma Rebellion also marked the last attempt to oppose the Meiji Government through force.

Of far greater historical significance was the demand made by other samurai leaders, who had also been members of the war party in 1873, that participation in government be expanded through the establishment of an elected assembly. In 1874, a group of samurai, led by Itagaki Taisuke (1837–1919) of Tosa, submitted a memorial to the throne attacking the absolutist Satsuma-Chōshū regime in the following terms:

> Present political power does not rest with the Emperor, nor with the people. It is monopolized entirely by one group of officials. If the absolutism of these officials is not corrected, it could mean the downfall of the nation. Moreover the only means of correction would be to establish an assembly elected by the people and to expand discussions concerning the country.

The government replied that it was too soon to consider giving "the people" a voice in political affairs. Actually, it is doubtful that any of the memorialists had in mind an electorate that would include more than a small percentage of the Japanese people. The memorialists were former samurai who espoused ideas of parliamentary democracy at this time primarily as a means to attack the Satsuma-Chōshū oligarchs in the Meiji Government. Although the people's rights (*minken*) movement they thus launched eventually became a campaign for full democracy, including universal manhood suffrage, it was by no means a "popular" undertaking in its origins.

One response of the government to the people's rights movement was to issue the press law in 1875 that caused dissolution of the Meirokusha. This and other laws repressive of the freedoms of speech and assembly were aimed at curbing the efforts by Itagaki and his allies to form political parties. Nevertheless, the emergent party advocates continued to press their demands, and, in the same year, 1875, Itagaki formed the first national political association, the Patriotic Party (Aikokusha). But it was not until 1881 that the *minken* people received a public commitment from the oligarchs that they would eventually be given the opportunity to participate in government.

In 1881, Ōkuma Shigenobu (1838–1922), one of the last of the non-Satsuma-Chōshū statesmen still in the government, was relieved of his position as the result of disclosures he made about corruption in high office. In the wake of Ōkuma's dismissal, the government secured an imperial edict promising a constitution and the opening of a national parliament within nine years, or by 1890. Although it may appear that Ōkuma thus forced a concession from the Satsuma-Chōshū oligarchs, in fact the latter had for long been considering how and when a constitutional form of government should be established in Japan, and the action of Ōkuma in 1881 probably did not appreciably alter their plans, although they may not have wished to reveal them publicly so soon.

The Meiji oligarchs were, by any criterion, extraordinarily capable and farsighted men who took a strongly pragmatic approach to problems. Once secure in power they did indeed tend toward the authoritarian in consonance with their samurai backgrounds. But one advantage of their functioning as oligarchs was that, immune from the everyday strife of elected politicians, they could concentrate on the pursuit of loftier goals for the betterment of Japan. They were committed to making Japan into a truly modern state, and national constitutions were an integral part of modernist thinking everywhere in this age. The man who assumed chief responsibility for writing the Meiji Constitution was Itō Hirobumi (1841–1909) of Chōshū. In 1882, he went to Europe to study Western constitutionalism, particularly as propounded by German theorists; and, in 1885, he became Japan's first prime minister upon the institution of a cabinet system of government.

Meanwhile, the people's rights advocates were also active, and both Itagaki and Ōkuma formed new political associations—the Liberal Party (Jiyūtō) and the Progressive Party (Shimpotō)—in preparation for the opening of a parliament (or Diet) within the decade. It is difficult to assess precisely the differences between the two major party lines established at this time. The works of Rousseau, Mill, and other Western political theorists had been translated into Japanese and were widely read and admired by the party people. French natural rights democracy seems to have appealed particularly to the Itagaki group, while Ōkuma and his followers espoused British utilitarianism. Moreover, whereas the Liberal Party came in general to represent agrarian interests, the Progressive Party tended to align it-self with the emerging class of urban industrialists. Yet, far more than any political creeds, specific issues, or class alliances, it was personal allegiance to the leaders themselves that provided the basis for party unity during this preconstitutional phase of the people's rights move-ment.

In addition to the political parties, an important source of burgeon-ing opposition to the Meiji oligarchy was the press. A number of the embryonic newspapers of the early Restoration period had been staffed by former Shogunate officials hostile to the new Satsuma and Chōshū leaders in the government. With the continued growth of a modern press, this opposition was taken up by journalists who were largely former samurai excluded from government by *han* cliquism. Many members of the emergent political parties, in fact, first got their start in journalism. Moreover, many newspapers founded in the early Meiji period were intended by their founders to serve as mouthpieces for specific political and social views, almost invariably of an anti-govern-ment tone. Hence, journalism in modern Japan was in its early de-velopment distinctly a journalism of protest, and it was to a great extent for this reason that the Meiji oligarchs so readily and frequently attacked journalists through the issuance of restrictive press laws.

The temper of the 1880's in Japan was markedly different from that of the 1870's. For the first decade or so following the Restoration, the Japanese had pursued with great, and often indiscriminate, en-thusiasm the remaking of their country on Western lines. In the 1880's, they not only modified their earlier, naïve admiration for the West, they began also to reassess and to find new value in their native traditions. For the oligarchs, it became incumbent to enunciate a coherent ideology for the state they were in the process of constitu-tionally fashioning. The way in which they did this can be seen most clearly in their policy toward education.

In its act of 1872, the Meiji Government had proclaimed the goal of universal primary education, and, during most of the remainder of the decade, it had sought to provide training to Japanese school-children that stressed practical subjects and encouraged Western-style individualistic thinking. But, by the beginning of the 1880's, the official attitude had changed, and the government now took deliberate steps both to reinstate traditional moral training in the schools and to redefine the aim of education to serve the state rather than the individual. The culmination of this new policy toward education was the issuance in 1890 of the Imperial Rescript on Education, a brief document that began as follows.

Know ye, Our Subjects!

Our Imperial Ancestors have founded Our Empire on a basis broad and everlasting, and have deeply and firmly implanted virtue; Our subjects ever united in loyalty and filial piety have from generation to generation illustrated the beauty thereof. This is the glory of the fundamental character of Our Empire, and herein also lies the source of Our education.[53]

From these few lines it is obvious that, after its earlier flirtation with the ideals of Western liberalism and democracy, the Meiji Government in its critical education policy had determined to indoctrinate a social ideology derived mainly from the Shinto-Confucian concepts that had evolved as a new orthodoxy of thought in the late Tokugawa period. Morality was once again to be based on such hierarchical virtues as loyalty and filial piety, and the ultimate object of devotion for all Japanese citizens was to be the throne, described elsewhere in the Rescript on Education as "coeval with heaven and earth." The new Japanese state was, in short, to be conceived as a great and obedient Confucian family with a father-like emperor at its head.

Nor was the government alone in its shift to conservatism in the 1880's. Even blatant Westernizers like Fukuzawa Yukichi began to have second thoughts about Japan's previously uncritical acceptance of everything Western in its rush to become civilized and enlightened. To a great extent, such second thoughts were simply the result of a more sophisticated view of the West. In their initial, excited response to the utopian ideals of liberal democracy, intellectuals like Fukuzawa had failed to temper their pro-Westernism by acknowledging that the Western powers themselves were pursuing baldly self-interested policies of world imperialism. Western theorists sought to justify these policies on the grounds of the social-Darwinist doctrines of Herbert Spencer: before the world could achieve a pacific stage of fully industrialized and enlightened civilization, it must continue to engage in a militant selection process that promised survival to the fittest races and nations.

It is to the credit of the Meiji oligarchs, who were usually far more realistic than their critics, that they always kept in mind the aim of enriching Japan in order to strengthen it militarily. In 1873, they had avoided armed intervention in Korea because it was too dangerous, but even then they envisioned a time when Japan would be able to compete for empire with the West. On the other hand, non-governmental intellectuals and the public in general did not, for the most part, come to accept the need for more statist-oriented policies and the open pursuit of nationalistic goals until the 1880's.

Overridingly the most important nationalistic goal of the 1880's and early 1890's was revision of the unequal treaties, and the repeated failure of the government to achieve revision contributed not only to growing skepticism about the West but also to the spread of conservative, Japanist sentiments. In one spectacular breakdown of treaty talks in 1888, Ōkuma Shigenobu, who had been drawn temporarily back into the government as foreign minister, lost a leg when a fanatical member of a right-wing organization threw a bomb into his carriage.

Symbolic to many Japanese of their frustrations and humiliation over treaty revision was a Western-style building in downtown Tokyo called the Rokumeikan or Deer Cry Mansion. Constructed in 1883 for the purpose of entertaining foreign diplomats and dignitaries, the Rokumeikan was the scene of many festive and gala entertainments, the most notoriously memorable of which was a masquerade ball thrown by Prime Minister Itō in 1887. Affairs like the 1887 ball in the Rokumeikan were regarded as the most conspicuous examples of how ludicrously even high-ranking Japanese could behave in their desire to prove to Westerners that they were civilized and knew the social graces. A decade or so earlier, such conduct would probably have been hailed as enlightened and progressive: It was a sign of the changed temper of the times that Itō and his ministers were disparagingly dubbed "the dancing cabinet."

It should not be supposed that the opposition to over-Westernization and the turn to conservatism in the 1880's was either universal or unthinkingly reactionary. Some extremely radical nationalists (like Ōkuma's assailant) did appear on the scene, but many prominent people remained highly committed to Westernization; and even those who most articulately called for a reassessment of traditional values more often than not advocated that Japan discriminately select what was appropriate for it from both East and West. The debate that emerged in the late 1880's over Westernization versus traditionalism was, moreover, conducted principally by the members of a new generation whose most impressionable years of intellectual growth had been spent during the epochal, but highly unsettling, period of transition from Tokugawa to Meiji. To a far greater extent than their elders, like the Meiji oligarchs and Fukuzawa Yukichi, they felt the intense cultural uncertainty of being torn between a Japan that had always represented the past and a West that invariably stood for the future.

Among those of the new generation who most fully embraced Westernization was Tokutomi Sohō (1863–1957).[54] The son of a wealthy peasant family of the Kumamoto region of northern Kyushu, Tokutomi received Western training as a youth in his native Kumamoto and later studied at the Christian university, Dōshisha, in Kyoto. In the mid-1880's, Tokutomi moved to Tokyo, where he took up a career as a writer and journalist. He organized a group called the

Min'yūsha (Society of the People's Friends), and in 1887 began publication of a magazine entitled *Friend of the People* (*Kokumin no Tomo*) to express the group's views.

Tokutomi, whose magazine soon achieved an enormous circulation, forcefully advanced his own opinions in books and articles on the progress of modern Japan. He criticized the kind of Westernization advocated by Fukuzawa and other enlighteners of the early Meiji period because it was directed only toward acquisition of the material aspects of Western civilization and not its underlying spirit. At the same time, Tokutomi pointed out the futility of pursuing the pre-Meiji ideal of "Eastern morals and Western technology," which was precisely what the Meiji Government seemed to be doing then in its policy of reinstituting Confucian moral training in the public schools. Under the new policy, Japanese students were expected simultaneously to learn modern, practical things and feudal morality. According to Tokutomi, the only possible choice for Japan, if it was to succeed in modernization, was to reject the Japanese past entirely and to pursue wholeheartedly both the material and spiritual aspects of Western civilization.

Tokutomi, who was strongly influenced by the writings of Herbert Spencer, justified his extreme position on the grounds that progress was a universal phenomenon. Hence, Westernization was actually another term for universalization. The features of modern civilization observable in the Western countries were the same that would appear in all countries as they advanced toward modernity. Japan already had many of these modern features and should seek to acquire the remainder as speedily as possible.

The principal challenge to the views of Tokutomi and the Min'yūsha came from the Seikyōsha (Society for Political Education), founded in 1888 by another group of young writers and critics. Publishing the magazine *The Japanese* (*Nihonjin*) in competition with the Min'-yūsha's *Friend of the People*, the Seikyōsha people attacked Westernization and called for "preservation of the national essence" (*kokusui hozon*). Their general position was perhaps best presented in the book *Truth, Goodness, and Beauty of the Japanese* (*Shin-zen-bi Nihonjin*) by Miyake Setsurei (1860–1945). Miyake, a student of philosophy who remained a rival of Tokutomi throughout their long, concurrent careers, asserted that, although a Spencerian-type of struggle among nations was unavoidable during the course of historical progress, the process of modernization did not lead inevitably to a universal kind of state. On the contrary, nations competed best by utilizing those special qualities that distinguished them from others. Like many members of the Seikyōsha, Miyake was much interested in physical geography and placed great store in the effects of geography and climate on the molding of racial characteristics and national cultures. To his thinking, diversity among peoples and nations was fundamental to progress in the world, and any attempt to reject national customs and indiscriminately adopt the ways of others could only be harmful. It was, in any event, clear that the Western countries were clinging tenaciously to their own particularistic national cultures, even while commonly pursuing modernization.

The advocates of preserving the national essence made many effective points in their arguments against the Westernizers, and, in theory, they provided the Japanese with a much-needed feeling of cultural worth after some two decades of breathtaking change within the ever-present shadow of the more advanced and "superior" West. A concomitant to the Seikyōsha movement, for example, was a renewal of interest in Japan's classical literature even at a time, as we shall see, when Japanese writers were first beginning to produce a modern literature under the dominant influence of the West. Ancient works, including collections of *tanka* poetry, were reprinted one after another, and especially great excitement was aroused over the rediscovery of Genroku literature. The prose of Saikaku, the puppet plays of Chikamatsu, and the poems of Bashō were resuscitated, annotated, and made available to a wide reading public.

Unfortunately, the concept of preserving the national essence, while emotionally stimulating, did not lend itself to very precise definition, and the Seikyōsha writers were never able to present a convincing program of action. Moreover, even though they were generally reasonable-minded people themselves, their views tended to provide fuel for the xenophobes and extreme nationalists; and, in subsequent years, as Japan embarked upon overseas expansion, preservation of the national essence became synonymous with ultra-nationalism.

Intertwined with the debate in the mid-Meiji period over such questions as the modern (Western?) spirit and Japan's national essence was the major problem of Christianity. The leaders of the Meiji Restoration had had little if any personal interest in Christianity, although some, like Itagaki Taisuke, the pioneer in the people's rights movement, conjectured that it might be an essential element in modernization. On the other hand, many of the intellectuals of the new generation of the 1880's and 1890's, including Tokutomi Sohō, were powerfully, and in some cases decisively, affected by Christian teachings.

The centuries-old ban on Christianity was not immediately lifted at the time of the Restoration. Not until 1873, after the Iwakura Mission observed how highly the Westerners treasured their religion, was it quietly legalized in Japan. Meanwhile, Western missionaries—particularly American and British Protestants—had already entered the country and begun their activities, including the compilation of English-Japanese dictionaries and translation of the Bible into Japanese. One field in which the missionaries performed especially valuable service was education. While the government concentrated on developing a national system of primary education, foreign missionaries and prominent Japanese independently established private schools to provide much of the higher training essential to Japan's modernizing program. Among the well-known private colleges founded about this time were the Christian university, Dōshisha, in Kyoto, and Keiō University and Waseda University in Tokyo, founded respectively by Fukuzawa Yukichi and Ōkuma Shigenobu.

Many of the youths most strongly influenced by Christianity were samurai from domains that had been on the losing side in the Restoration.[55] Restricted in the opportunities open to them in the new government, these youths sought alternate routes to advancement through the acquisition of Western training. When brought into direct contact with foreign Christian teachers, they were particularly impressed with the moral caliber and fervid personal commitment of most of these men. To the young and impressionable Japanese, the foreign teachers appeared to possess qualities of character very similar to the ideal samurai and Confucian scholars of their own traditional backgrounds. Indeed, many Japanese who converted to Christianity in the 1870's and 1880's seem to have viewed it as a kind of modern extension of Confucianism.

For their part, the American missionary and lay Christian teachers who came to Japan in the 1870's also responded with high enthusiasm toward their Japanese students. The faith of these men, who were imbued with the religious spirit of late nineteenth-century New England, was rooted in the belief that God's work on earth was to be carried out by individuals acting in accordance with a high moral code and the dictates of their Christian consciences. They were not particularly concerned with questions of dogma and abstract theology but wished to build strong characters; and they were quick to appreciate the features of good character, derived from the samurai code of conduct, that they detected in many of their students.

Tokutomi Sohō was one of a famous group of thirty-five Japanese youths, known as the Kumamoto band, who in 1875 climbed a hill in their native domain of Kumamoto in Kyushu and pledged themselves to Christianity and to propagation of the faith in order to dispel ignorance and to enlighten the people. These youths were students at a school for Western studies in Kumamoto conducted by Leroy L. Janes, a West Point graduate and former artillery officer in the American Civil War, and several of them went on to become distinguished spokesmen for Christianity in Japan. Although Tokutomi himself later renounced his formal ties with the church, he retained the Protestant Christian belief in "inner freedom" and in the individual's duty to use his independent conscience as a guide to social and political behavior. It was on the basis of this belief that he attacked the kind of Confucian morality the Meiji Government sought to inculcate in the primary schools from the 1880's on that called upon all Japanese to give blind and unquestioning loyalty to the state.

The influence of Protestant Christianity on Japanese who came to criticize the strongly statist policies of the government in the mid-Meiji period can be seen not only in independent intellectuals like Tokutomi, but also in many individuals who entered the socialist movement after its beginning in the 1890's. In fact, a number of the most prominent Christians in modern Japan have also been leading socialists. Still other Christians, however, were driven by the unfavorable climate for their views after the commencement of parliamentary government in 1890 to withdraw entirely from the arena of political and social criticism and to devote themselves to the private cultivation of their religion. The best-known example of these Christians was Uchimura Kanzō (1861–1930).

Uchimura, the son of a samurai, attended a Christian-influenced agricultural school in the northern island of Hokkaido and became a student of Dr. William S. Clark, an American lay teacher who, like Janes at Kumamoto, was successful in attracting young Japanese to the faith. Later, Uchimura went to the United States to study at Amherst, and it was there that he was converted to Christianity. In 1891, Uchimura created a sensation back in Japan when, as a teacher at the prestigious First High School in Tokyo, he refused to bow before a copy of the Imperial Rescript on Education. He was branded a traitor by some people, forced to resign his position for the offense of *lèse-majesté*, and became the target of polemical attacks that charged him with possessing allegiances incompatible with the responsibilities to emperor and nation required of subjects in the educational Rescript.[56] Uchimura thus became a victim of the shift in attitude on the part of the Japanese public and many intellectuals from the open and naïve internationalism of the 1870's to an illiberal, virulent nationalism. Although he worked for another decade or so in journalism, Uchimura eventually retired from public view to a life of private teaching and writing on religion.

Contrary to the assertions of his detractors, Uchimura did not embrace Christianity to the exclusion of national loyalty. He steadfastly proclaimed his devotion to the "two J's"—Jesus and Japan—and insisted that, just as Anglicans were essentially English Christians, Presbyterians were Scottish Christians, and Lutherans were German Christians, he was a Japanese Christian. Uchimura even founded a "non-church" (*mukyōkai*) movement in the attempt to deracinate Christianity from its alien institutions and traditions by eliminating its clerical organization and other ecclesiastical trappings, and to render it as much Japanese as Western. For his epitaph he wrote in English:

> I for Japan;
> Japan for the World;
> The World for Christ;
> And All for God.

Even when it enjoyed its greatest popularity in the Meiji period, Christianity could never claim as its own more than a very small percentage of the population of Japan (less than one-half of 1 per cent); and after the turn to conservatism in the late 1880's and 1890's, it lost any opportunity it may have had to become a major force in Japanese life. Moreover, even if it had not come to be seen as a threat to the statist views rendered newly orthodox in the Meiji Constitution of 1889 and the Imperial Rescript on Education, Christianity would have (and indeed has) suffered from sectarianism in Japan, a sectarianism that had been kept to a minimum by American Protestant missionaries in the palmy days of successful proselytizing during the first two decades of Meiji. Apart from its work in such fields as education and medicine and the profound influence it exerted on certain individuals, like the ones we have been examining here, Christianity has been of negligible importance in modern Japan.

The Meiji Constitution was written in secret by Itō Hirobumi and his colleagues and was presented to the Japanese people in 1889 as a gift from the emperor. It was based on a carefully considered mixture of conservative and liberal principles (with the former heavily outweighing the latter) that owed much to the constitutional theories of Germany, the Western country which the Meiji oligarchs had come increasingly to regard as most analogous to Japan in historical background and stage of modernization. The conservative character of the Constitution may, for purposes of illustration, be noted in several major areas. First, an appointive House of Peers was given equal lawmaking powers with an elective House of Representatives. Second, the personal liberties granted to the Japanese people were all made "subject to the limitations imposed by law"; in other words, such liberties were not to be inalienable but might be (and often were) restricted by government decree.

But the most strongly conservative feature of the Meiji Constitution was the great power it allowed the executive branch of government. This power derived in large part from omission: that is, from the deliberate failure to specify how the executive was to be formed and what were to constitute the precise limits of its authority. There was no provision at all, for example, about appointment of the prime minister, and no proviso about accountability of the other ministers of state in the cabinet to anyone except the emperor. Clearly, the oligarchs intended to retain firm control of the executive, and, after the opening of the first Diet in 1890, the party members in the House of Representatives found very little prospect that they would in the near future be able to participate significantly in the ruling of Japan. The oligarchs formed an extra-legal body known as the *genrō* or "elders," consisting at first entirely of the highest Satsuma and Chōshū leaders in government, and it was they who selected the prime ministers (from among themselves) and continued to dominate the affairs of state.

The socio-political orthodoxy that the oligarchs codified in the Meiji Constitution and the Imperial Rescript on Education is commonly called *kokutai*, a term that literally means the body of the country but is usually translated as "national polity." Based on the Shinto-Confucian concept (which we observed in the Rescript on Education) of Japan as a great family-state, *kokutai* held a special appeal for the Japanese people because of its glorification of the mystique of emperorship. The Japanese regarded their line of sovereigns—described in the Constitution as "unbroken for ages eternal" and in the Rescript on Education as "coeval with heaven and earth"—as a unique and sacrosanct institution that gave Japan a claim to superiority over all other countries in the world. For centuries, of course, the emperors of Japan had wielded no political power whatever, and during the Tokugawa period they were held virtual prisoners in Kyoto by the Shogunate. Nevertheless, the throne had served as an incomparably effective rallying point for nationalistic sentiment during the difficult and dangerous transition to the modern era. Although perhaps relatively ignored during the liberal euphoria of the 1870's, it inevitably drew the renewed attention of government leaders and conservative intellectuals in the 1880's. For nothing was more venerably Japanese than the imperial institution, and anyone wishing to revive traditional values, whether moral or cultural, was almost perforce obliged to start with recognition of the throne as the font of Japanese civilization. No simple explanation, however, can be given of the throne's role in modern Japan. For the most part the emperor has been held "above politics" and, with few exceptions his participation in governmental affairs has not been made public. But there can be no question that, as the living embodiment of *kokutai*, he was a potent symbol for radically nationalistic emotions in the period up through World War II.

A corollary to emperor glorification in the *kokutai* ideology was that, of all the peacetime occupations, government service was the most cherished because it meant, in effect, employment by the emperor. Although the Satsuma-Chōshū oligarchs continued to control the highest councils of state, a vast expansion of the bureaucracy during the final years of the nineteenth century created ample opportunities for good careers in government, careers that were avidly sought by youths of all classes. Tokyo Imperial University, moreover, was made a kind of orthodox channel for governmental preferment, further proof of the degree to which Japanese society and the aspirations of its members were subjected to state manipulation in the middle and late Meiji period.

Japanese prose literature by the time of the Meiji Restoration had sunk to an extremely low level. Tedious didacticism, bawdy comedy, and bloody adventure were the stock-in-trade of the authors of these years, and there was little prospect, in the absence of stimulation from outside, that the quality of their work would soon improve. But this remains conjecture, for the fact is that, within a few decades of the Restoration, Western influences had wrought a change in prose literature as profound as in any other area of Japanese culture during the modern era.

The most successful writer in the years immediately before and after the Restoration was Kanagaki Robun (1829–94), an *eddoko* or "child of Edo" who specialized in the traditional genre of "witty books" (*kokkeibon*). One of Robun's post-Restoration works was *A Journey by Foot Through Western Lands* (*Seiyō Dōchū Hizakurige*), in which he attempted to give a modern twist to Jippensha Ikku's famous story of two rogues frolicking their way down the Tōkaidō from Edo to Kyoto; another was *Eating Beef Stew Cross-Legged*, the parody on the aping of Western customs that we noted earlier in this chapter. A prime example of Robun's irreverent humor can be observed in the title of still another of his books, *Kyūri Zukai*. This title was phonetically the same as Fukuzawa Yukichi's *Physics Illustrated*; but, in the Sinico-Japanese characters used by Robun, it meant *On the Use of Cucumbers*. Such punning was of course frivolous, an adjective that may be applied to much of the work done by Robun and his fellow Edo authors. Although these men continued to hold the center of the literary stage for a while, they produced almost nothing that was memorable. The future of Meiji literature lay clearly in the assimilation of powerful artistic ideas and styles then being imported from the West.

In the first decade or so of Meiji, those Japanese writers and scholars interested in foreign literature devoted themselves mainly to the translation of famous Western works. An adaptation of *Robinson Crusoe* had, in fact, been completed even before the Restoration, and a Japanese rendering of *Aesop's Fables* existed as one of the few products of the old Jesuit Press that had survived the attempt by the Tokugawa Shogunate to eradicate all traces of contact with the Catholic Christian countries during the century from the 1540's to the 1630's. Among the earliest Western translations to appear in print in the Meiji period was Samuel Smiles's *Self-Help*, a book of success stories whose very title suggests the kind of subject matter that Japan's passionate new devotees of civilization and enlightenment were most likely to appreciate.

One of the first modern Western novels to be translated into Japanese was Bulwer-Lytton's *Ernest Maltravers*, the tale of a modern man's ingenuity and self-motivated drive to succeed (although the translator of this work saw fit to give it the erotically provocative Japanese title of *Karyū Shunwa* or *A Spring Tale of Flowers and Willows* in the hope of boosting its sales). For most of the first two decades of Meiji, Japanese translators of Western fiction concentrated overwhelmingly on the writings of British authors, a clear reflection of the enormous prestige in Japanese eyes of British civilization compared to that of any other country of the West. In addition to Bulwer-Lytton, prominent British authors translated into Japanese during the early Meiji period included Scott and Disraeli.

The Japanese were especially taken with tales of modern and "scientific" adventures, as can be seen in the popularity of Jules Verne's *Around the World in Eighty Days* and *A Trip to the Moon*. And from about the early 1880's on, largely in response to the movement for parliamentary government, they became infatuated with political novels. The translated writings of Disraeli and Bulwer-Lytton helped make respectable the practice of prose writing, which members of the ruling samurai class of the Tokugawa period had for the most part eschewed as vulgar; and during the 1880's many prominent members of the embryonic parties tried their hands at politically oriented novels. A good many of these novels dealt with the present, but others were set in such disparate times and places as ancient Greece, Ming China, France during the Revolution, and even a hypothetical Japan in the 173rd year of Meiji (A.D. 2040, 150 years after the opening of the first Diet in 1890).

Some idea of the growing consciousness in the 1880's of Japanese achievements and the anticipation that Japan would assume a more assertive international role can be seen in a passage from one of these political novels entitled *Strange Encounters of Elegant Females* (*Kajin no Kigū*), written in 1885 by Shiba Shirō under the nom de plume of the Wanderer of the Eastern Seas. Far from being an account of romance and passion, as the title would seem to suggest, *Strange Encounters* is the story of the Wanderer's investigation into revolutionary activities throughout the world. At the outset, he meets two strikingly beautiful European ladies, one Spanish and one Irish (although both graced by the author with Chinese names), at the Liberty Bell in Philadelphia. The three enter into serious discussion about matters of political repression and revolution and, even after the Wanderer departs for other foreign lands, the ladies periodically reappear to meet him on his travels. Although they are obviously in love with him, the Wanderer can think only of the need for promoting freedom and justice in the world. At one point, the Spanish lady encourages him by saying:

Now that your country has reformed its government and, by taking from America what is useful and rejecting what is only superficial, is increasing month by month in wealth and strength, the eyes and ears of the world are astonished by your success. As the sun climbs in the eastern skies, so is your country rising in the Orient. Your August Sovereign has granted political liberty to the people, the people have sworn to follow the Imperial leadership. So the time has come when, domestic strife having ceased, all classes will be happy in their occupations. Korea will send envoys and the Luchu Islands will submit to your governance. Then will the occasion arise for doing great things in the Far East. Your country will take the lead and preside over a confederation of Asia. The peoples of the East will no longer be in danger. In the West you will restrain the rampancy of England and France. In the South you will check the corruption of China. In the North you will thwart the designs of Russia. You will resist the policy of European states, which is to treat Far Eastern peoples with contempt and to interfere in their domestic affairs, so leading them into servitude. Thus it is your country and no other that can bring the taste of self-government and independence into the life of millions for the first time, and so spread the light of civilization.[57]

A major problem for both translators of Western books and writers of Western-inspired political novels was that of style. Tokugawa authors had employed several methods of writing, from the poetic use of alternating metrical lines of five and seven syllables to a style derived from Sinico-Japanese. The gap between these classical styles and the colloquial language of everyday speech was enormous, and the difficulty of devising a means to reproduce in Japanese the vernacular novels of the modern West taxed the ingenuity of the most dedicated of Meiji translators. As a result, most of the renditions of Western novels in the early Meiji period were not true translations at all, but rather were free adaptations of the original works. During the 1880's, a movement was begun to "unify the spoken and written languages" (*gembun-itchi*), and, toward the end of the decade, Futabatei Shimei

(1864–1909), author of Japan's first truly modern novel, was also the first successfully to bridge the gap between speech and writing. With continuing progress in education, growth of the mass media, and acceptance of the Tokyo dialect as the standard form of speech, the modern Japanese vernacular or *kōgo* was finally evolved, although it was not used widely by novelists until after the Sino-Japanese War of 1894–95, by the authors of primary school textbooks until 1903, or by newspaper reporters in general until a decade after that.

The man who more than any other made possible the writing of a modern prose literature in Japan was Tsubouchi Shōyō (1859–1935).[58] A graduate of Tokyo Imperial University and translator of the collected works of Shakespeare, Tsubouchi published an epochal tract in 1885 entitled *The Essence of the Novel (Shōsetsu Shinzui)*. In it he attacked what he regarded as the deplorable state of literature in Japan during his day:

> It has long been the custom in Japan to consider the novel as an instrument of education, and it has frequently been proclaimed that the novel's chief function is the castigation of vice and the encouragement of virtue. In actual practice, however, only stories of bloodthirsty cruelty or else of pornography are welcomed, and very few readers indeed even cast so much as a glance on works of a more serious nature. Moreover, since popular writers have no choice but to be devoid of self-respect and in all things slaves to public fancy and the lackeys of fashion, each one attempts to go to greater lengths than the last in pandering to the tastes of the time. They weave their brutal historical tales, string together their obscene romances, and yield to every passing vogue. Nevertheless they find it so difficult to abandon the pretext of "encouraging virtue" that they stop at nothing to squeeze in a moral, thereby distorting the emotion portrayed, falsifying the situations, and making the whole plot nonsensical.[59]

Tsubouchi insisted that the novel must be regarded as art to be appreciated solely for its own sake. He urged that Western, and particularly English, literature be taken as the model for a new kind of novelistic prose writing in Japan free of didacticism and devoted to the realistic portrayal of human emotions (*ninjō*) and the actual conditions of life. Even the supposedly enlightened authors of contemporary political novels dealt only with stereotypical characters who were motivated by the desire to "reward virtue and punish vice." Writers of the new fiction must seek to penetrate the wellsprings of individual behavior and reveal it, with candor, in all its manifestations.

Unfortunately, Tsubouchi, although a first-rate critic, was himself unable to produce the kind of modern novel that he so vigorously advocated. His book *The Character of Present-day Students (Tōsei Shosei Katagi)*, written in conjunction with *The Essence of the Novel*, deals with the lives and loves of students at Tokyo Imperial University in the early 1880's; but, despite Tsubouchi's efforts to delineate the psychological complexities of the students he was portraying, the work is very similar to the superficial character sketches and witty books of Tokugawa authors.

The kind of modern novel Tsubouchi had in mind was in fact written by his friend and disciple, Futabatei Shimei. Futabatei, born in Edo the son of a samurai a few years before the Meiji Restoration, studied Russian from 1881 until 1886 at a school for foreign languages sponsored by the Meiji Government. His extraordinary talent for languages enabled him to excel at the school and gave rise to his decision to become a full-time translator and writer. Futabatei's translations from the Russian of such authors as Turgenev, begun in the mid-1880's, were of prime importance in the literary history of the Meiji period; for they were the first renderings of Western literature into Japanese that can truly be called translations. In the free adaptations of other early and mid-Meiji translators, large sections were often either omitted or added and sometimes only the most essential plot of a book was retained. Beginning with Futabatei, Japanese translation of the literature of the West became a genuinely professional pursuit.

Immediately after finishing his studies at the foreign language school in 1886, the still-unknown Futabatei boldly called upon Tsubouchi to discuss the literary matters raised by the latter in *The Essence of the Novel*. Thus began a warm and lasting friendship between the two men that provided, among other things, the conditions necessary for Futabatei to embark upon the writing of the first modern Japanese novel, *The Drifting Cloud* (*Ukigumo*), published in installments between 1887 and 1889.

The Drifting Cloud is a realistic novel, written in a colloquial style, that has a unified and sustained plot and probes the feelings and psychological motivations of its principal characters. It is the story of Bunzō, a government clerk who lives in the home of his aunt and who loves and hopes to marry his cousin, Osei. As the story opens, Bunzō has lost his job, much to the disgust of the aunt, who has never been particularly fond of him and is now convinced that he is a failure. Bunzō's apparent inability to get ahead in a generation of Japanese striving madly to achieve the fame and fortune promised by modernity stands in sharp contrast to the prospects of Noboru, a colleague who has received a promotion just as Bunzō is fired. Clearly, Noboru is the new Meiji man, while Bunzō is a pathetic example of those who inevitably fall the victims of progress. When Noboru visits the aunt's home, he predictably causes new difficulties, for the aunt sees in him the ideal match for her daughter, and Osei herself, a flighty and superficial person, responds by rejecting Bunzō and entering into a flirtation with Noboru. Unfortunately, Futabatei's handling of the latter stages in the plot of *The Drifting Cloud* is clumsy and unconvincing. The Osei-Noboru flirtation peters out and, in the end, Bunzō, who has been immobilized by events, is encouraged by a mere smile from Osei to anticipate a reconciliation with her. For all its faults, however, *The Drifting Cloud* remains an epochal work that inaugurated realistic fictional writing in modern Japan.

While Tsubouchi Shōyō and Futabatei Shimei were thus taking the pioneer steps in creating a new fiction on Western lines, other writers, motivated in part by the strongly conservative, nativistic trend of the 1880's, sought to revitalize Japanese literature by means of its own tradition. The most influential of these writers emerged from a group called the Ken'yūsha (Society of Friends of the Inkstone), founded in 1885 by Ozaki Kōyō (1867–1903) and others, who were at the time still students at Tokyo Imperial University. Issuing a magazine with the facetious title of *The Literary Rubbish Bin (Garakuta Bunko)*, the members of the Ken'yūsha called for a literary renaissance through rejection of the styles of writing and themes, including the didactic and the "witty," that had held sway in Japan from the Bunka-Bunsei epoch earlier in the century, and restoration of the great prose standards of Genroku, particularly as found in the works of Saikaku.

Like the contemporary scholars of the "national essence" movement, the Ken'yūsha writers were not simply blind reactionaries. Ozaki, for example, thoroughly agreed with Tsubouchi's dictum (presented in *The Essence of the Novel*) that literature should be regarded as an independent art, not requiring justification on moralistic or other grounds. Ozaki believed, moreover, that the realism Tsubouchi sought in modern Western fiction was more readily and appropriately accessible to Japanese in the realistic writing of Saikaku. Ozaki's own novels, written in the style of Saikaku, were enormously popular and helped stimulate the rediscovery of Genroku literature that we have already noted. Yet Ozaki and the other Ken'yūsha writers, despite their appeal to readers in the 1880's and 1890's, contributed virtually nothing to the development of the modern novel in Japan. They were almost unchallengeably powerful in the literary world of the late 1880's and early 1890's, even to the point of controlling many of the most important outlets for fictional publication; but, upon the untimely death of Ozaki in 1903, their brand of "renaissance literature" quickly gave way to other kinds of modern fictional writing whose growth had been prefigured by the earlier work of Tsubouchi and Futabatei.

Japanese poetry, while subject to much the same pull between traditional and modern (i.e., Western) influences that afflicted prose literature and nearly all other aspects of culture in the Meiji period, had its own special problems. First, poetry had always been the most "serious" of Japanese literary pursuits and hence brought an infinitely more weighty tradition to the modern era than the slightly regarded practice of prose writing. Second, although constricting rules of diction and vocabulary could be broken, the special qualities of the Japanese language that so fundamentally determined what could and could not be done poetically (for example, rhyme could not be used as a prosodic device) prevented Japanese poets from emulating much of Western poetry. And finally, in Japan as in the West, poetry could not hope to compete in popularity with the novel as the dominant literary form of modernization.

To many early Meiji poets, the classical *tanka* was so buried in the past that there was little sense in even trying to exhume it. And, at any rate, both the *tanka* and the *haiku* were forms so limited in scope as to be useless for the expression of modern ideas and sentiments. Poets should instead turn their attention to the translation of Western poetry and to the development of new kinds of verse based on Western models. The first major step in this direction was the publication in 1882 of the *Collection of Poems in the New Style (Shintaishō)*, compiled by three professors of Tokyo Imperial University and consisting of nineteen translations from English and five original pieces by the compilers themselves. Like the political novels of the same time, much of the poetry written in the new style during the next few years dealt with the subjects of governmental and social reform.

Meanwhile, as a result of the conservative winds that had begun blowing forcefully by the middle and late 1880's, devotees of the older poetic modes, and especially the *tanka*, were given something of a new lease on life. The hidebound members of the traditional *tanka* schools, who had continued composing as though the Meiji Restoration had not happened, are of no particular interest to us; but other *tanka* poets actively sought to reform and reinvigorate their art. Perhaps the most noteworthy of these reformist poets (who first came into prominence during the 1890's) was Masaoka Shiki (1867–1902), a practitioner of *haiku* who did not seriously take up the *tanka* until about this time. Shiki was employed as a reporter on the staff of *Japan (Nihon)*, a magazine devoted, like Miyake Setsurei's *The Japanese,* to "preservation of the national essence"; and it was in large part because his editors began publishing *tanka* composed by members of the traditional schools as examples of a native art worth preserving that Shiki decided to speak out on *tanka* reform.

In addition to calling for freedom of poetic diction and the use of modern language, Shiki championed the concept of *shasei* or "realistic depiction." Furthermore, he deplored the fact that the *tanka*, from the time of the standard-setting tenth-century anthology *Kokinshū*, had been infused with an artificiality of wit and a fragility of emotion unsuited to the true spirit of the Japanese. Strongly endorsing the views of the Tokugawa period scholar of National Learning, Kamo Mabuchi, Shiki lauded the merits of the *Man'yōshū*. He saw in the poems of this earliest of anthologies such qualities as masculine vigor, directness of expression, and "sincerity" (*makoto*) that were in particular likely to be appreciated by his fellow countrymen in the expansive, imperialistic mood following Japan's startling military victory over China in 1894–95.

Much like the novelist Ozaki Kōyō, Shiki tried to find realism—apparently the most valued of "modern" aesthetic qualities—in the Japanese literary tradition. In fact, Shiki's advocacy of "realistic depiction" was, as Robert Brower has observed, "a quasi-scientific principle directly influenced by conceptions of illusionist realism in Western-style painting." [60] It appears that, with Shiki, we have still another example of the strong impulse on the part of so many modern Japanese scholars and artists (indeed, probably all of them during at least one phase or another of their careers) either consciously or unconsciously to relate to their own national past those features of modern culture that emerged in the West and that they admire and wish to utilize. But history is cruel to this impulse, for the unalterable fact is that the West evolved such things as modern realistic literature first and the Japanese will never know whether they could have done it independently.

In contrast to their relatively recent exposure to Western literature (that is, belles-lettres), the Japanese had had a rather long historical acquaintanceship with the visual arts, particularly painting, of the West. Unencumbered by a language barrier, the visual arts are obviously more amenable to cross-cultural transmission, although in the case of Japan this in fact meant simply that the inevitable clash between Japanese tradition and Western modernity could be precipitated even more readily and with greater abandon than it could in literature. At the same time, as Sansom has suggested, it is also possible that in the visual arts Japan's aesthetic heritage was better prepared than it was in literature to stand up against Western intrusion. [61]

The Jesuits had first introduced Western visual arts to Japan in the sixteenth century and had even trained Japanese artists in contemporary painting techniques. But the anti-Christian measures of the Tokugawa Shogunate had, of course, eliminated this and almost all other Western influences from the country during the mid-seventeenth century. Not until the rise of Dutch Studies about a hundred years later did knowledge of Western art again make its way into Japan. Subsequently, nearly all of the major, vital schools of painting in the late eighteenth and early nineteenth centuries were influenced to a greater or lesser degree by Western techniques. Some painters, like

Shiba Kōkan, went over entirely to the foreign medium and learned to paint in precise technical imitation of the Western manner. Curiously, however, the work of Shiba and other pioneer Western-style painters seems to have fallen into obscurity, and some artists in the last years of the Tokugawa Shogunate, after Japan had been opened by Perry, laboriously set about to learn Western painting on their own from the few foreign-language manuals they could acquire without being aware of what Shiba and his fellow proponents of Dutch Studies had already accomplished.

The most prominent person in the late Tokugawa and early Meiji efforts to develop and popularize Western art in Japan was Kawakami Tōgai (1827–81).[62] A moderately skilled artist in the *bunjin* or literati style of painting, Kawakami took up the study of the Dutch language sometime about the 1850's and soon turned his attention also to European painting. In 1857, he joined the Shogunate's Office for Barbarian Studies, the organization that also employed a number of the later members of the Meiji Six Society, and within a few years was appointed to head its newly established section on the study of painting. After the Restoration, Kawakami, who was primarily interested in the practical, scientific side of Western painting, was engaged by the Ministry of Education to develop teaching methods and to prepare training manuals on art for use in public schools. Among the innovations he sponsored was instruction in realistic drawing with pencils, rather than painting with the traditional Japanese ink-brush.

In 1876, the Meiji Government, continuing its policy of encouragement of Western-style art, opened the Industrial Art School (Kōbu Bijutsu Gakkō) and invited several Italian artists to provide training in painting, sculpture, and general methods of art. The most important of these was Antonio Fontanesi (1818–82), who during his stay of approximately two years in Japan made a profound impression on the students he taught, several of whom became outstanding Western-style painters in later years. So popular was Fontanesi that when he left for home in 1878, at least partly owing to a difference of opinion with his employers in the Japanese Government, a number of students withdrew from the school and founded a society for the furtherance of Western art, thereby inaugurating the first independent art movement of the modern era in Japan.

Fontanesi's departure was undoubtedly related to the beginning of a trend in the late 1870's and the 1880's away from Western art to a revival of interest in the traditional art of Japan. Coincidentally, in the very same year that Fontanesi left, 1878, another foreigner, the young American Ernest Fenollosa (1853–1908), arrived in Japan to begin a remarkable career as one of the two leading figures in the great resurgence of native art appreciation.

Fenollosa, a recent graduate of Harvard, was originally engaged to teach philosophy at Tokyo Imperial University, but before long he became an outspoken (and highly opinionated) admirer of Far Eastern, and particularly Japanese, art. Eventually, Fenollosa evolved a grand philosophical concept along the lines of "Eastern morals and Western technology," according to which he prophesied a Hegelian-type dialectical synthesis between the spiritual East and the material West that would advance the world to a new cultural plane. On a more immediate and practical level, Fenollosa, along with one of his students, Okakura Tenshin (1862–1913), began to take stock of Japanese art and to advocate ways in which it could be repopularized and perpetuated.

Traditional Japanese art and artists had unquestionably fallen on bad times during the early Restoration period. The two leading practitioners of the ancient Kanō school of painting, for example, were reduced to menial occupations in order to earn their livings. It was also because of the almost total lack of interest in native work in these years that Fenollosa and others were able to buy up at very low prices the vast number of art pieces that still constitute the core of many major Japanese collections in foreign museums today.

Fenollosa gave lectures to private groups in Japan extolling the glories of Japanese art and even pronouncing it to be superior to the art of the West. He and Okakura also founded a Society for the Appreciation of Painting (Kangakai) and urged the Meiji Government to sponsor training in the native artistic styles. Two results of their lobbying were the discontinuance of the Western-oriented Industrial Art School in 1883 and the substitution of brush painting for pencil drawing in public school art courses. But the greatest achievement of Fenollosa and Okakura was their role in the creation in 1889 of the government-backed Tokyo Art School (Tōkyō Bijutsu Gakkō), devoted exclusively to training in Far Eastern art. In 1886–87, Fenollosa and Okakura had traveled to Europe to study methods of art education and museum administration, and within a few years after their return, Okakura became head of the Tokyo Art School.

Of these two dynamic men who led the return to Japanese art in the 1880's, Fenollosa was by far the more inflexible. A transparent Japanophile so far as art was concerned, he also sought to impose on others his personal biases within the realm of Japanese art. For example, while he admired the Kanō school of painting, he viewed with distaste the literati movement of the middle and late Tokugawa period. Largely because of this preference on the part of a foreigner, it appears, no study of the *bunjin* painters was included in the curriculum of the Tokyo Art School.

Okakura, on the other hand, was very similar in sentiment to a number of his contemporaries who have been noted in this chapter, including the "national essence" intellectuals, the novelist Ozaki Kōyō, and the *haiku-tanka* poet Masaoka Shiki. All of these men were participants in the Japanist reaction of the 1880's and 1890's; and, although not all of them may have succeeded very well in their aims, they mutually aspired to revitalize Japanese culture and art by incorporating modern Western (or "international") elements into the native tradition and not by trying simply to reverse the course of progress. The tragedy for most of them was that this was no easy thing to do. A little Western "materialism" could rapidly dissipate a lot of Eastern "spiritualism."

In the case of the visual arts, the return to tradition led by Fenollosa and Okakura had been too radically launched, and within a few years the pendulum began to swing back to a position where both Western-style and Japanese art could co-exist in Japan in an atmosphere of relative tranquility and equal competition. The fiery Fenollosa returned to the United States in 1890, and paintings in the Western manner were prominently displayed along with Japanese works in an industrial fair held the same year. More important, it was about this time that a number of highly promising artists returned from periods of study in France, Italy, and other Western countries. Among these, the one who was to have the greatest influence in art circles and who may rightly be regarded as the true founder of modern Western-style art in Japan was Kuroda Seiki (1866–1924). An Impressionist who had studied for ten years in Paris, Kuroda caused a minor furor by publicly exhibiting a painting of a nude for the first time in Japan. His influence and popularity spread rapidly, and in 1896 he was invited to join the faculty of Okakura's Tokyo Art School, a clear recognition— however reluctantly given—that Western-style art was in Japan to stay.

Since very little specific attention has thus far been given to the development of traditional Japanese music, some general remarks should be made before examining the impact upon it of Western music following the Meiji Restoration.

To a great extent Japanese music evolved through the centuries in conjunction with—or, perhaps more precisely, as an auxiliary to— literature. This was particularly true from the medieval age on, when music was used as an accompaniment both to plays of the *nō* theatre and to the recitations of itinerant storytellers, who strummed their lute-like *biwa* as they chanted excerpts from such works as *The Tale of the Heike*. Music, of course, also became an essential ingredient of the two major dramatic forms of the Tokugawa period, *kabuki* and *bunraku*. Like the earlier *nō*, *kabuki* and *bunraku* were presentational rather than representational theatres and hence readily incorporated not only music but also miming, stunt-performing, and, in the case of *kabuki,* dancing. Although some purely instrumental, non-vocalized music was naturally performed (perhaps most notably on the *samisen* and the zither-like *koto,* an instrument of refined taste dating from very early times), much of the music of premodern Japan was quite clearly subordinated to lyrical singing, acting, and dancing, and to the recitation of libretti that possessed independent literary merit.

Probably the first public performance of Western music in Japan in modern times was the playing by Perry's naval band during its visit to Edo in 1853.[63] And as in the case of the conversion to Western-style clothing, it was the Japanese military that led the way in the adoption of Western music. Military units of the early Meiji period initially formed bands simply as part of their general reorganization along Western lines. But before long, these army and navy bands began giving frequent public concerts, and they became familiar fixtures at the ballroom dances and other Western-style social affairs held at the Rokumeikan in the 1880's.

In addition to military music, Christian church music was also prominently introduced to Japan in the early Meiji period. By far the most important form here was the Protestant hymn; and, as one authority has pointed out, many Japanese songs of the Meiji period tended to have a strongly "Christian" sound, just like the early nationalistic songs of missionary-influenced countries in twentieth-century Africa.[64]

It was in the public schools, however, that the most important measures were taken to advance knowledge and appreciation of Western music among the Japanese, and the pioneer figure in implementing these measures was Izawa Shūji (1851–1917). After a period of study in the United States, Izawa was engaged by the Ministry of Education in 1879 to prepare songbooks and to plan for the teaching of music in the public school system. Izawa's principal aim was to find some way of blending traditional and Western music in order to produce a new kind of national music for modern Japan. To accomplish this, he worked chiefly with an American, Luther Mason of Boston, and with members of the *gagaku* school of ancient court musicians. The choice of *gagaku* musicians as the Japanese specialists in the composition of "blended" music is particularly interesting, since it meant that Izawa and his associates chose to bypass the more recent and vital forms of "vulgar" music that had evolved in the Tokugawa period and to draw instead upon the rigidly conventionalized, albeit "elegant," musical tradition of at least a millennium earlier in Japanese history.

One notable product of the mixing of music in early Meiji (although not by Izawa) was the Japanese anthem, "Kimi ga Yo" ("His Majesty's

Reign"), composed in response to the desire to have a national song like the Western countries. The words for "Kimi ga Yo," taken apparently from the tenth-century poetic anthology *Kokinshū*, were first put to Western music by an English bandsman in the 1870's but were later adapted to a melody by a *gagaku* musician that was in turn harmonized and arranged for orchestra by a German, Franz Eckert.

However we may judge the efforts of Izawa to synthesize traditional and Western music, the most important result of musical training in public schools from his time on was to accustom successive generations of Japanese students to Western harmonies and modes, and thus to make possible Japanization of the classical repertoire of Western symphonic and chamber music. Today, Bach, Mozart, and Beethoven belong as much to the Japanese as they do to anyone else in the world.

Since the main orchestrated styles of native Japanese music were so closely associated with the theatre, the fate of the traditional theatrical forms after the Meiji Restoration has quite naturally determined their course as well. The *nō* theatre, a remnant of the medieval age, was antiquated even during the Tokugawa period and, despite the authorship of new plays by certain contemporary writers, remains a drama engulfed in history and aesthetic tradition to be admired primarily by connoisseurs and by students of the classical arts. Similar patronage continues to support the bourgeois puppet theatre. After a period of great flourishing in mid-Tokugawa times, *bunraku* declined steadily in popularity and, with the coming of the modern era and new demands for realistic portrayal, has had little hope of regaining any mass following.

Of chief theatrical interest in the early Meiji period was the development of *kabuki*. Much of the success of *kabuki* after the Restoration was owing to the efforts of the impresario Morita Kanya (1846–97) and the playwright Kawatake Mokuami (1816–93). After the overthrow of the Tokugawa regime brought to an end the many restrictions that the Shogunate had imposed on *kabuki* over the years, Morita moved his theatre from the outlying Asakusa (formerly the Yoshiwara) region to the central Tsukiji area of Tokyo. Built first in 1872 and reconstructed in 1878 after destruction by fire,[65] Morita's theatre gave rise to a new era in which *kabuki* enjoyed social respectability and was amenable to up-to-date, modernizing ideas.

One step taken to advance *kabuki* was the production of *sangiri* ("cropped hair") plays, especially by Mokuami, that dealt with current fashions and fads (although, apart from greater topical relevance, the *sangiri* plays were structurally much like the domestic pieces—*sewamono* —of traditional *kabuki*). Another type of new play was the *katsureki* or "living history," created after the rise of the people's rights movement in the 1870's. In the politically conscious atmosphere of the times, these plays represented an effort to stage realistic historical drama rather than the fancifully distorted quasi-history of earlier *kabuki*.

An even more significant innovation to emerge from the political ferment of the second and third decades of the Meiji period was *shimpa* or the "new school" of theatre, whose founders were actual participants in the political party movement. Chief among these was Kawakami Otojirō (1864–1911), a former *kabuki* actor and fervid political liberal of the day. Using current events and material from recently written political novels (including *Strange Encounters of Elegant Females* discussed above), Kawakami attempted to present plays of topical interest, which he further enlivened with special sound and lighting effects. The war with China in the mid-1890's provided a particularly fine opportunity for Kawakami, who was able to capitalize on heightened patriotic feelings by staging *shimpa* extravaganzas dealing with the fighting then in progress on the continent.

10

The Fruits of Modernity

JAPAN WENT TO WAR with China in 1894–95 over the issue, to put it euphemistically, of Korean independence. Korea had traditionally been tributary to China, a relationship that gave the Chinese a kind of protectorate over the foreign affairs of the peninsular, "hermit" kingdom. Victorious in 1895, Japan received, among other rewards, the colonial possessions of Taiwan and the Pescadore Islands. Moreover, by fully exposing the weakness and ineptitude of the Manchu Government, it helped precipitate an odious round of concession-grabbing by the Powers in China during the late 1890's that has been described as "the carving of the melon." The country that took the largest slice of the melon was Russia, whose increasing assertiveness from this time on in Northeast Asia led to a serious clash of interests and, finally, war with Japan. In its surprising triumph over Russia in 1904–5, Japan not only extended its empire through acquisition of the Liaotung Peninsula and Korea (formally annexed in 1910), but also vaulted into the ranks of the world powers. Thus, within a half-century, the "Meiji miracle" of modernization—made indubitable by the fine criterion of Japan's proven capacity to beat other major countries in war—had been spectacularly accomplished.

In the year Japan went to war with China, 1894, it also secured revision (effective in 1899) of its unequal treaties with the Western nations, thereby achieving a foreign policy goal that had become a national obsession. This achievement, along with Japan's many other advances in modern technology and the spectacular military victories that were soon forthcoming over China, fostered a universal sense of pride among the Japanese people. Despite the growing differences of opinion among intellectuals and government leaders (discussed in the last chapter) about methods of modernization and the cultural values proper to it, the Japanese were still capable in the mid-1890's of a remarkable unanimity of attitude toward national goals. No one, for example, vocally opposed the Chinese war; on the contrary, virtually all Japanese who spoke out publicly extolled its glories. That candid old Westernizer, Fukuzawa Yukichi, insisted, for example, that it would advance world culture, and even the devout Christian Uchimura Kanzō called the war a righteous undertaking. It seemed, indeed, to be almost a logical necessity for Japan, having become civilized and enlightened, to assume the responsibility for spreading the fruits of modernity to the still backward-thinking peoples elsewhere in East Asia.

One somber result of the Sino-Japanese War was China's further decline as a source of higher culture in Japanese eyes. Although the Meiji Restoration had rather abruptly shifted Japan's attention from China to the West as its chief foreign mentor, China's traditional prestige was still very high in Japan in the early 1890's, especially among many members of the conservative "national essence" movement. But the rhetoric of wartime propaganda, combined with growing contempt for Chinese ineffectuality in the field of battle, led most Japanese intellectuals and leaders to give less and less consideration to their millennia-old cultural ties to China. In the years following the war, some Japanese even conceived of a modern Japan benignly repaying its cultural debt to a decrepit China by aiding Chinese reformists and revolutionaries in their struggle against the alien and antiquated Manchu dynasty.

At the same time, the almost joyful unanimity of attitude with which the Japanese had entered the war with China was shattered in its aftermath. The "triple intervention" in 1896 of Russia, France, and Germany, forcing Japan to retrocede to China one of its main territorial booties from the recent fighting, the Liaotung Peninsula,[66] incensed many Japanese and made them more aggressively nationalistic than before. Other Japanese, appalled by the ugly spectacle of concession-grabbing that soon ensued in China, recanted their previous endorsement of war as a valid tool for civilizing and enlightening and became in varying degrees pacifistic. Observing, in addition, the factory layoffs and other economic dislocations and hardships that followed in the wake of the war, some of the latter also came to reject the capitalistic system of economic modernization that was evolving in Japan and espoused the doctrines of socialism.

It was thus in the period following the war with China that Japan was first truly exposed to those harsh ideological divisions of viewpoint that seem inevitably to accompany modernization. Yet, for better or worse in the long run, Japan as it entered this early phase of empire-building was spared much actual divisiveness by the authority of the oligarchs, who continued to hold a uniquely superior position within the Meiji Government.

The process by which the advocates of political parties gradually acquired power after the opening of the first Diet in 1890 can only be briefly sketched here. In the beginning, they could do little more than seek to harass the oligarchs by adopting obstructionist tactics. Not until after the turn of the century were the party people regularly taken into cabinets; and not until 1918 was a true party leader made prime minister. By then, most of the great Meiji leaders were dead and those few still alive, like Yamagata Aritomo (1838–1922) of Chōshū who, along with Itō Hirobumi, had been the most powerful of the oligarchs, enjoyed only a fraction of their former influence.

Scholars continue to debate whether the kind of party government that had evolved in Japan by the 1920's, ostensibly resembling in its major features the British political system, was or was not democratic. Even if regarded as democratic, the prewar form of party government was certainly extremely fragile, as was demonstrated by the relative ease with which it was crushed by the militarists in the early 1930's. Recent studies by Western scholars strongly suggest that, whatever else it may have been, "Taishō democracy" [67] was not populistic. In order to secure a measure of power from the Meiji oligarchs, the party leaders came to adopt what has been called the politics of compromise. In other words, they worked much harder at establishing a modus operandi with the oligarchs and other leading bureaucrats than at gaining popular support among the masses. By 1925, when universal manhood suffrage was finally adopted in Japan, there were two major parties. Both naturally sought to secure as large majorities in elections as possible; but there was in fact very little philosophical difference between them, and few if any party leaders were ever really motivated to "take the issues to the people." They were the members of a new kind of ruling élite who stood at the top of a still highly structured and even traditionalistic society, and in many ways they appeared as remote and unapproachable to the common man as rulers always had in Japan.

Although the socialist and other left-wing movements had very little practical success in the period before World War II, they constitute an important subject of study not only for an understanding of the origins of the left wing in Japan today but also because they have, quite understandably, always exerted a powerful influence on Japanese writers, artists, and intellectuals in general. One reason for the left wing's poor showing in the prewar period was the frequent governmental suppression to which it was subjected. For example, the first Socialist Party, founded in 1901, was banned on the very day that it declared its existence. Such treatment by the authorities soon led some socialist leaders to despair of ever achieving their goals by parliamentary means and to embrace more radical ideologies, such as syndicalism and anarchism. Interestingly, the split that occurred about the time of the Russo-Japanese War between those socialists who wished to continue their efforts to reform society from within and those who increasingly rejected legal, parliamentary tactics coincided roughly with the division between the Christians and non-Christians among them. By and large, the Christian socialists of this period, most of whom were fortified by the strong sense of moral purpose imparted by Protestant missionaries and teachers of the late nineteenth century, were unwilling to adopt revolutionary measures, but remained convinced that their programs could and should be implemented through the constituted governmental structure of Japan.

Probably the single most shocking event to the Japanese before World War II was the revelation in 1910 of an anarchist plot to assassinate the Meiji emperor. Scores of arrests were made and twelve men, most of whom were not actually privy to the plot, were executed. The severity of the government's "anti-radical" action at this time effectively stifled all left-wing activities, and it was not until after World War I that they were resumed.

Japan's participation in World War I on the side of the Allies was minimal; yet, as a result, it was able to enlarge its empire through the acquisition both of Germany's island possessions in the Pacific and the former German interests in North China. World War I also brought an unprecedented economic boom to Japan, which took over most of the Far Eastern markets temporarily abandoned by the European belligerents. Many economists, in fact, judge that it was about this time that Japan finally achieved economic modernity. However such modernity may be defined, Japan by World War I had obviously become a capitalist state of a highly monopolistic character. Much of the country's industry and commerce was controlled by a small number of financial combines or *zaibatsu*, whose managing families were plutocratically associated through marriage and other ties with leading members of the Japanese bureaucracy and political parties.

The Allies claimed to have fought the war "to make the world safe for democracy." And although Wilsonian idealism was largely ignored by the authors of the Versailles Treaty, who were mainly intent upon punishing Germany and furthering their own national interests, the postwar period was a time when Western-style democracy seemed clearly to be in the ascendant in the world. At the same time, the successful Communist revolution in Russia gave new hope to radicals and revolutionaries everywhere. Partly in response to this, and even as Taishō democracy flourished, the long-dormant left wing became once again active in Japan.

Probably the leading theoretician of Taishō democracy and what it might have been was Yoshino Sakuzō (1878–1933). An early convert to Christianity, Yoshino studied in Europe and the United States before assuming a full-time position in political thought on the faculty of Tokyo Imperial University in 1913. He persuasively expressed his aspirations for Japanese democracy in a series of articles for the magazine *Chūō Kōron* (*Central Review*), the most famous of which was "On the Meaning of Constitutional Government," published in 1916.

In essence, Yoshino sought to advance the cause of liberal democracy in Japan against oligarchic or plutocratic rule. He not only advocated universal manhood suffrage (which, as we have seen, was finally adopted in 1925), but also urged reform of the House of Peers and other appointive bodies in order to strengthen the power of the elective House of Representatives. Furthermore, Yoshino attempted to deal with the delicate question of the compatibility of democracy with the *kokutai* concept, which held the emperor to be theoretically the source of all state authority and power. While expressing his personal opinion that the emperor was quite unlikely to go against the sentiments or welfare of the people, Yoshino sought to clarify Japan's particular brand of democracy (within the outward form of a constitutional monarchy) by suggesting that the best Japanese word for "democracy" was *minpon*—literally, "the people are the foundation (of the state)"—rather than the more commonly used *minshu*, "the people are sovereign." Yet Yoshino's idea of the people as the foundation of the state, along with his frequent references to the "people's welfare," also had a strongly Confucian ring to it. Traditional Confucianists had always insisted that government be for the people, without for a moment considering the moral propriety of its also being of and by them.

In addition to the inspiration of the Russian revolution for the exceptionally radical-minded, specific developments in Japan during and after World War I appeared particularly favorable to the left wing as a whole. *Zaibatsu* exploitation and worsening labor conditions, for example, had brought on large-scale and militant industrial strikes in the cities, while in the countryside, where social conditions were little better than they had been before the Meiji Restoration, absentee landlordism had reached nearly the 50 per cent level. Moreover, the return of the European Powers to competition for the Far Eastern markets, combined with poor governmental planning, precipitated a sharp recession in the postwar period. The fall of silk prices was particularly distressing to farming families, many of which were greatly dependent on supplementary income from sericulture to make ends meet.

The reasons why, despite seemingly propitious conditions, the socialists and others on the left were able to achieve so little in practical terms following World War I deserve more attention than can be given here. But, for one thing, the structure of Japanese society was not conducive to their activities. The majority of Japanese were still farmers engaged in family-oriented, intensive agriculture and were highly conservative in outlook. Reverence for the emperor, and thus for the established order, was particularly strong among them. Even in the urban, industrial sector of the economy, many workers were held in paternalistic thrall by their employers and were simply not as socially and politically incitable as the members of a truly alienated proletariat. Despite occasional outbursts of anguish in such forms as strikes and riots over rises in the price of rice, the great staple of food consumption, both peasants and industrial workers by and large accepted their subordinate positions in life and obeyed the ostensibly unassailable authority of those above them.

This is not to suggest that the masses of prewar Japan were merely ignorant and docile. They were, in fact, almost universally literate, although their moral education, as we have seen, was heavily weighted in favor of the traditionalistic *kokutai* values. And any apparent docility was, I believe, actually a manifestation of how little revolutionary potential there was in prewar Japanese society. If the people were to be spurred into collective action, the appeal would at any rate have to come from the nationalistic, emperor-revering right and not from the left wing, which was primarily internationalist in outlook and was in particular opposed to those élitist privileges protected by the *kokutai* ideology.

We observed in the last chapter that the most powerful literary force in the late 1880's and early 1890's was the group of Ken'yūsha (Society of Friends of the Inkstone) novelists centered about Ozaki Kōyō, who believed that modern, realistic writing in Japanese should be modeled on the Genroku style of Saikaku. Although Ozaki and his companions remained popular favorites among the reading public through much of the 1890's, as Japan entered its age of parliamentary government and imperialist expansion, their prominence served largely to obscure the great diversity of creative activity and ferment of ideas among other writers in the literary world during this decade.

The danger in any survey of Japanese literature from the 1890's on is the temptation to classify writers according to various schools, such as the romantic and the naturalist, and thereby not only fail to do justice to the individuality of major authors but also to give the impression of a more orderly progression of literary trends than actually occurred. In literature, as in other cultural and intellectual pursuits, the achievement of modernity by Japan at the end of the nineteenth century and the beginning of the twentieth brought with it a complexity of outlook and activity that defies precise categorization. Even though it is helpful to apply labels to certain groups of writers because of important characteristics they shared, such labels should not be interpreted as fixed pronouncements on their places in modern Japanese literature.

One characteristic manifested by virtually all Japanese authors from Tsubouchi until at least the end of the Meiji period was their desire to describe man and his behavior as accurately and truthfully as possible. In this sense, all presumably regarded themselves as "realistic" writers, although obviously they differed greatly in their conceptions of what constituted realistic writing. Certain authors of the 1890's, often loosely called romantics, insisted, for example, that an accurate and truthful depiction of man could only be achieved through analyses of the psychological motivations and feelings of individuals and not simply by portrayals of certain types or categories of people. Behind this attitude lay the vexing problem of individualism in modern Japan. It is significant that many of the leading prose writers, poets, and critics of the most prominent journal of Japanese romanticism, *Bungakukai* (*The Literary World*, published in 1893–98), were either converts to or strongly influenced by Protestant Christianity, the only creed in late Meiji Japan that gave primacy to the freedom and spiritual independence of the individual. The absolutism embodied in the Meiji Constitution demanded strict subordination of the interests of the individual to those of the state; and the hopes of many intellectuals and artists that the people's rights movement might provide a legitimate channel for personal dissent were severely reduced, if not entirely dashed, when, from about the time of the Sino-Japanese War, the political parties began to abandon their strong opposition to the oligarchs and to pursue instead the "politics of compromise."

The feeling of frustration engendered by a society that placed such preponderant stress upon obedience to the group, especially in the form of filial piety toward one's parents and loyalty to the state, no doubt accounts for much of the sense of alienation observable in the works of so many modern Japanese writers. These writers have been absorbed to an unusual degree with the individual, the world of his personal psychology, and his essential loneliness. In line with this preoccupation, novelists have perennially turned to the diary-like, confessional tale—the so-called I-novel—as their preferred medium of expression.

Among the leading figures of late-nineteenth-century romanticism in Japan was Mori Ōgai (1862–1922), although his participation in this trend constituted only one phase of a long and varied career as writer, translator, and critic. A graduate of the medical school of Tokyo Imperial University, Mori spent the period 1884–88 studying medicine in Germany under the sponsorship of the Japanese army. Even after entering the literary field upon his return to Japan, he remained an army doctor, rising to the rank of surgeon-general before his retirement from active service in 1916.

Mori was the first major Japanese novelist to study the literature of a Western country at its source, and not surprisingly the dominant foreign influence on his writing was German. He produced the earliest quality translations from German literature in the late 1880's, shortly after Futabatei began his translations from the Russian, and, in 1890, he published his first novel, *The Dancing Girl* (*Maihime*). Based on Mori's personal experiences and labeled by him an *Ich Roman*, or I-novel, *The Dancing Girl* is the story of a Japanese student in Germany, Toyotarō, who has an affair with a German girl but who ultimately abandons her in order to return home and accept a position in the Meiji officialdom. In some ways, Toyotarō represents the exact opposite of Bunzō, the pathetic hero of Futabatei's *The Drifting Cloud*. Whereas Bunzō, a failure in the competition to get ahead in a rapidly modernizing Japan, also finds his hope for happiness in love threatened, Toyotarō rejects love for personal ambition.

Romanticism, which influenced many novelists and poets in the period up to the Russo-Japanese War, gave way shortly thereafter to the more clearly identifiable movement of naturalism. Stimulated in particular by the writings of Zola and Maupassant, the naturalists took their stand on the premise, derived from the philosophical positivism of nineteenth-century Europe, that man and society could be portrayed with scientific realism through careful observation and clinical recording of the most minute, mundane aspects of human behavior. The Japanese naturalist writers have been strongly criticized, however, for at least two major reasons: first, unlike the European naturalists, they concentrated almost entirely on the individual and made little attempt to relate him to the larger concerns of society; and second, by relying heavily on their own personal experiences to describe life as it really is, they were guilty of immense egotism. Yet, however much they may be criticized for their approach and methods, the naturalists certainly addressed with vigor the theme that has held greatest fascination for modern Japanese novelists: the innermost psychological and emotional life of the individual.

The Broken Commandment (*Hakai*) of Shimazaki Tōson (1872–1943), published in 1906, is generally regarded as the first naturalistic novel in Japan. Shimazaki, a convert to Christianity, had earlier been a contributor of romantic poetry to *Bungakukai*, and his emergence as a pioneer novelist of the naturalist school suggests that, despite the great differences between the two movements in the context of their historical development in Europe, romanticism and naturalism tended to merge in Japan, particularly in their mutually intense, egocentric concern for the individual. *The Broken Commandment* tells of Ushimatsu, a member of Japan's pariah class of *eta*, who has vowed to his father that he will never reveal his class origins. Even after he completes school and becomes a teacher, Ushimatsu maintains the secret in spite of a growing feeling of guilt that he should speak out and join others who are struggling to achieve social equality for the *eta*. In the end, Ushimatsu decides to reveal his identity; but, rather than join the fight for minority rights in Japan, he accepts the offer of a job on a ranch in Texas owned by another, expatriate *eta*. Unlike most other naturalistic novels, *The Broken Commandment* deals with a significant social problem, although any message that might be derived from Shimazaki's handling of it is largely vitiated by the improbable ending he has contrived.

Tayama Katai (1871–1930) was the second major writer of the naturalist school, and his 1907 novel *The Quilt (Futon)* was the earliest purely autobiographical work of the I-novel genre. Dealing with the unhappy love affair between a novelist and his young female pupil, *The Quilt* was for its time an especially daring revelation of the intimate relations between a man and a woman. To Tayama, personal confession was the most scientifically valid and "sincere" of literary techniques; and in his conscientious application of it throughout his career he, more than anyone, epitomized the real spirit of Japanese naturalism.

Although other authors began to react against naturalism shortly after it was established and popularized as a movement by Shimazaki and Tayama in the years immediately following the Russo-Japanese War, they in fact shared with the naturalists the important common desire to be free of the restraints of imposed moralism in Japanese society and to investigate at their will the sources of human behavior. One group of these authors, including Nagai Kafū (1879–1959) and his disciple Tanizaki Junichirō (1886–1965), became known as "aesthetics" or "decadents." Whereas the naturalists proclaimed a scientific interest in all aspects of life, no matter how trifling, such "aesthetics" as Nagai and Tanizaki were expressly concerned with the more unwholesome, hedonistic, and even bizarre patterns of conduct observable in man.

Nagai Kafū spent the years 1903–8 in the United States and France. His chief reaction to the United States seems to have been a mild distaste for the materialistic character of American life as he saw it. In France, on the other hand, the pleasures of Parisian life only intensified the sentiment that was to be the most persistent in Nagai's writings: nostalgia for the gracious and aesthetically cultivated ways of the past.

Back in Japan, Nagai's natural habitat was the demimonde and his guiding urge was to recapture what he could of the former life style of the floating world of Edo. Like the other Japanese aesthetics, he was preoccupied with women—especially the *samisen*-playing *geisha* type—and with the voluptuous delights they could provide. Ever nostalgic and sensual, Nagai appears constantly to have sought escape from the realities of modern Japanese society. Although he privately expressed outraged shock at the severity of governmental suppression of the anarchists accused in 1910 of plotting against the life of the Meiji emperor, it is doubtful that his escapism stemmed from any deeply felt despair over the restriction of personal freedoms in Japan. Rather, Nagai was drawn by temperament to seek his ideals and pursue his fantasies in the past. As Edward Seidensticker has put it: "Buildings had to be decaying, cultures ill and dying, if not dead, before he could really like them." [68]

Tanizaki Junichirō was a far more powerful and versatile writer than Nagai Kafū. Unlike Nagai, who was obsessed with the vanishing life of Edo, Tanizaki produced books on a great variety of subjects. Some, for example, are set in Japan's distant past, while others are intimately personal accounts, often of a highly erotic nature; still others, like his masterpiece, *The Makioka Sisters*,[69] are evocations of Japanese society. To many readers, Tanizaki was the most decadent of the decadent writers, a view they formed from the extraordinarily masochistic, sexually perverse behavior of so many of his characters. Nagai Kafū's heroes had, for the most part, simply used women or had taken what pleasures they could from them; but, in the writings of Tanizaki, men willingly debase and sacrifice themselves to the glorification of feminine beauty.. This is perhaps best seen in the recurrent theme of foot fetishism. Tanizaki's last—although by no means best—novel, *The Diary of a Mad Old Man* (*Fūten Rōjin Nikki*, 1961), deals exclusively with the passion of a sickly, withered, and impotent old man for his daughter-in-law, a former cabaret girl who humors him in return for monetary favors. The old man is particularly enamored with the girl's feet and even schemes to have imprints made of them on his tombstone so that he can lie in eternal abjection beneath them.

Another central theme in Tanizaki's work is the familiar conflict between East and West. For other Japanese, this was a conflict of philosophies or of an Eastern spiritualism as set against a Western materialism; but for Tanizaki it seems to have been primarily aesthetic. In his earlier writings he was, as he himself later lamented, excessively infatuated with the West and its modernity. As he approached middle age, he began to reassess and to appreciate anew the attractions of traditional Japan. In keeping with his ever-constant absorption with women, Tanizaki dealt most effectively with the pull of East and West in such novels as *Some Prefer Nettles* (*Tade Kuu Mushi*, 1928),[70] where an ostensibly Westernized man, unhappy in his marriage and accustomed to seeking physical gratification with a Eurasian prostitute, finds himself increasingly drawn to the old-fashioned, endearing femininity of the Kyoto beauty who is his father-in-law's mistress.

One of the greatest writers of the late Meiji and early Taishō periods, who was not associated with any particular movement or school, was Natsume Sōseki (1867–1916). Sōseki majored in English literature at Tokyo Imperial University and studied in England from 1900 until 1903. He subsequently lectured for a brief period at the university as the successor to Lafcadio Hearn, but devoted most of his time during the remaining years of his life to the prolific output of novels that has earned him the lofty position he holds in modern Japanese literature.

Natsume Sōseki's great theme was the loneliness and isolation of man, particularly the Japanese intellectual of his age, whose society had in recent decades rejected so much of the native tradition and had taken on so much of the scientific and industrial façade of the West that it had plunged itself into a great spiritual abyss. It is from Sōseki that we hear the most anguished cry over the failure of "Eastern morals" to keep pace with "Western technology" in the course of Japan's modernization. Man is by nature an isolated creature, yet how much more agonizing is his ordeal of loneliness when an impersonal and alien technology has destroyed the very fabric and continuity of his society.

In dealing with his subject of the solitary human ego, Sōseki used the familiar confessional technique of "fictional" self-analysis so favored by modern Japanese authors. In his finer novels, like *Kokoro* (1914), the impact of such self-analysis is one of almost overpowering intensity. *Kokoro* is a story of friendship between a youth and an older man (referred to by the respectful Japanese title of Sensei or "Teacher"). As the friendship between the two unfolds, we learn that some dark tragedy lies in Sensei's past, a tragedy that has left him with an utterly despairing, misanthropic view of life. The second half of the book is actually a novel within a novel, presented in the form of a letter that Sensei writes to the youth "confessing" the story of his past. It is the tale of a triangular love affair in which Sensei is overwhelmed with guilt for, in his mind, having betrayed his friend and rival and for having driven him finally to suicide. Later, however, Sensei considers the possibility that his friend (identified only as K) had some even more desperate reason for his ghastly act than failure in love:

> I asked myself, "Was it perhaps because his ideals clashed with reality that he killed himself?" But I could not convince myself that K had chosen death for such a reason. Finally, I became aware of the possibility that K had experienced loneliness as terrible as mine, and wishing to escape quickly from it, had killed himself. Once more, fear gripped my heart. From then on, like a gust of winter wind, the premonition that I was treading the same path as K had done would rush at me from time to time and chill me to the bone.[71]

In fact, Sensei does commit suicide after completing the confessional letter to his young friend. And he does so at a time, in the year 1912, of particular poignancy both for him and for the Japanese people:

> . . . at the height of the summer Emperor Meiji passed away. I felt as though the spirit of the Meiji era had begun with the Emperor and had ended with him. I was overcome with the feeling that I and the others, who had been brought up in that era, were now left behind to live as anachronisms.[72]

Perhaps even more moving to the Japanese people than the death of the Meiji emperor was the double suicide shortly thereafter of General Nogi Maresuke (1849–1912) and his wife, who chose, in accordance with an ancient custom, to follow their sovereign in death. Shocking as such an act may seem to foreigners, it was viewed by most Japanese at the time as one of absolute purity and selflessness and worthy of their highest admiration. Nogi had been a hero of the Russo-Japanese War, the conflict that made Japan a world power and put the stamp of success on its efforts at modernization. Yet even in the afterglow of that success, Nogi, whether it was his precise intent or not, made the most forceful of all possible appeals to his fellow countrymen not to forget the great national heritage of the past. Among those most profoundly affected by his death was Mori Ōgai, who from this time on devoted himself chiefly to the writing of novels that dealt with Japanese history.

It should not be thought that all writers of the late Meiji and early Taishō periods were pessimistic or skeptical about the values of a modernized Japan. On the contrary, a new group of authors, known as the "White Birch" writers from the title of the magazine *Shirakaba* that they began publishing in 1910, had already appeared on the scene to voice cheerful and idealistic sentiments about the course of Japanese society, sentiments that were more in keeping with the advent of Taishō democracy. The White Birch writers were for the most part younger men from excellent families; indeed, their nominal leader, Mushanokōji Saneatsu (1885–   ), was descended from the Kyoto aristocracy. They regarded themselves as cosmopolites whose interests were in the furtherance of international, rather than simply national, art. Mushanokōji, for example, was singularly unimpressed with the purported significance of Nogi's suicide as a reaffirmation of the vital spirit that had traditionally permeated Japanese life and culture.

The White Birch writers took particular exception to what they regarded as the excessively gloomy outlook and plodding ways of the naturalists. Instead, they affirmed their own faith in the positive value of individualism and the expectation that it would thrive in Japan as elsewhere. They also tended to preach a Tolstoian kind of humanism, and dabbled to varying degrees with ideas of social leveling. Mushanokōji even went so far as to establish in Kyushu in 1919 a "new village," whose inhabitants were expected to live in idyllic tranquility and communal brotherhood. But, by and large, the humanism of the White Birch writers, who were secure in their own élitist social status, was more intellectual than practical. The most powerful advocacy of radical social change in this period came from the group of proletarian writers who emerged in the early 1920's along with organized Marxism in Japan.

The Japanese Communist Party was founded in 1922 and from the start was beset with great difficulties. Not the least of these was the inability of its members to agree on ideological matters. Some Marxists, for example, asserted that, since the Japanese Government was a fully bourgeois-dominated, capitalistic regime, efforts should be made to precipitate its overthrow by the proletariat. Others insisted that Japan had still not experienced a bourgeois revolution, and that it would be necessary to eliminate the many feudal elements in Japanese society before any consideration could be given to a proletarian take-over. Even if there had been ideological agreement, the Communist movement stood virtually no chance in prewar Japan, for popular sentiment was hostile and the authorities were unrelentingly harsh. With the approach of the 1930's and mounting Japanese involvement in military adventurism on the continent, the movement was ruthlessly destroyed.

The Taishō period in general, and the years following World War I in particular, witnessed the emergence of a truly mass or popular culture in Japan. Further advances in public transportation, communication, higher education, publishing, and journalism were among the factors that contributed to the widening of opportunities, especially for middle-class urban dwellers, to participate in a new kind of up-to-date "cultural life." Like much of the movement for civilization and enlightenment in the early Meiji period, many aspects of this post-World War I pursuit of a cultural life appear to have been little more than frivolous imitations of Western habits and fads. The addition of one or two rooms decorated and furnished in the Western manner could, for example, transform a mere house into a "cultural home." And, while "modern girls" could be seen strolling the Ginza with permanent waves and shortened hemlines, "modern boys" sported "all back" hairdos and dark-rimmed, Harold Lloyd glasses. Even the great earthquake that wrought a holocaust of destruction in Tokyo in 1923 ironically helped to advance the popular culture; for in the process of the city's reconstruction it was provided with a greatly increased number of bars, cafés, and other places of leisure and entertainment where the "modern" generation could meet and socialize.

Unlike the age of civilization and enlightenment, when the West represented an exciting but bewildering kind of utopia and only a relatively few people could really partake of it, the evolution of a mass culture in the 1920's not only affected (by definition) virtually all Japanese, it also engendered in them a more cosmopolitan outlook and a stronger sense of internationalism than they had ever had before. Perhaps the greatest spur to this newly internationalist sense was the boom in foreign sports that occurred about this time. American baseball became the national mania that it still is today in Japan, and such leisure sports as golf and tennis also gained steadily in popularity. Japanese athletes, moreover, became increasingly prominent in Olympic competition. The good showing of Japanese swimmers at the Paris Olympics in 1924 even set off a round of pool-building in public schools.

Although not always used for edifying purposes, the phonograph and the radio both contributed greatly to the new spread of culture, particularly in making available for the first time to all Japanese the sounds of Western music. Among the *interi* or "intelligentsia," it became fashionable to discuss the merits of, say, the playing of Kreisler or the singing of Caruso.

One of the most popular mediums of mass culture in the 1920's was the motion picture. The first foreign "movie" was shown in Japan in 1894; a few years later, the Japanese began making movies of their own; and by the post-World War I period Japanese studios were producing a steady flow of films to meet the increasing demand for them by the movie houses that were proliferating throughout the country. The earliest commercial movies made in Japan were little more than records on film of stage productions of *kabuki* and its modern variant, *shimpa*. In the absence of any innovative methods, much of the popularity of these movies with audiences depended on the emotive skills of the *katsuben* or "narrators," who provided the voices for the characters on screen. Not until such techniques as the close-up, the cut-back, and the capturing of "fast action" were introduced about the time of World War I through the works of D. W. Griffith did film-making become a potentially important form of art in Japan.

Most of the films produced to meet the demands for mass entertainment in the 1920's were, needless to say, of very little artistic merit; indeed, a great many were of the bombastic *chambara* or samurai "swordplay" type, the equivalent of the stereotypical American Western. Still, some people sought to do original work and became pioneers in a tradition of serious film-making that has earned much international recognition in recent years, particularly for the way in which Japanese directors have used the motion picture as a means to express their native, highly refined aesthetic tastes.

In contrast to the flourishing of motion pictures in Japan, efforts from the early years of the twentieth century to establish a modern Japanese theatre or drama (*shingeki*) achieved nothing comparable to the great distinction and commercial success of contemporary theatre in the West. The two main streams of the *shingeki* movement date from the founding in 1906 of the Literary Association (Bungei Kyōkai), one of whose organizers was the novelist and critic, Tsubouchi Shōyō, and in 1909 of the Liberal Theatre (Jiyū Gekijō) of Osanai Kaoru (1881–1928). Tsubouchi regarded *shingeki* as part of the overall attempt made from at least mid-Meiji times on to reform Japanese literature and theatre in general, and is remembered, in this phase of his career, primarily for his experiments in combining scenes from Shakespeare on the same programs with *kabuki* plays. Osanai and his supporters, on the other hand, completely rejected traditional Japanese theatrical forms, with their characteristic mixture of music, dance, and acting, in favor of the representational, essentially "spoken" theatre of the modern West. As one scholar has observed:

> The enthusiastic followers of Osanai, who eventually assumed almost exclusive leadership in the *shingeki* world of the following decades, considered Shakespeare and the Western classics before Ibsen at the same level as *nō* and *kabuki*. They considered these to belong to a world without any connection with the vital problems of modern man—a world where dance, music, the stylization and professionalism of the actors could provide entertainment on a commercial basis for nonintellectuals, but not the discussion and the message of a new world to come needed by intellectuals for a rapid modernization of the country.[73]

From its inception, *shingeki* relied heavily on the production of translated Western plays, with Osanai and the progressive stream of the movement favoring in particular the works of Ibsen, Chekhov, and Gorki. Moreover, the *shingeki* people tended to lean strongly to the left in their social thinking. This became especially apparent in the late 1920's and 1930's, when *shingeki* became so openly "proletarian" that it eventually came under attack from the newly emergent militaristic leaders of Japan. The relative lack of success of *shingeki* before World War II may be attributed, therefore, to several reasons: its failure to produce a significant repertoire of original plays, its tendency to use the stage for ideological propagandizing, and the official suppression that this propagandizing incurred.

The Manchurian Incident of September, 1931, is generally taken by the Japanese to mark the beginning of the phase of "fascism" in their country that led to the Pacific War and, ultimately, to crushing defeat in 1945. Although most Western scholars are reluctant to apply the essentially European concept of fascism to developments in Japan during this period, it is clear that, under the pressure of international and domestic crises, the form of parliamentary democracy that had gradually evolved in Japan from the mid-Meiji period on disintegrated rapidly before the rise of the military, who succeeded in establishing an oppressive police state by the middle and late 1930's.

Even during the heyday of Taishō democracy, the climate in Japan had scarcely been hospitable for left-wing political and social movements. Though parties of a non-revolutionary, social-democratic character were allowed to exist and to participate in elections, the Communist Party, as noted, was harshly suppressed. After their advance to power in the 1930's, the military became increasingly less tolerant toward any doctrines that went against the orthodox views of state, views that were set forth for the edification of the Japanese people in 1934 in a tract entitled *Kokutai no Hongi* or *The Fundamental Principles of Our National Polity*. Japan was a sacred land, ruled by a godlike (although isolated and non-acting) emperor. Its citizens were the members of a great family headed by the emperor, and they were expected to serve the state with unquestioning loyalty. The military in particular was not to be criticized, for it had the holy mission of expanding Japanese influence abroad and it was, in any case, answerable only to the emperor (which meant, for practical purposes, that it was answerable to no one).

Culturally, the period of the 1930's and the Pacific War was one of general aridity. The suppression not only of proletarian authors and playwrights, but even of professors with abstruse, scholarly views that were deemed incompatible with the national polity effectively muted much of the literary and academic worlds. One of the few significant developments was the rise to prominence of a group of authors, including Kawabata Yasunari (1899–1972),[74] who were called "neo-sensualists" and who attacked the excessively scientific, clinical approach to literature of both the proletarian and naturalist schools and called for a return to purely artistic values and emotional sensitivity in fictional writing. But to a great extent this period of mounting militarism and impending cataclysm was a time when most Japanese manifested an intense passion for diversionary and escapist entertainment labeled by its critics as a conglomeration of "the erotic, the grotesque, and the nonsensical." Included within this category were dance halls and girlie revues, the yoyo, "baby golf," crossword puzzles and mahjong.

Little need be said here about the Pacific War. Following their surprise attack on Pearl Harbor in December, 1941, the Japanese scored a series of spectacular victories that secured a vast imperial hegemony over the western Pacific and much of Southeast Asia, a hegemony that was not seriously challenged for more than a year. But, from 1943 on, the Allies, who had given priority to the European theatre of war, turned the tide of fighting inexorably against Japan. And, by August, 1945, after American planes had dropped atomic bombs on Hiroshima and Nagasaki, Japan lay in ruins, a totally and unconditionally defeated country with many of its citizens facing imminent starvation.

Succor came to the Japanese from their former foes, especially the United States, which from the beginning monopolized, under General Douglas MacArthur, the Allied Occupation of Japan. The Occupation, lasting until 1952, stripped Japan of its empire and instituted sweeping reforms (many of which have since either been reversed or significantly modified) in virtually every major sphere of Japanese social, political, and economic life. Among the Occupation reforms was the promulgation of a new constitution, based on thoroughly Anglo-American principles, that abolished the old *kokutai* ideology by declaring Japan a republic, guaranteeing certain inalienable personal liberties, and reducing the status of the emperor to that of a British-style "symbol of state."

However the Occupation may ultimately be judged, it was certainly an extraordinary event in world history in which a country with a great and ancient heritage, never before defeated in war, was subjected to the absolute will of a foreign power intent upon "demilitarizing and democratizing" it. In the early *apure* (*après-guerre*) years of the Occupation, the Japanese, spiritually and physically exhausted from their wartime ordeal and the overwhelming shock of defeat, could do little more than passively accept the reformist dictates of their conquerors who, if not always wise, were at least humane.[75] But with the advent of the Cold War in the late 1940's the character of the Occupation changed, and Japan came to be treated less like a former enemy than as an essential ally to be revitalized and strengthened in order to join the "free world" in its struggle to contain the spread of Communism in Asia.

Since the end of the Occupation in 1952, Japan has enjoyed an economic resurgence that has been nothing short of miraculous and that has brought it to a level of material prosperity undreamed of in the prewar period. In the process, however, Japan has made little effort to assert itself once again in the arena of international political affairs. Rather, its perennial rulers of the conservative Liberal-Democratic Party have been content to accept U.S. military protection and to give at least tacit support to American foreign policies in Asia and elsewhere (although the American rapprochement with the People's Republic of China, begun in 1971, will doubtless force Japan to assume a more independent role in the world, politically and diplomatically).

It is beyond the scope of this book to attempt to deal with the great diversity of Japanese cultural activities in the contemporary world. In the major fields of higher culture, Japan is as much a participant in internationalist trends as any other modern country. At the same time, the Japanese continue to draw, either consciously or unconsciously, on their own deeply rooted cultural traditions, perhaps most notably their extraordinary aesthetic sensitivity. This is as apparent, for example, in the internationally acclaimed films of Kurosawa Akira (1910–   ) as in the novels of Mishima Yukio (1925–70), the most cosmopolitan of recent Japanese writers.[76]

Mishima committed suicide in November, 1970, in a sensational, indeed grandly theatrical, manner; and it is doubtful that there will ever be an end to speculation about it. Many people have debunked Mishima's stated reasons for taking his life as he did. But surely there is some significance in the fact that he chose to destroy himself in the time-honored samurai fashion (by *seppuku* or disembowelment) and that, before dying, he exhorted Japan in the name of the emperor to reject the pernicious "progress" of recent times and to return to earlier, more traditional values and ways.

The suicide of Mishima has certainly not drawn the sympathetic response from his countrymen that General Nogi's did in 1912. A quarter-century after Japan's militarist era and the debacle of 1945, Mishima's act may appear, instead, as a bizarre and anachronistic bit of samurai bravado or, at best (if we accept his last exhortation at face value), as a kind of *cri de coeur* that men of many countries have made during the past two centuries against the cultural and spiritual debasement of industrial modernization. Yet, such a *cri de coeur* continues to hold special poignancy for the Japanese—still the only non-Western people to achieve full modernity—as a reminder of the far greater discontinuity between past and present for them than for Europeans and Americans. Despite their remarkable national progress in the last century, the Japanese remain strongly enthralled by their own unique heritage and uncertain, as they have been since Perry's squadron first arrived in 1853, of their moorings in the cultural gulf that still separates East and West in the modern world.

Notes

1. Quoted in Ryusaku Tsunoda, Wm. Theodore de Bary, and Donald Keene, eds., *Sources of Japanese Tradition* (New York: Columbia University Press, 1958), p. 8.
2. Another term for this form of poetry is *waka*, or simply "Japanese poem."
3. Quoted in Donald Keene, ed., *Anthology of Japanese Literature* (New York: Grove Press, 1955), p. 76.
4. *Ibid.*, pp. 37–38.
5. *Ibid.*, pp. 46–47.
6. *Ibid.*, p. 60.
7. G. B. Sansom, *Japan, A Short Cultural History* (New York: Appleton-Century-Crofts, 1931), p. 228.
8. Keene, ed., *Anthology of Japanese Literature*, p. 80.
9. Quoted in Earl Miner, *Japanese Poetic Diaries* (Berkeley: University of California Press, 1969), p. 26.
10. Donald Keene in Tsunoda, de Bary, and Keene, eds., *Sources of Japanese Tradition*, p. 180.
11. Donald Keene, ed., *Anthology of Japanese Literature*, pp. 90–1.
12. *Ibid.*, p. 59.
13. Keene, ed., *Anthology of Japanese Literature*, pp. 67–68.
14. Lady Murasaki, *The Tale of Genji*. Translated by Arthur Waley (New York: Modern Library, 1960), pp. 22–23.
15. Ivan Morris, tr. and ed., *The Pillow Book of Sei Shōnagon* (New York: Columbia University Press, 1967), Vol. 1, pp. 7–8.
16. *Namu Amida Butsu* or "Hail Amida Buddha!"
17. Tsunoda, de Bary, and Keene, eds., *Sources of Japanese Tradition*, pp. 202–3.
18. Quoted in Donald Keene, *Japanese Literature* (New York: Grove Press, 1955), p. 78.
19. Keene, ed., *Anthology of Japanese Literature*, p. 196.
20. From the *Shinkokinshū. Ibid.*, p. 194.
21. Tsunoda, de Bary, and Keene, eds., *Sources of Japanese Tradition*, p. 193.
22. Later in the century imperial princes were substituted for the Fujiwara.
23. Donald Keene, tr., *Essays in Idleness: The Tsurezuregusa of Kenkō* (New York: Columbia University Press, 1967), p. 23.

24. *Ibid.*, p. 70.
25. Following a Chinese practice, the medieval Japanese designated five Zen temples in Kyoto and five in Kamakura as the leading Zen institutions of their respective cities.
26. Donald Keene, Nō, *the Classical Theatre of Japan* (Tokyo: Kodansha, 1966), p. 25.
27. During the *shite's* absence from the stage, there is a *kyōgen* (discussed below) in which the priest speaks to a man of the locality and learns more about the history of the Shrine in the Fields.
28. Matsukaze is the *shite* and Murasame is a companion (*tsure*).
29. Donald Keene, ed., *Twenty Plays of the Nō Theatre* (New York: Columbia University Press, 1970), pp. 31–32.
30. Keene, *Anthology of Japanese Literature*, pp. 315–16.
31. Competitions in the arrangement of flowers and in the identification of different types of incense were also popular.
32. "Ami" was taken from the first two syllables of the name Amida.
33. C. R. Boxer, *The Christian Century in Japan*, 1549–1650 (Berkeley: University of California Press, 1951), pp. 207–8.
34. Scholars estimate that male literacy in Japan by the end of the Tokugawa period was more than 40 per cent, a figure that compares favorably with, and in many cases is higher than, European literacy rates for the same period.
35. Sōtatsu, Kōrin, and the group of painters they influenced are known as the Rimpa school.
36. "*Uki*" can be written with two characters, one meaning wretched and the other floating; "*yo*" means world.
37. I have used Ivan Morris's translations for the titles of all the Saikaku works mentioned here.
38. Ihara Saikaku, *The Life of an Amorous Woman and Other Writings*, edited and translated by Ivan Morris (New York: New Directions, 1963), pp. 124–25.
39. *Ibid.*, pp. 202–3.
40. The term *bunraku* is taken from a famous puppet theatre, the Bunraku-za, established in Osaka in the nineteenth century. Another term for the puppet theatre is "*jōruri*," adopted from the name of Princess Jōruri, a character who appears in some early puppet plays.
41. Donald Keene, *Bunraku: The Art of the Japanese Puppet Theatre* (Tokyo: Kodansha, 1965), p. 31.
42. Donald Keene, tr., *Major Plays of Chikamatsu* (New York: Columbia University Press, 1961), pp. 51–52.
43. Keene, ed., *Anthology of Japanese Literature*, pp. 369 and 371.
44. The Forty-Seven Rōnin were a group of vassals who in 1702 avenged the death of their daimyo lord in what has become the most celebrated vendetta in Japanese history.
45. The word "mirror" in traditional Chinese and Japanese Confucian thought means the use of history as a "reflector" of proper and moral ways of governance.
46. Honda Toshiaki is the subject of Donald Keene's entertaining and informative book, *The Japanese Discovery of Europe*, 1720–1830 (revised ed. Stanford, Calif.: Stanford University Press, 1969).
47. Harold G. Henderson, *An Introduction to Haiku* (New York: Doubleday, 1958), p. 86.
48. *Ibid.*, pp. 89 and 101.

49. The imperial seat was at this time moved to Edo and the city renamed Tokyo or "Eastern Capital."
50. Tsunoda, de Bary, and Keene, eds., *Sources of Japanese Tradition*, p. 644.
51. Donald Keene, *Modern Japanese Literature* (New York: Grove Press, 1956), p. 31.
52. Fukuzawa Yukichi, *An Encouragement of Learning*, translated by David Dilworth and Umeyo Hirano (Tokyo: Sophia University, 1969), p. 1.
53. The Rescript is translated in full in John K. Fairbank, Edwin O. Reischauer, and Albert M. Craig, *East Asia, The Modern Transformation* (Boston: Houghton Mifflin, 1965), p. 276.
54. In this discussion of Tokutomi and the "new generation," I have utilized Kenneth B. Pyle, *The New Generation of Meiji Japan* (Stanford, Calif.: Stanford University Press, 1969).
55. The following comments on Christianity in the Meiji period have benefited from my reading of Irwin Scheiner, *Christian Converts and Social Protest in Meiji Japan* (Berkeley: University of California Press, 1970).
56. Another incident that occurred about this time involved a professor at Tokyo Imperial University, Kume Kunitake, who was dismissed from his position for writing an article in which he called Shinto a primitive form of heaven-worship.
57. From a passage given in G. B. Sansom, *The Western World and Japan* (New York: Knopf, 1958), p. 414.
58. An excellent monograph dealing with Tsubouchi and Futabatei Shimei and containing a translation of the latter's *The Drifting Cloud* is Marleigh G. Ryan, *Japan's First Modern Novel: Ukigumo of Futabatei Shimei* (New York: Columbia University Press, 1967).
59. Keene, *Modern Japanese Literature*, p. 57.
60. Robert H. Brower, "Masaoka Shiki and Tanka Reform" in Donald H. Shively, ed., *Tradition and Modernization in Japanese Culture* (Princeton, N.J.: Princeton University Press, 1971), p. 418.
61. Sansom, *The Western World and Japan*, p. 404.
62. For a discussion of Kawakami, see John M. Rosenfield, "Western-Style Painting in the Early Meiji Period and Its Critics," in Shively, ed., *Tradition and Modernization in Japanese Culture.*
63. For the following remarks on music in the Meiji period, I have relied in particular on William P. Malm, "The Modern Music of Meiji Japan" in Shively, ed., *Tradition and Modernization in Japanese Culture.*
64. *Ibid.*, p. 260.
65. The present Kabuki-za in Tokyo, however, is still another building, erected by others in 1889.
66. Japan regained this territory after defeating Russia in 1905.
67. The Taishō emperor, Meiji's son, ascended the throne in 1912. The reign period to which he has given his name was 1912–25.
68. Edward Seidensticker, *Kafū the Scribbler* (Stanford, Calif.: Stanford University Press, 1965), p. 49.
69. Tanizaki's title for this book was *Sasame Yuki (Thin Snow)*, but it has been translated into English by Edward Seidensticker as *The Makioka Sisters* (New York: Knopf, 1957). It deals with the decline of an Osaka merchant family in the period before World War II.
70. Junichirō Tanizaki, *Some Prefer Nettles*, translated by Edward G. Seidensticker (New York: Knopf, 1955).

71. Natsume Sōseki, *Kokoro*, translated by Edwin McClellan (Chicago: Henry Regnery, 1957), pp. 240–41.

72. *Ibid.*, p. 245.

73. Benito Ortolani, "Fukuda Tsuneari: Modernization and Shingeki" in Shively, ed., *Tradition and Modernization in Japanese Culture*, p. 486.

74. Among the novels of Kawabata, who received the Nobel Prize for literature in 1968, are *Snow Country* and *Thousand Cranes*.

75. One of the leading literary spokesmen of the *apure* period was Dazai Osamu (1909–48), whose best-known novel, *The Setting Sun*, deals with the decline of an aristocratic family in the years immediately following the war.

76. A number of Mishima's novels have been translated into English. Among them are *The Temple of the Golden Pavilion, After the Banquet,* and *The Sailor Who Fell from Grace with the Sea.*

Glossary

aragoto "rough business" style of *kabuki* acting
biwa Japanese lute
bugaku ancient court dance
bummei kaika civilization and enlightenment
bunjin "literati" artists
bunraku the puppet theatre
bushidō "the way of the warrior"
cha-no-yu the tea ceremony
chōka "long poem"
chōnin townsman of the Tokugawa period
daibutsu great buddha
dengaku "field music"
dōbōshū "companions" or art connoisseurs of the Ashikaga Shogunate
dogū earthen figurine of the Jōmon period
dōtaku bronze "bell" of the tomb period
emaki horizontal, narrative picture scroll
fudai daimyō vassal or hereditary daimyo of the Tokugawa period
fukko return to antiquity
fukoku-kyōhei "Enrich the country and strengthen its arms"
fusuma sliding door
gagaku "elegant music" of the Japanese court
garan plan of a Buddhist temple compound
gembun-itchi movement to "unify the spoken and written languages"
genrō body of governmental "elders"
giri duty
haikai "light verse" of the Tokugawa period
haiku seventeen-syllable poetic form
han daimyo domain
haniwa terra-cotta figurine of the tomb period
heimei quality of "openness and candor" seen in the *haniwa* figurines
jidaimono historical play
kabuki plebeian theatre
kagura Shinto music

kakekotoba "pivot word" of poetry
kakemono vertical, hanging scroll
kami Shinto deity
kamikaze wind of the gods
kana Japanese syllabary
kanga Chinese picture
katsureki "living history" play of modern *kabuki*
kogaku-ha Ancient Studies School of Tokugawa period Confucianism
kōgo vernacular Japanese
kokkeibon "witty book"
kokugaku-ha National Learning (Neo-Shinto) School of the Tokugawa period
kokusui hozon "preservation of the national essence"
kokutai national polity
kōshoku erotic
koto Japanese zither
kugutsu puppeteer of the late Heian and Kamakura periods
kyōgen light or comic theatre of the Muromachi period
magatama curved jewel of the Japanese imperial regalia
makoto sincerity
mappō latter days of the Buddhist law
michiyuki theatrical "lovers' journey"
minken people's rights
miyabi courtly refinement
mono no aware a "sensitivity to things"
monogatari tale
monomane acting technique—the "imitation of things"
mukyōkai "non-church" movement
namban literally, "southern barbarians"—form of culture
nembutsu invocation in praise of Amida buddha
nikki diary
ninjō human feelings
nishiki-e "brocade," multi-colored woodblock print
nō classical theatre of the Muromachi period
okashi lightness or wit
onnagata female impersonator of the *kabuki* theatre
raigō pictorial representation of the coming of Amida at the time of death
rangaku Dutch Studies
rekishi monogatari historical tale
renga linked verse
ri reason or principle
rōnin masterless samurai
sabi aged or antique
samisen Japanese banjo-like musical instrument
sangiri "cropped hair" play of modern *kabuki*
sansui landscape (literally, "mountains and water")
sarugaku "monkey music"
satori Buddhist enlightenment
sewamono contemporary or domestic play of the puppet and *kabuki* theatres
sharebon "amorous book"
shasei realistic depiction
shimai climactic dance in a *nō* play

shimpa "new school" of theatre of the Meiji period
shin mind
shinden architectural style of the Heian period
shingeki modern theatre
shingon true words
shishi men of high purpose
shite protagonist of a *nō* play
shoin domestic architectural style of the medieval age
shōji sliding door covered with translucent rice paper
sonnō-jōi "Revere the Emperor! Oust the Barbarians!"
sui chic
tanka short (thirty-one syllable) poem
tatami rush matting
tennō emperor
tokonoma alcove
torii entranceway to a Shinto shrine
tozama daimyō "outside" daimyo of the Tokugawa period
tsū savoir faire
tsure "companion" of a *nō* play
uji clan
ukiyo-e "pictures of the floating world"
uta-monogatari poem-tale
wabi poverty
wabicha classical tea ceremony stressing "poverty" aesthetic
wagoto "soft business" style of *kabuki* acting
waki subordinate actor of a *nō* play
yomihon historical novel
yūgen mystery or profundity
zuihitsu miscellany or "running brush"

Selected Bibliography
of English-Language Books Consulted

BOXER, C. R. The Christian Century in Japan, 1549–1650. Berkeley: University of California Press, 1951.

BROWER, ROBERT H., and EARL MINER. Japanese Court Poetry. Stanford, Calif.: Stanford University Press, 1961.

COVELL, JON CARTER. Under the Seal of Sesshū. New York: De Pamphilus, 1941.

DAZAI, OSAMU. The Setting Sun. Translated by Donald Keene. New York: New Directions, 1956.

FUKUZAWA YUKICHI. An Encouragement of Learning. Translated by David Dilworth and Umeyo Hirano. Tokyo: Sophia, 1969.

HENDERSON, HAROLD G. An Introduction to Haiku. New York: Doubleday, 1958.

IHARA, SAIKAKU. The Life of an Amorous Woman and Other Writings. Edited and translated by Ivan Morris. New York: New Directions, 1963.

KAWABATA, YASUNARI. Snow Country. Translated by Edward G. Seidensticker. New York: Knopf, 1956.

KAWABATA, YASUNARI. Thousand Cranes. Translated by Edward G. Seidensticker. New York: Knopf, 1959.

KEENE, DONALD, ed. Anthology of Japanese Literature. New York: Grove Press, 1955.

KEENE, DONALD. Bunraku: The Art of the Japanese Puppet Theatre. Tokyo: Kodansha, 1965.

KEENE, DONALD, tr. Essays in Idleness: The Tsurezuregusa of Kenkō. New York: Columbia University Press, 1967.

KEENE, DONALD. Japanese Literature. New York: Grove Press, 1955.

KEENE, DONALD, tr. Major Plays of Chikamatsu. New York: Columbia University Press, 1961.

KEENE, DONALD. Modern Japanese Literature. New York: Grove Press, 1956.

KEENE, DONALD. Nō: The Classical Theatre of Japan. Tokyo: Kodansha, 1966.

KEENE, DONALD. *The Japanese Discovery of Europe, 1720–1830.* Revised edition. Stanford, Calif.: Stanford University Press, 1969.

KEENE, DONALD, ed. *Twenty Plays of the Nō Theatre.* New York: Columbia University Press, 1970.

KONDO, ICHITARO. *Japanese Genre Painting: The Lively Art of Renaissance Japan.* Translated by Roy Andrew Miller. Tokyo: Tuttle, 1961.

KUCK, LORAINE. *The World of the Japanese Garden.* New York: Walker-Weatherhill, 1968.

LANE, RICHARD. *Masters of the Japanese Print.* New York: Doubleday, 1962.

MALM, WILLIAM P. *Japanese Music and Musical Instruments.* Tokyo: Tuttle, 1959.

MICHENER, JAMES A. *The Floating World.* New York: Random House, 1954.

MINER, EARL. *Japanese Poetic Diaries.* Berkeley: University of California Press, 1969.

MISHIMA, YUKIO. *After the Banquet.* Translated by Donald Keene. New York: Knopf, 1963.

MISHIMA, YUKIO. *The Sailor Who Fell from Grace with the Sea.* Translated by John Nathan. New York: Knopf, 1965.

MISHIMA, YUKIO. *The Temple of the Golden Pavilion.* Translated by Ivan Morris. New York: Knopf, 1958.

MORRIS, IVAN, ed. *Modern Japanese Stories.* Tokyo: Tuttle, 1962.

MORRIS, IVAN, tr. *The Pillow Book of Sei Shōnagon.* New York: Columbia University Press, 1967.

MORRIS, IVAN. *The World of the Shining Prince.* New York: Knopf, 1964.

MURASAKI, LADY. *The Tale of Genji.* Translated by Arthur Waley. New York: Modern Library, 1960.

NATSUME, SŌSEKI. *Kokoro.* Translated by Edwin McClellan. Chicago: Henry Regnery, 1957.

PAINE, ROBERT T., and ALEXANDER SOPER. *The Art and Architecture of Japan.* Baltimore: Penguin Books, 1955.

PYLE, KENNETH B. *The New Generation of Meiji Japan.* Stanford, Calif.: Stanford University Press, 1969.

RYAN, MARLEIGH G. *Japan's First Modern Novel: Ukigumo of Futabatei Shimei.* New York: Columbia University Press, 1967.

SANSOM, G. B. *Japan, A Short Cultural History.* New York: Appleton-Century-Crofts, 1931.

SANSOM, G. B. *The Western World and Japan.* New York: Knopf, 1958.

SCHEINER, IRWIN. *Christian Converts and Social Protest in Meiji Japan.* Berkeley: University of California Press, 1970.

SEIDENSTICKER, EDWARD. *Kafū the Scribbler.* Stanford, Calif.: Stanford University Press, 1965.

SHIVELY, DONALD H. *Tradition and Modernization in Japanese Culture.* Princeton, N.J.: Princeton University Press, 1971.

TANIZAKI, JUNICHIRŌ. *Diary of a Mad Old Man.* Translated by Howard Hibbett. New York: Knopf, 1965.

TANIZAKI, JUNICHIRŌ. *Some Prefer Nettles.* Translated by Edward G. Seidensticker. New York: Knopf, 1955.

TANIZAKI, JUNICHIRŌ. *The Makioka Sisters.* Translated by Edward G. Seidensticker. New York: Knopf, 1957.

TERRY, CHARLES S., ed. *Masterworks of Japanese Art*. Tokyo: Tuttle, 1956.
TSUNODA, RYUSAKU, WILLIAM T. DE BARY, and DONALD KEENE, eds. *Sources of Japanese Tradition*. New York: Columbia University Press, 1958.

Index

Index 227